Bruce Crowther

Captured on Film

Bruce Crowther

Captured on Film

The
PRISON
Movie

B.T. Batsford Ltd. London

ISBN 0 7134 6115 2

Typeset by Lasertext Ltd, Stretford, Manchester
and printed in
by
and bound by
Courier International Ltd, Tiptree, Essex

for the publishers
B. T. Batsford Ltd
4 Fitzhardinge Street
London W1H 0AH

Frontispiece:
Dana Andrews has no one but himself to
blame when he contrives to be put behind bars
for murder in *Beyond Reasonable Doubt* (1956).
Ostensibly, it is just to gain publicity for an
abolitionist campaign. But, only he knows that
he really did commit the crime and deserves
what's coming to him.

Contents

═ Acknowledgements ═

I am grateful to Dave Tuck for his knowledgeable assistance, helpful criticism and pertinent advice. He helped greatly in developing the original idea. I would also like to express my appreciation to Dave Dalton for his help with my research. Nevertheless, any errors of fact that might appear are my responsibility alone and all opinions expressed are mine.   B.C.

Credits

Some of the illustrations in this book come from stills issued to publicize films made or distributed by the following companies: A & M; Allied Artists; Alpha; Associated British; Brent Walker; British Lion; Brooksfilms; Bryanston; Centaur; Columbia; Corona-General; Decla-Bioscop; EMI; Ealing; Euro France-di Laurentiis; Fantasy; First National; Globe; Group W; Hammer; Hecht-Lancaster; Jalem; Malpaso; Merton Park; MGM; Mirisch; Mutual; Palace; Paramount; Polytel; Radio; Rank; Reliance; RKO; Hal Roach; Scotia-Barber; Tomorrow Entertainment; Triton; Twentieth Century-Fox; United Artists; Universal-International; Virgin; Warner Brothers.

Pictures are reproduced by courtesy of Derek and the late Pat East, Hilton Tims, Ann Caves and the Stills, Posters and Designs Department of the British Film Institute. The photograph of the author on the jacket is by Phill Clarkson.

Although every attempt has been made to trace the present copyright holders of photographs, the author and publishers apologize in advance for any unintentional omission or neglect and will be pleased to insert the appropriate acknowledgement to the companies concerned in any subsequent edition of this book.

I am grateful to the Edinburgh University Student Publications Board for permission to reproduce the extract on page 70 from 'Stone Womb (an epitaph)' originally published in *Breakout* by Pat Arrowsmith. I also wish to acknowledge the extracts from *San Quentin: the Story of a Prison* by Clinton T. Duffy and Dean Jennings reproduced on pages 10 and 11 and published originally by Doubleday, McIntosh and Otis and Peter Davies.

Under siege after a revolt of inmates, one of the prisoners in The Birdman of Alcatraz **(1962) doubles up as he catches a blast from a guard's gun.**

Prologue

The wind was whipping spray off the choppy waters of San Francisco Bay but no one in the boat heading through the mist towards the flashing red and white lights on the island thought about the weather. The thoughts of everyone on board were concentrated on what awaited them on the island; a few minutes in a rocking boat were incidental.

When the boat docked beneath the sign that read, UNITED STATES PENITENTIARY, the new arrivals scrambled ashore and were herded up steps towards the grey stone buildings of Alcatraz.

Inside, the building was cleaner than they had expected and the sharp smell of fresh paint assailed their nostrils. For a few moments there was an almost imperceptible relaxation among the new arrivals; one or two even risked a whispered word with a neighbour. Along the way they passed a tanned, leathery-faced elderly man incongruously wearing a baseball cap and windcheater.

Suddenly, a squad of heavily-armed uniformed men hurried into sight and conversation stopped abruptly. Far away in the echoing vastness, orders were shouted and soon their own guard was chivvying them into the dining hall.

The smell of paint was even stronger here. How could anyone eat with that tangy odour in the air? Then, all thoughts of food and even of their own reason for being here vanished as one of their number spotted a familiar face. Seated at one of the long trestle tables was a burly man in prison uniform. A name was whispered from person to person and suddenly, daringly, one of the new arrivals broke away and scurried to the big man's side. He grinned amiably and, emboldened now, others followed their eager companion. Their guard glowered but did nothing to prevent them clustering around the big man who even signed one or two autographs before more orders were yelled and he had to leave the dining hall. The new arrivals drifted back to their guard, a little shamefaced at their recent excitement, and listened as the guard explained what was happening here on this unseasonably chilly July morning in 1980.

A motion picture was being made, which accounted for many things: the fresh paint; the armed guards who were really film extras; the leathery-faced man in the baseball cap was a Native American named Clarence Carnes who long ago had been imprisoned here and had taken part in a bloody escape bid; the burly man at the dining table was actor Telly Savalas who was playing the role of one of Carnes's long dead companions.

The motion picture company had been granted permission to film here so long as it was not necessary to halt the regular tours of Alcatraz, which are conducted under the stewardship of guards – sorry, guides – employed by the United States National Parks Department.

For the visitors, the presence of a motion picture company was no detriment to their enjoyment. Indeed, the fact that parts of the prison had been repainted, even to the sign in the dining room announcing today's menu, the fact that uniformed prisoners and armed guards were everywhere re-enacting a real life uprising that had taken place 34 years ago, the presence of Clarence Carnes, all added spice to a visit to a prison which is as much a part of American folklore as the Alamo.

*

It was during that 1980 visit to Alcatraz, which vividly demonstrated a curious intermingling of fact and fantasy, of history and folklore, of real people and actors, of prison life and prison movies, that the seeds of the idea culminating in this book were first sown.

It is because of this constant mixing of fact and fiction that *Captured on Film* is about more than just prison movies; it is also about those real prisons and their inmates that gave rise to Hollywood's fictions.

This writer has not been to prison but, on that visit to Alcatraz, as the doors of Cell Block D closed, plunging him and the other temporary occupants of Cell Number 10 into stygian darkness, he could not help but contrast this with the very different kind of darkness in which he has spent many hours comfortably watching movies unfold their fantasies.

Those moments in the Hole at Alcatraz, fleeting though they were, brought to the surface strange fears and uncomfortable emotions. So much so that it is hard not to conclude that most of the people who make prison movies haven't the least idea what imprisonment is really like. Real life prisoners may know better, but only rarely do they get the chance to make movies. Come to think of it, judging from some of the movies that have been made, maybe the wrong people are being sent to prison.

No attempt has been made here to create an encyclopaedia. A glance through the lists of American movies that are set in prison, or have significant scenes behind bars, or that use the effects of imprisonment as a springboard for their tales, reveal a total of around 3,000 in the past 90 years. In addition to all these there are the westerns and, as every front-row cowboy knows, it is rare for a western movie not to have at least one scene set in the town jail. In these pages, therefore, there appears only a personal selection of movies and readers will doubtless know of many that are not featured in the text. For the most part, films are here because of their importance, or their relevance to real events. In a few cases they appear because they are so bad they are hard to overlook.

Prison movies are predominantly American although in certain areas, notably the prisoner-of-war movie, the British take a more significant role. The dominance of Hollywood and personal choice are both reflected in the movies featured in *Captured on Film*.

In addition to the movies there is much here about the reality of prison. As already indicated, the author has not been to prison and therefore such information has been gained second hand. I hope this position will not change but, as some of the appalling miscarriages of justice that unfold in these pages will demonstrate, not even the most law-abiding of us is entirely safe.

Introduction

Writing in the *Daily Telegraph* in November 1988, Judge Stephen Tumim reflected upon his first 12 months as HM Chief Inspector of Prisons and commented that he would never again 'sentence someone to custody without an image of the sort of life to which he is being consigned.' The judge was echoing remarks made some 40 years earlier by a Los Angeles District Attorney who had transgressed and went to the very jail to which he had sent hundreds of his fellow citizens. On his release, the District Attorney observed that if he were ever in office again he 'would hesitate about sending so many men to prison. It is far more terrible than people realize . . . .'

That two officers of the court in both Great Britain and the USA should learn of the reality of prison life long after they had begun sending men there as punishment raises disturbing questions. What did they think it was like? Didn't anyone tell them? Hadn't they ever been to the movies?

Prison as a subject for movies captured the imagination of movie makers and audiences from the earliest days of popular cinema. In 1905, *The Ex-Convict* was a salutary little tale of an ex-con who can support his family only by stealing. Fortunately for him, in the romantically melodramatic fashion of the time, the house he robs is the home of a little girl whose life he had earlier saved. Whether or not audiences for this film understood the rather fuzzy moral is open to question, but movie makers loved this corny little coincidence and used it over and over again in future years.

However, films like *The Ex-Convict* and *Escape from Andersonville* (1909) barely hinted at the possibilities and in the 1920s prison movies or movies with prison-related plots proliferated. That decade alone saw some 250 such movies emerge from Hollywood. The reason for the enthusiasm of the mass audience is speculative and may have been little more than a morbid desire to see what went on behind those cold grey walls and iron bars.

The reason for the flood of prison movies that came in the following decade is a little easier to explain. The massive audiences for prison movies in the early 1930s were responding eagerly to a variation on a currently popular theme. These prison movies were simply an off-shoot of the gangster movie genre.

Gangster movies of a sort had also been around for a long time but as a genre they really began at the tail end of the silent era with *Underworld* (1927). It was the coming of talking pictures that same year that gave the incipient genre the boost it needed. Apart from such obvious contributions to the excitement of these movies as the clatter of machine-guns, the clash of breaking glass and the screech of automobile tyres, there was the saltily entertaining dialogue. Screen gangsters rattled out terse epithets and wisecracks at one another and at the cops. This did not accurately reflect the way real-life gangsters spoke; indeed, first-hand reports suggest that many real-life gangsters had vocabularies considerably more restricted than some latterday screen idols whose off-screen unscripted dialogue consists of animal grunts. However, real-life gangsters took their cue and were soon speaking the way the movies claimed they did. Audiences loved it all, happily overlooking the often slimy reality which lay behind the fictions they saw on the screen.

The casting of exciting actors in the roles of criminals contributed to the false glamour that surrounded the gangsters. This came about because Hollywood had painted itself into a corner. With only rare exceptions, movies had spelled out a simplistic pecking order. The top-billed male actor played the hero, the male villain had to be content with, at best, second-billing. Indeed, if the hero had a 'best friend' (and he usually did) the villain would slide down a peg or two. The fact that heroes were played by stars led to a simple correlative: Star roles were heroic. Gangster movies awkwardly upended this fact of movie life.

The stars of these movies (or in some cases, their soon-to-be stars) were men like Humphrey Bogart, Edward G. Robinson and James Cagney. According to those earlier standards of Hollywood entertainments, the characters with whom audiences should have identified in, say, *Little Caesar* (1930) and *The Roaring Twenties* (1939) were, respectively, Douglas Fairbanks Jr and Jeffrey Lynn. Given unredeemably limp roles to play, both actors all but vanished beneath bravura performances from 'criminals' Robinson and Cagney.

The stars therefore continued to appear to audiences as heroes; the fact that they were portraying characters more villainous than the 'heavies' of earlier movies spread confusion. If stars were playing gangsters, then gangsters must surely be heroes. Even if, in real life, gangsters were robbing, cheating, corrupting and killing, in the movies they were surrounded with an aura of artificial glamour. It wasn't long before a similarly putative aura clung to the real-life gunmen and gang lords.

True, very few screen gangsters lived beyond the closing credits, but even in their depiction of such deaths movie-makers fudged issues. The reason why so many screen gangsters died in the last reel was a result of the dilemma faced by makers of gangster movies who tried to accommodate the imposition of self-censorship. Hollywood's self-regulatory body, the Hays Office (which had begun life in 1922 as the Motion Picture Producers and Distributors of America, Inc and had created a 'production code' in 1930), called for a criminal never to be shown benefiting from his crimes.

In practice, what usually happened was that a screen criminal was allowed to get away with just about everything up to and including murder only to pay the ultimate price in the closing scene. Unfortunately, such screen deaths were far from being the salutory lesson they were supposed to be. For many in the audience, being shot to death after having enjoyed a fine old time living high off the hog with unlimited money and all the things this could buy: fancy clothes, fast cars and even fancier and faster women, appeared to be a not unreasonable price to pay.

Prison was only rarely an intrinsic part of the regular gangster movie; like death from a cop's bullet, prison hung in the air as an imprecise threat to the liberty of the movies' heroes. But by the 1930s, film-makers had long known of their audience's interest in the tightly enclosed world of prison. With the added benefit of sound the few years between the start of the decade and the repeal of Prohibition saw numerous prison movies stumble out into Hollywood's daylight.

Most entries in this particular cycle of prison movies were little more than gangster films transposed from the city streets to the close confinement of a cell block and they took with them many of the same problems for film-makers.

Not least of these problems was in placing a heroic mantle around the shoulders of a brutal criminal. Just as gangsters were heroes and the opposing forces of law and order the villains, so in prison movies the convicts were the good guys and their guardians were the baddies.

In an attempt to justify what was essentially an unjustifiable role, prison guards in the movies were often portrayed as brutal and corrupt thugs. It says much for the power of the movies that the prison service in America and in Britain today has yet fully to live down this depiction.

Such topsy-turvy morality was tolerated, even applauded, thanks to Prohibition, the law of the land between 16 January 1920 and 5 December 1933, which made any citizen who wanted a drink a potential, and often an actual, criminal. Although movie-makers seldom took the trouble to try, it was easier to excuse a man in prison than a gangster in the streets. After all, a prisoner could be there through a miscarriage of justice, and many movie prisoners were; but there was no excuse for a criminal on the outside laying waste to all around him with a Thompson sub-machine-gun.

Unfortunately, if not entirely unexpectedly, movie-makers did not take the opportunity to redress the balance of good versus evil. The wrongfully convicted man was only rarely played by a star. Instead, the stars took the meatiest roles and, just as in gangster movies, this meant that they were the bad guys who paid the price of their misdeeds by going to the electric chair or being gunned down attempting an escape. Once again it was a case of the individual, with whom audiences were expected to identify, losing a battle with the might of the State, a battle in which the physical odds were stacked unfairly against the criminal while the moral odds militated against the State.

It was in this ambivalent atmosphere that the first of the classic prison movies appeared.

Hoods and Hit Men: Gangsters in Prison

'Nobody escapes, nobody ever escapes.'
(Brute Force)

The prison movie was given a welcome boost by riots at Dannemora and Auburn prisons in New York state in 1929, which were followed by an intense public debate on the issue of penal reform. The following year, 1930, saw a rush of minor prison movies, among them *Numbered Men*, and one that became a prototype for countless others over succeeding decades – *The Big House*.

Directed by Mervyn LeRoy, *Numbered Men* was shot on location at San Quentin and had the stereotypical wrongfully convicted man (played by Raymond Hackett) sent to prison where he meets his star-system superior Conrad Nagel. At the appropriate moment, this noble soul takes the rap for the kid who can then go free to marry Mary, his faithful childhood sweetheart (played by Bernice Claire), who has, betimes, narrowly avoided the murky intentions of an escaped con (Ralph Ince). *Numbered Men* is really rather uninspired but it served as a useful dry run for Mervyn LeRoy who would later direct a classic of the genre.

The cast of *The Big House* is a mixture of second string actors and unknowns with the principals, Chester Morris and Wallace Beery, turning in performances they seldom, if ever, bettered.

At the start of *The Big House* the audience is regaled with a guided tour of what it is like to enter prison as the camera follows new arrival Kent Marlowe (Robert Montgomery) who is photographed, fingerprinted, kitted out, and gradually dehumanized until he becomes just another numbered man among a mass of numbered, regimented, anonymous, blank-faced men facing soul-destroying incarceration.

The movie's audience, who are representatives of a society that expects people to come out of prison having had a hard time and thus be deterred from doing anything that will put them back inside, should have been in full and hearty agreement with this treatment of criminals. The way the movie is handled has the reverse effect. Marlowe has killed, but only accidentally, and lacks the will to survive the brutalities inherent in the system. As the story progresses the audience's sympathies, which at first are concentrated on Marlowe, are manoeuvered into blanket support for all the cons and then are stacked squarely behind just one man, John Morgan (played by Morris), a gutsy forger. The audience may still be on the 'wrong' side but Morgan is, at least, guilty of so-called victimless crimes. Even the ending is morally uneasy as Morgan eventually gains his release by preventing fellow-con Butch Sch-midt (Beery) from killing guards during an uprising. Thus, Morgan is made to appear to be a good guy when in fact he is a bad guy who happens to be not quite as bad as some of the others. This is blatant manipulation of the audience but it is concealed because *The Big House* is a well-constructed and well-acted movie, skilfully directed by George Hill from an Academy Award-winning screenplay by Frances Marion.

It was not the first time and it most certainly wasn't the last, but audiences for *The Big House* were set up to accept the unacceptable with insolent ease. The white-collar criminal who represented the 'good' in prison is one who has returned time and again in the movies where, as in real life, he generally comes off much better than his heavier-handed fellow criminals.

Most of the soon-to-be-familiar stereotypes were firmly established in *The Big House*: the 'square John', a con with his own standards of honesty and a natural leader of men; the 'rat', a squealing informer; the well-meaning but ultimately ineffectual warden (even if he was here based upon San Quentin's John Holohan); the bullying, sadistic guard, and the unrepentant con whose conduct inside the walls is little different to that which sent him here.

Most significant of all of *The Big House*'s contributions to the movies is that rearranging of normal attitudes towards law and order which caused audiences to root for the bad guys and helped create a cockeyed attitude towards law enforcement and the treatment of offenders.

The Big House had many imitators and its title spawned a number of similar entries in the prison and crime movie lists, among them *Mutiny in the Big House* (1939), which was based loosely on the real life exploits of Father Patrick O'Neil. In October 1929, O'Neil helped halt a prison break at Canon City, Colorado, in the course of which seven guards and five inmates perished. Awarded the Carnegie Medal for bravery, O'Neil's story was a natural for the movies who instantly implanted a few easily recognized stereotypes: a weak-willed

forger named Johnny (Dennis Moore), who had earned himself 1–14 years for passing a dud $10 cheque, and Red, the lowering heavy (Barton MacLane). The movie simplifies its plot to a Manichean struggle between the heavy and Father Joe (Charles Bickford) over who will win the soul of the weakling. It wasn't just students of psychology in the audience who guessed how it would all turn out in the end.

The following year Hollywood had another fling at the heroic chaplain tale, this time in *Men Without Souls* (1940), which has Father Tom Storm (John Litel) talking 'good' convict Johnny (Glenn Ford) out of killing the chief warder. When the warder is killed anyway, everyone assumes it was Johnny. Everyone except Father Tom, of course. The fact that the movie has a heavy named Blackie, played by Barton MacLane, should, however, alert any member of the audience who hasn't himself spent the previous decade in the slammer to the identity of the probable culprit.

Prison, in most 1930s movies, is a place of unfair or inhuman punishment, seldom is it shown to be a correctional establishment. In place of rehabilitation is confinement, oppression and fear. Neither is there much evidence of reforming zeal in these movies. Certainly, some of the prisoners in *The Big House* and its imitators find a kind of nobility, but this comes from within themselves and not as a result of externally imposed correction.

Among the few movies to suggest that official rehabilitation is possible is *The Criminal Code* (1931) in which a young man, Robert Graham (Phillips Holmes), is sent down by a crusading District Attorney after an accidental killing. DA Brady (Walter Huston) later becomes warden of the prison and begins to see things in a different light, aided by the fact that his daughter Mary (Constance Cummings) loves poor Robert. The potential for prison to harden the tyro criminal was present in the stage play from which the movie sprang. There, at the final curtain, Robert kills the brutal guard captain; in the movie, Captain Gleason (DeWitt Jennings) is killed by the psychotic Galloway (Boris Karloff) who has already done away with his fellow stereotype, Punch, the weasely stool-pigeon (Clark Marshall).

Hollywood liked the story so much it took a couple more flings at it. In 1938 Walter Connolly took the Huston role in *Penitentiary* while in *Convicted* (1950) it was Broderick Crawford's turn. In this version the kid was played by Glenn Ford with Dorothy Malone as the DA's daughter and Millard Mitchell making an effective Mallowby, the tough but square John.

While the existence of brutally-run prisons is demonstrably a fact of life in enough cases to cause righteous anger, it is far from being always the truth. Thus prisons, like the men who guard them, have frequently had an unjustifiably bad time in the hands of movie-makers.

Prison guards rarely have a movie angled from their side. An exception is *Prison Warden* (1949) in which Victor Burnell (Warner Baxter) is appointed to clean up corruption, but both he and the plot are hamstrung by a contrived relationship between his wife, Elisa (Anna Lee) and her former lover, Al Gardner (Harlan Warde), now a convict in her husband's charge. Clearly uneasy at being on the side of the righteous, this was not a formula Hollywood chose to repeat.

Contrastingly, prisons themselves, the actual bricks and mortar, concrete and steel, have attracted rather a lot of fascinated attention from film-makers. Among the American prisons that became as legendary in the movies as they are in real life are Sing Sing, San Quentin and Alcatraz.

Sing Sing took its name from the village in upstate New York where the prison was built in the 1820s. Elam Lynds, who had started out in the prison service as controller of Auburn prison in New York state, had a simple code: 'In order to reform a criminal you must first break his spirit.' Lynds put his theory into cruel practice and eventually so dismayed the authorities that he had to be moved on from Auburn. He was given the task of supervising the building of Sing Sing and then running it. Under Lynds' harsh rule Sing Sing became the most feared prison in the country and so many evils

were perpetrated under the despotic eye of its warden that the villagers of Sing Sing changed the name of their community to Ossining to avoid being tarred with the same brutal brush. A firm believer in the lash, Lynds introduced several techniques with which the American prison system was plagued for the next century and a half (and in places still is).

Lynds clearly did not belong to the school of thought that decreed that prison was a place to which men were sent 'as' punishment and not 'for' it. Among his methods were the rule of silence, solitary confinement and the whipping of prisoners for the most trivial of infringements. The lash may not have survived quite so long as did the other punishments but it certainly lasted long enough to make the name of Elam Lynds and the prison he built at Sing Sing hated and feared. It adds nothing to the reputation of the man or his prison that his eventual dismissal from the prison service came about not because of his sadistic treatment of convicts but because he was caught with his fingers in the till.

Some 70 years after Lynds' resignation, the great prison reformer Thomas M. Osborne became warden of Sing Sing, succeeded a few years later by Lewis E. Lawes who continued the uphill task of instigating prison reforms. Lawes commented on the problems he faced by declaring, 'Bit by bit, one reform at a time, the memory of Captain Lynds is being scrubbed out of the stones at Sing Sing.'

Lewis Lawes was warden of the prison for 21 years, retiring in 1941, but found time to write plays and books, some of which provided the basis for movies. His autobiographical book, *20,000 Years in Sing Sing*, provided a resonant title for the 1932 movie that starred Spencer Tracy as gangster Tom Connors.

As usual, the audience for *20,000 Years* was manipulated; this time by having the gangster-hero voluntarily submit to the death penalty. The movie thus shows that a man, even a hardened criminal like Connors, can achieve a kind of spiritual nobility in the manner in which he goes to his death.

The prison warden, Mr Long (Arthur Byron),

operates an 'honour system' wherein prisoners are tested by being allowed out, in Connors' case to visit his dying girlfriend, Fay (Bette Davis). Once on the outside Connors, who has hitherto been a tough nut earning himself a spell in solitary, kills a man. His victim is Finn (Louis Calhern), the man responsible for sending Connors to the pen, thus setting up the crime as 'justifiable' homicide. Improbably, Connors then upholds the honour system and ensures that the public does not lose faith with the reforming warden by returning to face death in the electric chair. Maybe movie audiences of the day were taken in by this selfless heroism. Today, Tom Connors' actions bear all the hallmarks of a deranged personality with an overpowering death wish.

When the movie was remade in 1940 as *Castle on the Hudson* (UK: *Years Without Days*), with John Garfield in the Tracy role, certain important changes took place in the ambience although the storyline, structure and many scenes are almost identical. This time the hero, Tommy Gordon (Garfield), who has gone down for a 25–30-year stretch for a jewel store robbery, is also released on parole. But in the end, he goes voluntarily to the electric chair to shield his girlfriend who has killed Tommy's

Always the visitor, almost never the visited. Ann Sheridan made sure a long parade of convicts got the most out of their visiting privileges. Here she is trying to convince dubious guards to let her in to see John Garfield in Castle on the Hudson **(1940).**

crooked lawyer, Ed Crowley (Jerome Cowan). Tommy's attitude is therefore less narrowly defined than was Tom Connors'. In going to the chair to save a woman rather than a philosophical ideal, he is more romantic and in keeping with the gradual shift Hollywood was unwittingly making towards the doomed heroes of the mid-1940s' *films noirs*.

If San Quentin did not have quite the same reputation for evil as its East Coast counterpart, it was certainly not regarded by its inmates as a holiday home by the Pacific.

San Quentin was notorious for its 'lime cell', a cell coated with lime hosed down to cause a discharge of chloride of lime which burned the occupant's hair, as well as the tender linings of his nose and throat. Other grim devices were the 'derrick', a hoist on which the prisoner was hung by his arms, which were bound behind his back, thus applying severe strain to the muscles and internal organs; the 'San Quentin overcoat', a tightly-wrapped canvas shroud into which a man was strapped for hours at a time, and the infamous San Quentin dungeons.

Another famous reforming warden, Clinton T. Duffy, first saw the dungeons when he worked at San Quentin as a clerk in the administration office. His description, in his autobiographical account of his years in the prison, evokes the grim appearance of this tomb of the living dead. Duffy had gone into the dungeons while carrying out a census of the prison's population and found there:

> a black tunnel about fifty feet long, with seven small cells on each side. The ancient mass of rock and concrete had the musty odour of a tomb; no sunlight had touched its mouldy walls for almost ninety years, and the foul air had no place to go, for there were no windows and the cell doors were hand-forged iron. Each cell was nothing more than a niche cut into the stone, and the walls and floor were bare. There was no light, no bed, no ventilation, no toilet facilities, not even a bench. There were sometimes three or four men in one cell, and there was no place to sit except a triangular block of concrete in one corner. Prisoners slept on the damp floor, with one blanket if they were lucky, and they got bread and water at the whim of the guards.

I had to use a flashlight to take my notes, and for weeks afterwards I was haunted by the memory of the shrunken faces I saw in the dim light, the smell of the living dead, the drip-drip of moisture from the vaulted ceiling.

When Duffy was appointed Acting Warden in 1940 he immediately closed the dungeons and, to make sure they could not be reopened if his appointment was not confirmed, he had the cell doors ripped out.

Such conditions were not exactly the stuff of prison movies of the 1930s as Warden Duffy also commented when he saw a movie ostensibly located at San Quentin:

I saw a warden who was a pawn in the hands of a scheming guard. I saw that all the prisoners except the hero were cruel, moronic characters who shuffled around in sloppy clothes which had large black numbers stencilled on them. The men were busy all day and night plotting all sorts of violence, and they talked from the sides of their mouths in some sort of underworld slang . . . The guards were vicious and clubbed prisoners whenever they felt like it.

San Quentin (1937) stars Humphrey Bogart, whose angular proletarian face was ideally suited to stereotypical preconceptions about what criminals should look like. He plays Joe 'Red' Kennedy, a hardened con whose rehabilitation is sought by Captain Stephen Jameson (played by Pat O'Brien, the one-man stereotypical good guy of countless gangster and other crime movies of the era). Joe's escape from San Quentin is urged on him by Lieutenant Druggin (Barton MacLane, who was the black obverse of O'Brien's shining coin), who convinces the con that Jameson has designs on his sister. Later, after he has shot and injured Jameson, Joe decides to return to prison but is mortally wounded. Having already fulfilled its commitment to the Hollywood code, the movie then lays on repentance with a trowel and has the dying convict urge his fellow cons to help Captain Jameson with his plans for prison reform. None of this – from the ease with which Joe breaks out of jail to his sudden transformation into a creature of noble sensibilities – is very convincing.

A later movie with the same title, *San Quentin* (1946), stars Lawrence Tierney as reformed con Jim who comes to the aid of Warden Kelly (Harry Shannon) when he comes unstuck with one of his rehabilitation schemes. Kelly takes a group of cons to speak at a San Francisco newspaper club where another supposedly reformed con, Nick Taylor (who else but Barton MacLane), uses the occasion to launch an escape bid. When Kelly is wounded and others are killed it falls to Jim to go after the bad guy. (Just what the cops are doing during all these amateur-night heroics is anybody's guess.)

Whichever of the two movies bearing the name of San Quentin is considered, it isn't surprising that Warden Duffy was unimpressed.

The 1930s saw the beginning of a growing list of iconographic actors whose presence provided a useful shorthand for film-makers. Among such icons were Barton MacLane as the tough con or bullying guard; Charles Bickford, equally suitable as the square John or the well-meaning warden or chaplain, and Humphrey Bogart who became familiar as the ruthless con determined not to be broken by prison, even if resistance cost him his life.

Bogart followed *San Quentin* with other prison and prison-related movies including *Dead End* (1937), *Crime School* and *Angels with Dirty Faces* (both 1938), and *You Can't Get Away With Murder* (1939) in which he takes the role of Frank Wilson, a hardened criminal (what else?) whose exploits lead him to prison along with young offender Johnnie Stone (Billy Halop, one of Hollywood's currently popular Dead End Kids). Wilson has previously killed a shopkeeper leaving Fred Blake (Harvey Stephens) to take the rap. In the breathlessly enclosed world of Hollywood, Fred's sweetheart is Johnnie Stone's sister, Madge (Gale Page).

The piling up of coincidences convinces Wilson that prison will cause Johnnie to crack and reveal information about the killing he has perpetrated but for which Fred is destined to take his seat in the electric chair. Wilson plans an escape, intending that Johnnie will die in the attempt. Although the escape bid fails Wilson does kill the kid who, in true Hollywood tradition, manages to use his last breath to finger Wilson for the earlier murder. The innocent man is freed, Wilson goes to the chair, and audiences were left to go home safe in the knowledge that right will out, even if it takes a petty hoodlum like Johnny Stone to correct the lethal blunders of state and national law enforcement agencies.

Its simplistic views of what was right and what was wrong with the legal and prison systems suggested that *You Can't Get Away With Murder* was the work of someone unfamiliar with the real life world of prison. However, it was in fact based upon a stage play, *Chalked Out*, co-written by Lewis E. Lawes who at the time was the reforming warden of Sing Sing. It would seem that Warden Lawes was less cynical of Hollywood's view of prison than was his San Quentin counterpart, Warden Duffy.

Sing Sing and San Quentin may have been decidedly unromantic places but the same cannot be said for Alcatraz, a West Coast prison whose name conjures up more myths and fantasies than all the other prisons in America put together.

Prisoners on Alcatraz were subject to strict

Ben Gazzara is just one of many actors to bring Al Capone to life. In Capone **(1975) he bears an uncanny resemblance to the failing hoodlum.**

discipline but, thanks to the reforming zeal of wardens in other places, the date of its inauguration meant that the worst excesses of the old San Quentin and Sing Sing were missing. Nevertheless, the employment of a code of silence, long hours locked up in the cells and the extensive use of solitary confinement and 'the Hole' made Alcatraz a name to be feared by convicts.

Over the years Alcatraz had several notable inmates and, despite its claims of impregnability, numerous escape bids. The stories of several of these prisoners and their lives, and deaths, on the Rock became the subject of true-life movies but most of these individuals, their brief moment of movie glory apart, were largely unknown to the general public.

This could not be said of one prisoner on the Rock between 1934 and 1939 who was known to just about everyone who had ever read a newspaper or seen a movie anywhere in the world. He was Al Capone, a Brooklyn-born son of an immigrant family, whose sense of right and wrong was buried deep enough to have allowed him to become a success in any area of big business he might have chosen to follow. In fact, he decided to employ his extraordinary and ruthless talents in a life of crime and by 1932, when he was sent to jail for income tax evasion, he controlled a lawless multi-billion dollar empire centred upon Cicero, a suburb of Chicago.

The reason for the authorities' decision to transfer Capone from prison in Atlanta, Georgia, to the Rock when Alcatraz opened as a civil prison in 1934 is speculative but appears to have been more a public relations exercise than an actual necessity. Capone was unlikely to attempt an escape and, anyway, by 1934 his personal power was already diminishing. In Alcatraz any remaining authority he might have had plummetted. Without his army of thugs to protect him he was pushed around by some of the Rock's genuine hard cases, one of whom, a Texan bank robber named James Lucas, stabbed him with a pair of hair-cutting scissors. In addition, Capone's mental and physical health began to deteriorate (he had syphilis).

After the attack by Lucas, Capone was moved from Alcatraz to San Pedro prison, then to Terminal Island, then to Lewisburg from where he was eventually released to live out his life at his Miami mansion.

In one of the numerous Hollywood versions of Capone's story, *Al Capone* (1959), starring Rod Steiger in the title role, the Lucas attack (which was precipitated because Capone pushed ahead of the bank robber in the barber shop queue) was translated into something much more dramatic with half a dozen cons setting about the former gang lord.

An Edward G. Robinson feature from 1937, *The Last Gangster*, took a look at a 'might be' tale of a former gang boss trying to pick up the pieces of his empire after release from prison. Although he had previously incarnated a Capone-figure to great effect (in *Little Caesar*) and would again with similar success in *Key Largo* (1948), this was not one of Robinson's better efforts.

The 'last gangster' Robinson plays is gang boss Joe Krozac who goes to prison for ten years on a tax fraud rap and is sent to Alcatraz. (The movie is set in 1927 although Alcatraz did not open as a civil prison until seven years later; neither were the authorities using book-keepers as a means of nailing big time villains as early as this.) While Joe is doing time his wife, Talya (Rose Stradner), has a child and becomes the subject of sympathetic newspaper articles by Paul North (James Stewart). Rose divorces Joe, marries Paul, and beats it to the middle of nowhere, even giving the baby the name North Jr in her efforts to shake off her past.

When Joe finally gets out of the joint he tries to rejoin his old gang but is harshly shown that this is an error of judgement. He goes in search of his son (played by Douglas Scott) but on seeing how he is growing up a credit to his adoptive father and reformed mother Joe backs off. When Joe is gunned down by rival mobster Frankie 'Acey' Kile (Alan Baxter) he dies clutching his son's school merit badge.

When, 35 years later, the Corleone family came to the screen in *The Godfather* (1972) to prove, in case it needed proving, that Joe Krozac had not been the last of his kind, such token sentimentality was still prevalent, but neither Don Corleone nor his son Michael would have been as easily put off as was poor old Joe.

Somewhat more successful was Edward G. Robinson's *Black Tuesday* (1954) in which he was again a big time criminal intent on engineering his escape from prison where he is awaiting execution. Robinson plays Vincent Canelli who is due to die on 'Black Tuesday', New Jersey's official day for hanging up its dirty washing. Canelli's girlfriend, Hatti Cumbest (Jean Parker), kidnaps Ellen (Sylvia Findley), the daughter of prison guard John Norris (James Bell) who is thus persuaded to help in Canelli's escape. The gangster takes along another death row con, Peter Manning (Peter Graves), not for altruistic reasons but because Manning has stashed away the loot from his last robbery.

During the escape bid, another escapee, Joey Stewart (Warren Stevens), kills Norris and eventually the cons hole up in a warehouse with a motley selection of hostages including Ellen, newspaperman Frank Carson (Jack Kelly), a doctor (Victor Perrin) and a priest (Milburn Stone). Thus well-equipped for any eventuality, Canelli prepares to take on the world but first he has to persuade the doctor to operate on Manning who has been wounded but who insists on going alone to recover the hidden money. The police tail Manning back to the warehouse, surround the place, and turn up the heat. Canelli threatens to kill his hostages if the cops won't play ball and actually does kill a guard (from fairly well down the cast list and thus expendable). Manning is then stricken with an unaccountable attack of conscience that prompts him to kill Canelli. This act of improbable nobility is then topped by Manning's decision to go down to the police facing either summary justice or a long walk on some future Black Tuesday.

All of which has drifted some way from Al Capone, whose legend was still strong enough in 1962 to allow a movie, *Alcatraz Express*, to be built around his transportation to the prison. Here, Neville Brand plays the gang lord with

Robert Stack repeating his TV role as book-keeper-turned-gangbuster 'Untouchable' Eliot Ness.

Back in 1930s Hollywood, the third member of the great triumvirate of gangster movie icons (the others being Bogart and Robinson) was James Cagney. In a string of movies he was either in prison, recently out, or about to go back in again. The sheer dynamism of the actor was such that confinement was anathema and careful plotting to evade custody was equally unsuitable. What Cagney did superbly well was to slam-bang his way out of, over the top of, or straight through any obstruction in his path be it cop, guard or prison wall.

In *Each Dawn I Die* (1939) Cagney was a newspaper reporter wrongfully committed to prison, while in *Angels With Dirty Faces* (1938) he was a 'there but for the grace of God' hoodlum. But there were no redeeming features about his characters in two late gangster movies, *White Heat* (1949) and *Kiss Tomorrow Goodbye* (1950). In each film he played an out-and-out villain and while his Ralph Cotter, an escaped convict, in the later film might well qualify as one of the blackest of all movie villains, it is his Cody Jarrett in *White Heat* that most sticks in moviegoers' memories. The most powerful of the scenes in which this psychotic, mother-fixated homicidal maniac dominates the screen is set in prison. Jarrett has gone inside on a minor rap to avoid arrest on a more serious charge. While in prison he learns that his mother, the only person who can calm him out of the blinding headaches that periodically attack him, has died. In an extraordinary display of bravura acting, Cagney clambers up onto the table and then stamps crazily across the massive dining hall scattering dishes, cons and guards every whichway before being overpowered. The movie might not have too much to do with prison, but the dining hall scene is a superb cinematic moment.

White Heat includes a cop who is sent to prison in the guise of a crook in order to worm his way into the confidence of a criminal. This notion had formed the basis for *Public Hero Number One* (1935) in which Sonny Black

(Joseph Calleia) is the gangster, a member of the Purple Gang, which is the target of cop Jeff Crane (Chester Morris). Hollywood liked this idea, too, and remade it as *The Get-Away* (1941) with Dan Dailey as Black and Robert Sterling as Jeff Crane.

The effect on prisoners of the impending execution of a fellow inmate is an area offering highly-charged drama and it is one moviemakers have not overlooked. Perhaps the most gripping examination of this facet of prison life came in a stage play by John Wexley, which was made into a movie in 1932 and again in 1959. The first time around *The Last Mile* starred Preston Foster with Mickey Rooney playing the central role in the remake (Spencer Tracy played the role on stage). In both versions the mounting tension in the prison – and especially along Death Row – was played with all-stops-out hysteria, contrasting uneasily with the eerie calm of recent TV documentaries that have studied the same subject now that certain states in America have reintroduced the death penalty.

In the 1932 version of *The Last Mile* Richard Walters (Howard Phillips) is convicted of a murder he did not commit and manages to establish his innocence in time to gain a reprieve. In the play he went to the chair quite early on, thus leaving the field clear for tough con Mears. In the movie Mears (Foster) has to be content with starting a riot and walking deliberately into a hail of bullets at the end.

In the 1959 version of the movie, Walters is played by Clifford David while Rooney assaults the part of Mears with frenzied glee. The balance of the audience's emotions is unforgivably manipulated by making all nine men on Death Row likable (in Rooney's hands even the sadistic Mears has a kind of repellent fascination) while the guards are uniformly callous. Death Row warden Callahan (Leon Janney) is particularly unpleasant until he faces death when, predictably, he falls apart at the seams of his prison blues.

One major problem for film-makers working on prison movies is the apparently narrow scope of the subject. The manner in which the

Henry Fonda went behind bars in 1937 for You
only Live Once and he was still doing time in
1976 in The Last of the Cowboys.

convicts. A strong cast of second-string actors,
including Neville Brand, Emile Meyer and Leo
Gordon, were joined by some non-actors playing themselves. A first-rate screenplay by Richard Collins is aided by the brisk uncluttered
direction of Don Siegel, the whole helped by a
commendable absence of stereotypes.

Brand appears as Dunn, a long-term prisoner
who plans a riot not with escape in mind but in
the hope of securing better conditions. Dunn is
helped by The Colonel (Robert Osterloh) who
is intellectually opposed to the riot but goes
along with the plan in order to help his friend
keep Mad Mike Carnie (Gordon) in check.

The three conspirators overpower an inex-
perienced guard, take four more hostages and
free other cons on the block. Dunn begins his

Neville Brand (r), whose prison movie record
was second only to Barton MacLane's, serves
notice on Emile Meyer in Riot in Cell Block
Eleven (1954).

makers of both versions of *The Last Mile*
responded to the constraints of the tightly
enclosed world of prison, by using inner tensions to build their drama (even though in both
versions they went over the top), is a solution
not everyone could accept. Thus the prison riot
becomes a major feature of many movies,
allowing as it does the introduction of two-way
violence and even an element of adventure.

Inside the Walls of Folsom Prison (1951)
enjoyed the best of two worlds being set in the
present with a reforming warden, Mark Benson
(David Brian), putting the prison to rights but
containing a substantial flashback which
remembers a riot 30 years before during the
reign of sadistic warden Rickey (Ted de
Corsia). The rioters are led by Charlie Daniels
(Steve Cochran) and the riot ends in the wholesale slaughter of the cons.

One of the best of the riot movies resulted
from the first-hand experience of prison life
gained by producer Walter Wanger. Jailed in
the early 1950s for shooting and injuring his
actress wife's agent, Wanger turned his brief
incarceration to good effect. *Riot in Cell Block
Eleven* (1954) remains a good, solidly constructed movie that never overstates its case
(for reform) while effectively conveying the
deep-seated but frustrated anger felt by many

negotiations with the warden (Meyer) who is a reformer and generally in sympathy with the con's demands even if he disapproves of his methods. The warden is equally disapproving of the methods for ending the riot advocated by Haskell (Frank Faylen), the state governor's representative.

As the riot spreads through the prison, police are moved in, prisoners are killed and when Mad Mike wrests control of the riot from Dunn, and on the other side the warden accedes to Haskell's plan to dynamite their way in, matters are clearly moving towards a messy end. Then, in a sudden but realistic change of pace, the state governor agrees to the prisoners' demands and the riot fizzles out.

Later, the state legislature vetoes the governor's proposal, the prisoners' demands are forgotten, and Dunn faces a further 30 years as instigator of the riot. The warden's assertion

that the riot has, at least, brought the need for reform to wide public attention ironically underlines the futility of the whole exercise.

Riot in Cell Block Eleven is an unsensationally angry film but is also unsentimentally compassionate and it must be conceded that producer Walter Wanger's brief incarceration in prison did him some cinematic good (especially so when it is realized that the same spell in the slammer encouraged him to make *I Want to Live* four years later).

Riot (1968) was shot in an Arizona state prison, which helped create a patina of realism. The movie also benefits from strong central performances by Gene Hackman and Jim Brown in a tale that uneasily presaged events a few years later at Attica prison.

Based upon a book by ex-con Frank Elli, which was in turn based upon real events in Minnesota a few years before, *Riot* features a phoney confrontation designed to conceal a planned escape. Red Fletcher (Gene Hackman) leads the riot, aided by an initially unwilling Cully Briston (Jim Brown), Surefoot (Ben Carruthers), a homicidal Native American, and Bugsy

In the late 1960s and 1970s both sides of prison riots took advantage of the posibilities offered by media-hyping. Here Gene Hackman talks to the press in Riot **(1968).**

Charles Bickford (c) complains about the chow to Hume Cronyn while fellow con Sam Levene (r) looks on. From the way Ray Teal (rear) is fondling his club he obviously believes that Brute Force (1947) is better than the soft approach.

(Mike Kellin). The cons plan to break out when attention is diverted by the riot, intent on using an old and previously unused tunnel. Not surprisingly, the riot gets out of hand as soon as the cons are out of their cells.

The warden (played by a real life prison warden, Frank A. Eyman) does his best but is hindered by his superiors and eager media people sent out to cover the story. Before being restored to confinement following a great deal of bloodshed, much of which appears to be unnecessary, the prisoners make their escape bid but Red and Surefoot fall out with lethal results. Only Cully, the one who did not really want to be a part of the scheme, makes it to the outside and, it would appear, is still out there somewhere.

Unlike *Riot in Cell Block Eleven*, which largely avoided stereotypes and sensationalism,

Riot overflows with both. Among the former are a sadistic guard, a naïve psychiatrist (a contradiction in terms one hopes), and a rampantly homosexual medical orderly. Among the sensational elements are the establishment by the rioting prisoners of a homosexual brothel and a court that tries, convicts and summarily punishes individuals who have contravened the prisoners' own 'laws'. Such behaviour, allied as it is to several vicious killings by cons, undermines any sympathy the audience might feel for the prisoners. The balance is further tilted towards favouring the authorities when, at the movie's end, the guards show remarkable restraint when putting down the riot.

The riot towards the end of *Brute Force* (1947) is not a means by which prisoners seek to register complaints at their treatment, neither is it a means to conceal a stealthy escape. Instead, the riot is part of a doomed full-frontal attempt to break out of a place that is, literally, a lethal environment for the cons.

An uncompromisingly bleak view of prison life, *Brute Force* has no illusions about whose side it is on. The cons are heroically led by Joe Collins (Burt Lancaster), and include such sympathetic fellows as Gallagher (Charles Bickford) and Soldier (Howard Duff), while the senior guard is Munsey (Hume Cronyn), a sadistic Nazified bully who deadens the sound of the beatings he administers by playing appropriately Wagnerian music on his gramophone. The other principal members of the prison's administration are a weak warden (Roman Bohnen) and a drunken doctor (Art Smith), by now well-established prison movie stereotypes. Another stereotype, the informer among the cons who gives away his fellow inmates' plans, here meets one of the stickiest ends in prison movies when he is forced by an encircling group of blow torch-bearing fellow convicts into the bed of a drop hammer, which promptly stamps out his life.

Although a generally strong movie, *Brute Force* suffers from a failing of many prison movies of its kind – the romantic flashback. Each of the cons is in stir primarily as a result of feminine wiles. Soldier has tangled with the military police over his Italian wife, Gina (Yvonne De Carlo) and the behaviour of her fascist father; Tom Lister (Whit Bissell) embezzled to buy Cora (Ella Raines) a mink coat; Spencer (John Hoyt) is a victim of Flossie (Anita Colby). As for Joe Collins, he plans to escape because he is in love with Ruth (Ann Blyth) who cannot face a critical operation without him by her side.

The closing sequence of *Brute Force*, the riot and the ensuing escape attempt, inevitably leads to the deaths of most of the would-be escapers and Munsey who is tossed from a gun tower by the mortally wounded Collins.

The weakness in *Brute Force* demonstrates the fact that these movies, largely dominated by men, gave film-makers a problem in how best to introduce the glamour and sexual titilation they believed their audiences could not do without and which many felt was a prerequisite for good box-office returns.

Women had also been an awkward encumbrance for makers of gangster movies. In those films, women were usually seen either as a pure and honest out-of-reach dream of the gangster, or as hard-boiled floozies ready to snap a garter at the opening of a well-filled wallet. Occasionally women were used with rather more imagination. Ann Dvorak was Francesca, the object of Tony Camonte's incestuous lust in *Scarface* (1932), and after *Public Enemy* (1931), Mae Clarke spent the rest of her career trying to live down the moment when James Cagney mashed half a grapefruit into her face.

In prison movies the use of women was rarely as inspired, though often just as sexist. A way out for those film-makers who lacked the courage of their own convictions, to say nothing of their characters' convictions to an all-male institution, was the introduction of the faithful little woman – wife, girlfriend, mother – on the outside. Sometimes these characters appeared in introductory scenes leading to the hero's incarceration; mostly, and less convincingly and often disruptively to the movie's narrative flow, they appeared in the form of flashbacks.

A British movie that had a marked impact upon popular perceptions of prison life is *The Criminal* (1960). A tough gangster, Johnny Bannion (Stanley Baker), is sent down for three years for his part in a racetrack blag and on his release promptly starts up where he left off. After another robbery Bannion is arrested again when his disaffected girlfriend, Maggie (Jill Bennett), tips off the police. Back inside for 15 years, Bannion is prepared to sit out his term, knowing that the latest bundle of loot is safe and that his new girlfriend, Suzanne (Margit Saad), will wait for him. But Bannion's old pals, led by Mike Carter (Sam Wanamaker), spring him in the hope that he can be persuaded to take them to where the money is hidden.

The prison scenes are effectively realized although the American tradition of cells filled with stereotypes is maintained, to say nothing of a vicious chief warder (performed with malicious glee by Patrick Magee).

Another British prison movie, *The Pot Carriers* (1962), offered a harsh indictment of the essential futility of confining men in a grim, squalid and meaningless microcosm of society. The movie, sustained by an excellent performance from Ronald Fraser as Redband, should have left no one in any doubt that the

The notice behind warder Edward Judd speaks volumes about prisoners' rights. However, Stanley Baker and Margit Saad, in The Criminal (1960), appear to be speaking Standard Domestic Squabble.

prison system was clearly on the road to nowhere, a place it reached less than two decades later.

As has been suggested, the eventual decline of gangster movies was largely a result of built-in flaws. The severely self-limiting factor of having a violent criminal as hero was one such flaw and this was overcome by having the actors concerned, notably James Cagney, change sides without any appreciable adjustments to their manner of dress, speech or the number of people they might kill in the course of a movie. Humphrey Bogart also changed sides but while Cagney could readily don the persona of a gun-toting G-man, Bogart was more at ease in the guise of a crusading news-paperman or district attorney. The criminals these men pursued became, for a time, the lat-terday equivalents to the faceless, black-hatted baddies of a thousand horse-operas. But then a new breed of gangsters and tough cops breezed into the movies.

The new wave of gangster movies concen-trated less on individuals and more on the cor-porate structure of organized crime. The Mafia movie now became a popular successor to the machine-gun movie of the past. Movie-makers made the shift without ever managing, if indeed they ever tried, to shake the impression that they admired the characters they created. The already clouded dividing line between good and evil became even less distinct and by 1972 and *The Godfather* it was virtually impossible to find a major crime movie in which any of the leading characters had a single redeeming feature.

The new style, tough-cop movie, was simi-larly uneasy in its disposition of redeeming qualities. Although the new kind of cop was (usually) honest, he was also ruthlessly violent. Led by Richard Widmark's *Madigan* (1968) and followed by the likes of Charles Bronson, Clint Eastwood and Burt Reynolds, they blasted their way through assorted criminals with scant regard for the letter of the law. Although Madi-gan was relatively moderate in his use of gun law, the propensity for violence of the charac-ters played by such successors as Eastwood's Harry Callahan bordered upon the psychotic. These cops made Cagney, Bogart and other earlier counterparts seem positively limp-wristed.

There was to be no cycle of films featuring tough and fearlessly lethal prison guards. Although the movie cop was rescued from obli-vion by violence, the prison officer had no such luck. It was a different story for the prisoner, however, and a variation on old themes resur-faced.

Big House USA (1955) adopted the currently popular pseudo-documentary style in tracing the crime (a kidnapping), its investigation and the arrest and conviction of Jerry 'The Iceman' Barker (Ralph Meeker). Sent to Cascabel Island prison (a real place despite its romantic-sound-ing name), Barker is sucked into an escape bid masterminded by Rollo Lamar (Broderick Crawford) who wants Barker along because only he knows where the ransom money from the kidnap is hidden (sounds familiar).

The Steel Jungle (1956) finds Ted de Corsia as racketeer Steve Martin comfortably running his business from behind bars, while *Revolt in the Big House* (1958) has another big-time hoodlum locked up and still lording it over everyone in sight. This is Lou Gannon (Gene Evans) who plans a mass breakout intending to slip quietly away while the cons are massacred by the guards he has thoughtfully alerted. Lou's plans are sabotaged by his Mexican cellmate, Rudy (Robert Blake), who tips off the cons after being knifed and when Lou heads for the hills by way of a subway it is he who perishes in a hail of bullets.

Although made in the late 1950s, *Revolt in the Big House* has barely moved on, showing, as it does, its complement of stereotypes (including a wild-eyed psychotic, played by the glori-ously manic Timothy Carey, and a sturdy warden, played by Emile Meyer, who had been there before). The movie is rescued from banality, however, by its small-budgetted set-ting, tellingly restricted to the cell block and exercise yard.

Ironically enough, prison proved to be a genuine refuge for some gang lords and their minions when things became too hot on the outside. Thus, Vito Genovese, head of one of the nation's biggest Mafia families, was in the same joint at the same time as Joe Valachi, who was busily singing about the rackets to the FBI. This tale reached the screen in *The Valachi Papers* (1971) with Charles Bronson as Joe and Lino Ventura as Don Vito, who puts out an open contract on his fellow inmate for $100,000. Thanks to Bronson's habitual stoic screen pre-sence, his character manages to avoid, here at least, the usual movie assumption that stool-

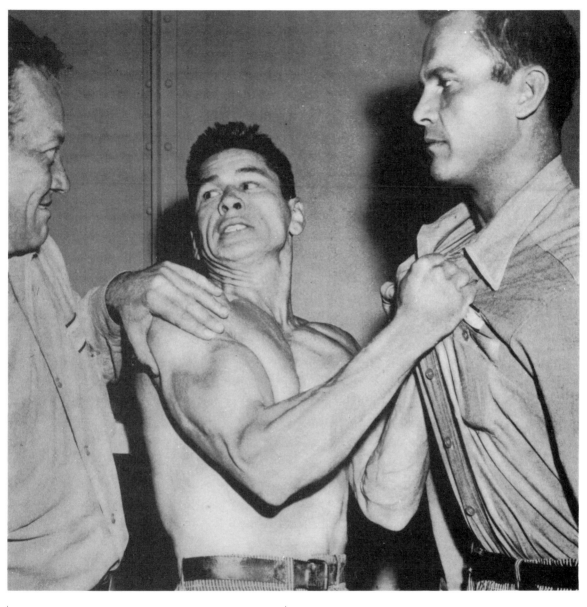

**William Talman (l) and Charles Bronson (c)
persuade Ralph Meeker to escape from the**
Big House USA **(1951).**

pigeons are bad guys even when the people they're ratting on are a thousand times worse. Popular movie opinion (and real life too) seems to hold that, however horrendous a man's crimes, he deserves to be treated with honour – especially by his evil soulmates. Heigh-ho, it's a funny old world.

By the mid-1980s, the gangster movie was among the most popular forms of movie. This was especially so in the video market and even came in for parody in *Johnny Dangerously* (1984), in which gangster Johnny Kelly (Michael Keaton) is hounded into prison by Assistant District Attorney Tommy Kelly (Griffin Dunne), his kid brother (shades of Cagney and O'Brien).

Michael Keaton goes into his dance in gangster parody Johnny Dangerously **(1984).**

While languishing on Death Row, Johnny learns that his brother is about to be killed; he escapes, saves Tommy's life and decides to go straight running a pet shop in New York City. The movie even risks using clips from *The Roaring Twenties* in its closing moments. The movie's star is an engaging young man and hence the latterday youth audience has no difficulty in identifying with him and doubtless sympathized with him when he went inside.

Back in the 1930s, however, the convict as hero proved to be steadily more difficult to swallow. Despite this, prison movies of that decade continued to be made, even gaining in strength and importance through a shift in focus. At first this ran concurrently with the gangster-inspired cycle, but in these other prison movies the hero was a mistreated man, either through the already clichéd miscarriage of justice or through unfair or inhumane treatment in prison. Such movies pointed out flaws in the system and sometimes deliberately strove to become society's conscience and force changes. Once in a while, they actually succeeded.

2

Hopeless Cases and Lost Causes: Social Reform in Prison

'The men who commit crimes are hard men,
and their punishment must be hard.'
(I Am a Fugitive from a Chain Gang)

Prison as a place in which common criminals, such as thieves and murderers, are held as a form of punishment or penitence or, hopefully, correction and rehabilitation, has been a part of American and British society for less than 300 years.

Before then such criminals in England, be they highwaymen, pickpockets, footpads or poverty-racked men, women and children stealing to avoid starvation, were liable to be punished by death or maiming, public flogging or, as attitudes began to soften and if they were lucky, by transportation for life. Prison for these criminals was merely a place where they might be held while awaiting trial or the execution of sentence. Prison as a long-term place of detention was not for them but instead was usually home to members of the middle and upper classes who had fallen into bankruptcy and debt or had conspired against the State.

The class barriers so implied are still with us today as comparisons between the fate of so-called white-collar criminals and that of their blue-collar counterparts will show.

As attitudes towards criminals in the Old World slowly softened and changed, there appeared in the New World a much more enlightened view of crime and its punishment. Towards the end of the eighteenth century,

Quakers in Philadelphia turned their local jail into a place of confinement in the hope that correction would ensue and that the prisoners, newly penitent, would one day be fit to rejoin society. Soon, other 'penitentiaries' were built elsewhere in the New World but the 'Philadelphia system' quickly had a much less enlightened rival. During the first quarter of the nineteenth century a prison was built at Auburn in New York state wherein miscreants paid for their crimes by hard labour.

Perhaps it wasn't surprising that in get-up-and-go America, the profit-making potential of this second system attracted more interest and spread rapidly. Unfortunately for the convicts, the methods adopted by the warden of Auburn, the sadistic former army captain Elam Lynds, who believed in breaking a criminal's spirit, also spread to the prisons following Auburn's example. Maybe matters had improved since the days when an eight-year-old waif in London might be hanged for stealing bread but the treatment of prisoners had a long way to go.

Such reforms as were possible during the second half of the nineteenth century and the first quarter of the twentieth century were severely limited, owing in part to public indifference (after all, convicts were not supposed to enjoy life in prison) and to entrenched interests. Not least among these was the profitability of certain aspects of convict labour.

When Hollywood, a community with a prevailing interest in making a fast buck, cashed in on public interest in any burning issue of the day it did so by churning out a string of movies. As so often happened when Hollywood did something for all the wrong reasons, some of these fast-buck movies became classics of their kind. There was, however, a still small voice murmuring in the ears of some movie-makers, a voice that stirred them to create movies with a conscience.

Hollywood's first important period of social conscience movies came late in the 1930s as the facts of the Great Depression struck home to more and yet more ordinary citizens. The film industry's motives for this unusual outbreak of conscience appear mixed but high among them is the fact that it was undergoing one of its sporadic outbreaks of self-consciousness coupled with an urgent desire to be taken seriously and not dismissed as just a dream factory.

The decision to make such movies must have come hard as to do so meant an almost inevitable brush with poverty, an area of life the film industry tended to avoid like the plague (and for much the same reason – the fear of contagion).

Among the most rewarding exceptions was Preston Sturges's *Sullivan's Travels* (1941), which traces the fictional steps of a Hollywood movie director who tramps the roads to discover what life is like for the underprivileged. But Sullivan (Joel McCrea) comes unstuck and is accused of his own murder. Sneered at by the authorities who judge this man by his raggedy clothes (courtesy of his studio's wardrobe department), he is sent to a prison farm. There, he spends time in the farm's equivalent to a regular prison's hole. This is described succinctly in the screenplay:

SWEATBOX IN THE WOODS
It is a little structure not quite high enough to stand up in, not quite wide enough to sit down in. There is a small door within the door to give the man water.

There is a telling scene in *Sullivan's Travels* in which the movie director is taken along with a group of other convicts to a black church where, when the service is over, a film show is held. The fact that these men are thought fit only to associate with the black community, in the South just another of society's outcasts, is effectively understated. Sullivan also discovers in this scene a value in the movies that he never understood from his Hollywood vantage point. At first the other prisoners and then, he too can laugh at the antics on the screen. He realizes, perhaps a shade glibly, that the movies can ease pain and frustration and, for a few minutes at least, tug aside the suffocating blanket of suffering that shrouds so many lives.

Sullivan's Travels, however notable, was an exception to Hollywood's general rule. Particularly in its golden years, when every product of the dream factory seemed to outbid every other in the density of its coating of glitz, Hollywood shied away from showing poor people simply being poor. The poor were okay on-screen just so long as they were also cute. Prison movies, like the crime movies from which they stemmed, brought with them an uncomfortable correlation between poverty and the working classes.

Class distinctions might not be the first thing that leaps to mind in considering crime but, statistically, there is powerful evidence to demonstrate that the great divide exists as much in criminal behaviour and the manner in which criminals (whether convicted or merely suspected) are treated as in any other area of human activity.

The most common crimes in the twentieth century are robbery, burglary, larceny and theft. It is self-evident that the most common perpetrators of these crimes are poor – otherwise why would they bother? As for the criminal's class status: American statistics from the early 1970s show that while 17 per cent of the population outside prison were occupied in either manual labour or in service industries these same categories provided 43 per cent of the prison population. White-collar workers outside prison were 41 per cent of the population, inside they represented only 14 per

Paul Muni (l) contemplates the unrelenting horror of life on a 1920s Georgia prison farm. Despite the public uproar when I Am a Fugitive from a Chain Gang **(1932) was released, it was a long time before the authorities changed their style.**

cent. There is no good reason to suppose there has ever been a significant variation in these statistics.

Nevertheless, despite many reservations among studio heads (and some studios never did get around to dealing with the poor and huddled masses outside their fancy palaces) the poor were given some attention during the outburst of social conscience movies that illuminated the late 1930s. Some of these were also prison movies and while such tales continued to appear throughout the next few decades, sometimes erring on the side of the do-gooders, sometimes looking at other social issues through prison movies, perhaps the most

important of them all was a forerunner by several years of that late 1930s collection.

I Am a Fugitive from a Chain Gang (1932) was based upon the true account of extraordinary events in the life of an unemployed World War I veteran named Robert Elliott Burns. Apprehended for his part in a grocery store robbery (which netted less than $6 for the three perpetrators), Burns was sentenced to a 6- to 10-year term on a Georgia chain gang. In 1922 Burns escaped, travelled north, and under a new name began a new life and rose to prominence in Chicago as a publishing executive. In 1930 he was identified and voluntarily returned to Georgia after being promised by state officials that his case would be treated leniently and he would be pardoned. The state reneged on these promises and Burns was sent back to the chain gang. He escaped again and this time went to New Jersey where he wrote magazine articles that told not only his story but also recounted the appalling manner in which convicts were treated on chain gangs in Georgia. It was when these articles were published in book form, under the title *I Am a Fugitive from a Georgia Chain Gang!*, that Burns's story came to the attention of Warner Brothers. The resulting movie shook a nation complacent in its belief that convicts got only what was coming to them.

The movie that emerged from Warner Brothers' studios pulled few punches, the screenplay being reasonably faithful to Burns's book (which is, in fact, rather awkwardly episodic in its construction). The screenplay, by Howard J. Green, Brown Holmes and Sheridan Gibney, traces the ex-soldier's return from the War (renamed James Allen for the movie and portrayed by Paul Muni), the refusal of his prewar employer to take him on again, and his agreement to take part in a robbery at a time when he is flat broke and living in a doss house in Atlanta, Georgia. After his conviction for his largely unwitting part in the robbery, James Allen is sent to a chain gang where his induction is followed in harrowing detail by the camera. The shackling of the new prisoner's legs, the chaining together of men during their daily labour, at night as they sleep in squalid bunkhouses, and as they move painfully from camp to work-site, are bad enough but then, through James Allen's treatment, audiences experienced everything else chain gang prisoners suffered: appalling food, almost non-existent sanitary arrangements, harsh brutality of the guards who beat a man for offences as trivial as failing to ask permission to wipe sweat from his brow. And each day ends with a prisoner being picked out, almost at random, and whipped until he is a bloody, unconscious wreck.

With the help of a black convict, Sebastian (Everett Brown), James Allen devises a scheme to escape. With accurate blows of his sledgehammer, Sebastian distorts the shackles on Allen's legs so that when the moment is right he can slip his feet out of them and take to the woods and swamps that surround the camp.

In the movie the escaped convict becomes an engineer who builds bridges (a more visually compelling occupation than the real man's work). Marie (Glenda Farrell), the young and attractive proprietress of the rooming house where he lives learns of his true background when she secretly opens a letter to him from his brother and insists that he marry her, intent it seems on battening on to a potentially successful breadwinner. (In real life the lady was neither especially young nor attractive and was rich enough to start Burns off on a prosperous career first as a realtor and then as a publisher.) When Allen meets another attractive young woman, Helen (Helen Vinson), a chorus girl (in real life a part-time waitress and taxi-dancer with delusions of becoming a concert violinist), their affair forces an inevitable confrontation with his wife, which in turn leads to her contacting the authorities in Georgia who have him arrested.

During his second escape, which is aided by a fellow prisoner, Bomber Wells (Edward Ellis), James Allen dynamites a symbolic bridge separating him from his pursuers just as Bomber dies from gunshot wounds. On the

As late as 1950 the imagery of the Chain Gang **was still potent.**

run and fearful of all authority, the escaped convict visits Helen to say goodbye for ever.

In an emotive final scene she pleads with him as he backs slowly away from her:

Can't you tell me where you're going? [He shakes his head.] Will you write? [He shakes his head.] Do you need money? [He shakes his head again, still backing away.] But you must, Jim! How do you live?

As the sound of an approaching car is heard Allen backs out of sight into the surrounding darkness and his disembodied voice speaks the movie's last line: 'I steal.'

These closing moments of the movie were so dramatically effective that several people subsequently claimed credit for them with one, director Mervyn LeRoy, suggesting he was inspired by the accidental blowing of a fuse just as Paul Muni spoke his final line. In fact, this scene appears in the movie exactly as written in the screenplay, the only difference being that there are then two further short scenes before the closing title, scenes which were edited out of the final cut.

Another scene that artfully indicates the effect of the chain gang on long-term prisoners is when one convict, Barney Sykes (Allen Jenkins), is released. His legs freed from iron shackles for the first time in years, Barney shuffles across the yard as though he were still chained. Clearly, Barney will never be able to shake off the 'prison waltz' and it will remain with him for the rest of his life.

Later, as Barney hitches a ride on an undertaker's wagon, he casually strikes a match on a coffin. Death no longer has much meaning. Indeed, as a convict remarks, completion of sentence apart, death is the only way out of there.

Despite a few relatively unimportant changes in status and motivation of some minor characters, the movie is substantially in accord with Robert E. Burns's book which was in its turn generally accurate. Perhaps not surprisingly, some of the author's understandable bitterness at his treatment spills over in the form of some unnecessary special pleading.

With Burns's story already generally familiar, thanks to his magazine articles and suc-

cessful book, the movie attracted big audiences and the fugitive gained a great deal of public sympathy. It all went down very badly, however, with state officials in Georgia who once more instigated attempts to have Burns extradited from New Jersey to complete his sentence. The New Jersey state governor ordered a special hearing at which Burns was represented by the nation's most famous lawyer, Clarence Darrow. The hearing revealed so many alarming facts about the chain gang system in Georgia that the state governor refused Georgia's extradition request. Other states joined New Jersey in condemning Georgia, which did nothing to help the paranoiac disapproval with which Burns was regarded in the South. Attempts to have Burns extradited continued for several more years and it was not until 1945, when the Georgia chain gang system was officially ended and 13 years after the movie's release, that his sentence was commuted by Governor Ellis Arnall to the time he had already served. A pardon was deemed impossible because he really had taken part in the original $6 robbery.

There is little doubt that the publicity Robert E. Burns received as a result of the movie was a significant factor in focusing public attention on an iniquitous system of punishment. This prompted an examination not just of his case but of the widespread use of chain gangs throughout the South where the prison service was still geared to using convict labour in much the same way as slaves had been used generations before on plantations. Nevertheless, the extent to which the movie really affected the prison system should not be overstated (as it often is); the fact that chain gangs were still used in Georgia, the state which received the most adverse publicity, for a further dozen years or so clearly shows that the prison service was not as sensitive to socially conscious movies as their makers and advocates might have hoped.

Also released in 1932, another chain gang movie, *Hell's Highway*, is rather more pointed in its delineation of the corruption that allowed convict labour to be used for private financial gain. Another important difference in *Hell's Highway* is in the character of its protagonist. Unlike the Robert E. Burns figure, Duke Ellis (played by Richard Dix) is a hardcore criminal who attracts no general sympathy for the fact that he is a convict but draws a response from audiences only because of the treatment he suffers at the hands of the prison authorities. Thus it is the treatment of offenders held within the system that is under attack, not the system itself.

When a contractor to whom convicts have been hired demands a 50 per cent uplift in their work rate, the guards use the lash and the sweatbox. Here the sweatbox is much worse than in *Sullivan's Travels*; feet bound and restrained by a leather collar, one man slowly strangles to death. In another scene, a deaf and dumb convict is shot because he does not hear an order.

Duke Ellis is given some redeeming features and prevents his young brother, also on the chain gang, from joining in a probably doomed

The funeral cart was the only sure way out for many chain gang prisoners in the Deep South. Richard Dix (second from l) doesn't think much of the odds of getting off Hell's Highway **(1932).**

escape attempt (the original ending had Ellis going to certain death).

Hell's Highway is commendably free from most stereotypes although there is one, Matthew the Hermit (Charles Middleton), a religious fanatic who provides a few moments of relief from the relentless grind. Unusually for its time, *Hell's Highway* has a substantial number of blacks in the cast, thus accurately conveying the probable racial mix on a Southern chain gang. One of the black cons (Clarence Muse) is allowed a line that underlines the authorities' attitude towards convicts, black or white, when a guard urges that a mule be removed from the burning sun: 'Mules cost a lot and convicts cost nothing.'

Understandably overshadowed by the much more famous movie, *Hell's Highway* may be an example of Hollywood's ability to cash in on issues in the public eye, but it also demonstrates how even a rather sloppily constructed film can generate interest in social problems when framed in the context of a prison movie.

Road Gang (1936) finds two youngsters on a chain gang but James Larabee and Bob Gordon (David Woods and Carlyle Moore Jr) have the kind of good luck only the movies can bring. A crusading newspaperman picks up their case and they are freed as he ably cleans up corruption among the authorities that permit exploitation of labour gangs.

Blackmail (1939) bears a striking resemblance to *I Am a Fugitive from a Chain Gang* in its tale of John Harrington (Edward G. Robinson), a man sentenced to a chain gang for a crime he did not commit. John escapes, changes his name to John R. Ingram, marries Helen (Ruth Hussey) and becomes a successful oil man. He is found by William Raney (Gene Lockhart) who admits to the original crime for which John was convicted and promises he will confess to the law, but only for a price. Raney's price is John's oil well but once the deed is transferred Raney tips the cops and John goes back to the gang. After being subjected to torture, John learns that his wife and son are now destitute. He escapes again, with help from Moose McCarthy (Guinn Williams), and fires the oil well to force a confession from Raney.

For all its lack of originality, *Blackmail* succeeded in keeping important issues before the public, as did a number of prison movies which bordered the area of the social problem film. Some of these adopted that perennially favourite storyline: an ordinary law-abiding citizen finds himself in prison through force of circumstance rather than as a result of his own deliberate criminal intent.

One form of this tale which was strong enough to withstand several remakes (and heaven knows how many variations on the theme) tells of a man who kills another in self-defence, goes to prison and there finds himself hardened by his surroundings, itself another form of self-defence, and as a result becomes involved in another killing.

A subtle variation examines the effects of wrongful imprisonment upon a man who is not an ordinary law-abiding citizen but is a real criminal who just happens, for once, to be innocent of the crime of which he is accused. This variation was taken to its bleak limits in *You Only Live Once* (1937), a grim tale of a three-time loser, Eddie Taylor (played by Henry Fonda), who is suspected of complicity in a crime simply because he has already served three terms in prison for crimes he really did commit. The irony of Eddie's latest brush with the law is that he is entirely innocent and is the victim of a mistaken eye-witness. Once the machinery of the law lurches into motion, however, no one questions the accuracy of the identification. Eddie was guilty before, therefore he must be guilty again if only to sustain the ordinary citizen's stereotypical belief in the impossibility of rehabilitating hardened criminals.

You Only Live Once benefits from director Fritz Lang's alien viewpoint. As he did in several major works in his native Germany and later during the flowering of Hollywood's *film noir*, Lang stands aside from the prevailing view of society, observing with detachment the inept and bigoted manner in which men handle their lives and the lives of others. As he follows the vain attempts of Eddie and his wife, Joan (Sylvia Sidney), to rebuild their shattered lives,

Lang never quite allows runaway cynicism to overstate his case. Instead he points to all the human prejudices that trap the ex-con in a cage from which he can never escape, a prison far worse than any in which he has previously done time.

Eddie's story ends without any of the upbeat moralizing which characterized many Hollywood movies of its time. On the run from police and citizens who are implacably intent on sending him back to prison, Eddie refuses to believe the ineffectual priest who comes to tell him he has been pardoned. In a panic Eddie fires his gun and kills the priest. Society finally has Eddie where it wants him, where it has, all along, believed he truly belongs. As the police close in on Eddie and his wife, who has insisted on staying with him in his futile attempt to escape the inevitable, society – the movie's audience – sees the scene through the cross-sight of the police gun that will end the lives of the persecuted couple. The implication is unmistakable; it isn't some faceless servant of society who kills Eddie Taylor, it is us.

A much less hopeless view of the plight of the ex-convict is taken in two films made two years after *You Only Live Once*, both of which star John Garfield, a solidly proletarian actor with whom blue-collar audiences could readily identify. Indeed, as a youth, Garfield had a few brushes with authority and spent some time at a special school for problem children.

In *They Made Me a Criminal* (1939) Garfield plays the role of Johnny Bradfield, a boxer with no illusions about the corruption of the fight game and of the society in which he moves. Airily concocting an imaginary idyllic home life for the benefit of the press, Johnny rides high as a popular champion. But when his manager kills a reporter who threatens to expose the reality of Johnny's life – which revolves around women and booze – the boxer's fragile world falls apart. On the run for the crime, he takes refuge at a rehabilitation centre for juvenile delinquents. Learning that the centre is having to close through lack of funds, Johnny arranges to fight at a local arena even though this will reveal his true identity to a pursuing cop.

Unlike the ending of Eddie Taylor's life, Johnny Bradfield's ends happily, if highly improbably, when the cop lets him go having seen how the juveniles are becoming less delinquent through the boxer's example and the local (and, of course, beautiful) social worker is also on his side.

The second of the two John Garfield movies, *Dust Be My Destiny* (1939), also has an improbable ending but reaches it by a route Eddie Taylor would have recognized and envied. Just out of prison, although apparently innocent, Garfield's character, Joe Bell, is arrested for vagrancy while looking for work. Sentenced to three months at a convict labour camp, Joe is soon in conflict with the warden whose antagonism stems from his belief that the lower social orders are morally inferior. The warden's sudden death, although accidental, panics Joe and he escapes. Just as Eddie Taylor's wife stood by her man so Joe's girlfriend, Mabel (Priscilla Lane), remains faithful to him. Eventually, however, convinced that Joe will have a fair hearing only if he will surrender to the police, Mabel informs on her lover. Earlier hints of class consciousness are now made clear as the prosecution bases its case on Joe's position on the social ladder but the jury, representing ordinary men and, by implication, the movie's audience, rally round and find him innocent. The movie's belief in the jury adopting a 'there but for the grace of God go I' view of the case is naïvely touching but probably warmed the hearts of the audiences as they spilled out onto the streets when the movie was over. Just how they behaved when they were next in a jury room is anybody's guess.

A book by Lewis E. Lawes, warden of Sing Sing, formed the basis for *Invisible Stripes* (1939), a movie that stars George Raft and Humphrey Bogart as a pair of ex-cons. Raft plays Cliff Taylor whose younger brother, Tim (William Holden), is already on the downward path Cliff has followed to its bitter end. Despite his own problems, Cliff, who is trying to go straight, decides to give his brother practical help in the shape of money with which to start a new life. Unfortunately, the only way Cliff can

get his hands on cash is to return to crime which he does by joining up with his old cellmate Chuck Martin (Bogart), an active and seemingly successful small-time crook. When Tim is suspected of crimes his brother has committed on his behalf the movie's makers have Cliff do the right thing – by Hays Office standards – and go down fighting in a barrage of bullets which also leaves Chuck Martin dead. Unsatisfactory though the movie is in most respects, it does at least start out with the right intentions by squarely stating the problems facing former prisoners trying to get along in a society that adopts certain presumptions about them.

James Cagney wasn't left out of this kind of reforming zealotry. In *Each Dawn I Die* (1939) he plays Frank Ross, a reporter who is railroaded for trying to blow open the rackets that are strangling his city. Once in the joint Frank quickly develops into a hardened con under the tutelage of Hood Stacey (George Raft) whom he helps escape during a court hearing. Double-crossed and left behind, Frank plots a massive jail break but backs out. He is saved by the intervention of Stacey who, dying, convinces the man who originally framed Frank to admit the truth.

1939 also saw MGM's 'Crime Does Not Pay' series, which included *They All Come Out*, which details the efforts of the Federal Bureau of Prisons to rehabilitate convicts. A straightforward documentary-style account, the film features the stereotypical hard nut Clyde Morgan (Bernard Nedell) and the young, malleable first-timer Joe Cameron (Tom Neal) who plays ball with the system. Shot in various state prisons, including Atlanta and Alcatraz, the movie's main interest lies in the fact that it is the first directorial effort of Jacques Tourneur who later became a major *film noir* stylist.

A different kind of social conscience is evident in *The Defiant Ones* (1958), an early example of the string of equal rights movies that Hollywood made as blacks slowly ceased to be death at the box-office. Unlike so many of these movies, which sprinkled naive liberalism around as though it were the answer to all ills, *The Defiant Ones* is not merely worthily well-

meaning but was also well made and, for its day, has been well thought out. If society's prejudices do not come under scrutiny as closely as latterday civil rights advocates would like, it was ahead of its time.

The film stars Tony Curtis and Sidney Poitier as two convicts, John 'Joker' Jackson and Noah Cullen, whose escape from a prison truck in the Deep South is clearly foredoomed. Not only are the two convicts chained together but they hate one another; Curtis hates Poitier because he is black, and is hated in return because of that unreasoning hate. Thus prejudice has already started its work by creating further prejudice. With this in mind, the guards are not unduly worried about the prisoners' escape. One casually sums up their situation 'They'll kill each other before they can get fifty miles.'

But the mutual jeopardy of the two convicts begins to have an effect as they struggle to escape from a slippery-sided clay pit. When Cullen almost drowns as they cross a river in flood, Jackson saves him, observing, 'I didn't pull you out. I just stopped you pulling me in.' Robbing a country store, they are found and almost lynched by the townspeople but Big Sam (Lon Chaney Jr), an ex-con himself, frees them. All this mutual jeopardy doesn't stop the two from scrapping with one another, until one of their fights is halted when they find themselves under the gun of a small boy.

The Kid (Keith Coughlin) takes them home, a lonely farm, where his mother, a young widow (Cara Williams), helps them break the chain which has thus far bound them to one another. They prepare to go their separate ways; the widow gives Noah directions that will lead him to certain death in a nearby swamp but when Joker learns of this he finds that despite the breaking of the literal bond there are still more powerful bonds which he cannot sever. He saves Noah but is shot by the Kid. Eventually reaching a railway line, the black convict scrambles aboard a train but his wounded white companion cannot make it. Noah jumps

Paul Winfield's imprisonment in Sounder **(1972) could have been the end for his impoverished family but his young son, Kevin Hooks, helps pull them through.**

from the train and the movie ends as he comforts his friend as the police close in.

Although the ending, especially the singing by Poitier of an old song about an escaped prisoner, 'Long Gone', does not go down well in today's more cynical atmosphere surrounding race relations this momentary weakness is carried by the strengths of what has gone before.

The mirrored sunglasses of the guard symbolize the anonymously implacable face of authority in Cool Hand Luke **(1967). Morgan Woodward (l) takes aim while Paul Newman and George Kennedy (r) look on helplessly.**

The plight of poor black Americans is movingly portrayed in *Sounder* (1972) which also touches upon the calamitous effect prison can have upon the family of a convicted man. Here, Nathan Lee Morgan (Paul Winfield) is put away for stealing food for his family and while he serves his year's hard labour, during which he is is injured and thus faces even bleaker times ahead, his young son, David (Kevin Hooks), grows up quickly. The fortitude with which Nathan's wife, Rebecca (Cicely Tyson), confronts the cards life has dealt betrays no flicker of resentment although, heaven knows, the kind of woman she represents had more than enough cause.

Prison farm chain gangs also feature in *Cool Hand Luke* (1967), a movie which did not set out to heighten the nation's conscience but followed a longstanding tradition of showing how

a man can redeem himself by drawing upon his own inner resources. Here, redemption for Luke Jackson (Paul Newman) develops out of his gutsy determination not to submit his will to any man's whether such stubbornness leads to his suffering a fearsome beating in a fight with a much stronger fellow con or even to his death.

Luke's refusal to conform earns him fierce retribution from the guards headed by the chillingly sadistic captain (Strother Martin). Luke's sheer cussedness eventually wins him the admiration of fellow con Dragline (George Kennedy) with whom he fights a bloody battle. Despite being beaten by a much stronger man, Luke simply will not lie down and this helps move him into top-John position, a role enhanced in the eyes of the other cons when he wins a bet to eat 50 hard-boiled eggs.

When Luke's mother, Arietta (Jo Van Fleet), visits him she is too weak to climb from the back of a truck and her later death spins him into a frenzy. Chained up and subjected to a 'break him' campaign, Luke eventually begs for mercy but the shattering of the other cons' illusions is only temporary. He escapes with Dragline but his companion tips the guards, partly to save Luke from his hell-bent course towards self-destruction, and partly to gain clemency for himself. Dragline fails, and Luke, whose crime was stealing the coin-filled tops of parking meters, is shot to death.

Based upon the novel by Donn Pearce, who served time on a prison camp for safe-cracking, *Cool Hand Luke* depicts a foredoomed life that provides an uplifting message for the central character's fellow inmates and, perhaps, to the wider audience, although Luke's obsessive rebelliousness seems a touch out of place when set in the context of his sentence – he's only there for two years.

This wilful determination to do 'hard time' makes Luke the kind of stereotypical self-destructive rebel the movies know very well and used often in prison dramas. The fact that they are much less thick on the ground in real life acts as no deterrent to their continuing appearance on the screen.

Rebellion of a sporting kind has made an appearance in a number of prison movies in both America and Britain in which an implied curative quality is granted such diverse sports as running, American football and boxing.

In *The Loneliness of the Long Distance Runner* (1962) the protagonist, Colin Smith (Tom Courtenay), is a rebellious youth whose attitude towards society has resulted in his ending up in a Borstal institution. The governor of the Borstal (Michael Redgrave) belongs to the social class that believes in the mysteriously curative value of sports and cold showers. When Smith shows an aptitude for long-distance running ('we had plenty of practice in running away from the police in my family') the governor encourages him to develop his gifts. Using a forthcoming contest between the Borstal and a local public school (in England, unlike America, this term denotes a private school out of the reach of the working classes) as the focal point of his reforming zeal, the governor hopes for victory but Smith has other ideas.

Up to this point Smith has been a model prisoner; not because he is being rehabilitated, as the governor thinks, but because it makes life easier. However, the class divide has scarred him and although he arrives at the finishing line far in front of the other competitors, Smith stops short of the tape. He stands, staring at the governor, as his rivals cross the line ahead of him.

Smith's continued rebellion demonstrates his awareness of something the governor will never understand: in real life the boys from the public school will always be first across the line. In real life it is class which counts; skill and ability have nothing to do with success.

In *The Loneliness of the Long Distance Runner*, which is based upon an Alan Sillitoe story, the transient freedom of running was a metaphor. Too good to be used only once.

In *The Jericho Mile* (1979) a gifted athlete, Rain Murphy (Peter Strauss), is serving a life sentence and occupies his time steadily improving his performance on a track inside the walls of Folsom prison. Through his friendship with a black inmate, R. C. Stiles (Richard Lawson), Murphy alienates other white prisoners including drugs baron Dr D (Brian

Dennehy) and only the blacks and chicanos will help when the coach from a nearby university wants a better track built for this potential world beater to train on. Like Colin Smith, Rain Murphy is a rebel and although he eventually achieves an Olympic qualifying time he passes up the chance to go to the Games knowing that the appearane of freedom this will offer is illusory. At the end of the Olympics, win or lose, he will go back to prison. The symbolism of the title is ironic; it will take more than a fanfare of sporting trumpets to blow down these walls.

Shot inside a real prison under the direction of Michael Mann and with inmates as extras and appearing in several minor speaking parts (and being paid the going Screen Actors' Guild rates), *The Jericho Mile* has a raw vitality and powerful verisimilitude in many areas, not least in its crackling dialogue, which in turn baffled audiences and gave them a new form of slang to use in real life. An example of the former is the answer given by Rain Murphy when he is asked where his friend Stiles is: 'Transferred down from cue. Some sucker tried to turn him out. Stiles waffed 'em.'

The best known example of the new slang that found its way into common usage after the release of *The Jericho Mile* is 'Stop goin' up in my face' and its countless derivatives which have found their way into TV commercials and, that ultimate accolade of contemporary literature, the car bumper sticker.

The Longest Yard (1974, released in Britain as *The Mean Machine*) ably uses the potential for violence in American football. Paul Crewe (Burt Reynolds), a former top-ranking football player, has fallen out with his ex-wife and is sent to jail for stealing her car. The prison warden, Rudolph Hazen (played by Eddie Albert), pressurizes Crewe into forming a team from among the inmates to give the guard's squad someone to play against. The prisoners' team, known by the cons as The Mean Machine, are a tough lot and well aware of the way they can turn the forthcoming football game into an occasion for getting in a few blows against the system. But Crewe has been offered a parole by Warden Hazen if the guards' team wins the national

He may be Boss of the Mean Machine but he's still a con. Burt Reynolds in The Longest Yard **(1974).**

semi-pro championships. Crewe is in a dilemma; if his team loses the guards will rub it in, if his team wins the warden will make life miserable.

With the guards fielding a brutal exponent of the worst the game can offer, the prisoners take a beating. Crewe's team-mates realize that he has been looking out for number one but then, as the football field takes on the appearance of the aftermath of a small war with bruised and broken bodies everywhere, Crewe, like Colin Smith and Rain Murphy, accepts the reality of his place in society. Whether the warden's team wins or loses, the parole he has been offered is not guaranteed. It is not his due but rests entirely on the whim of the warden. Like the protagonists of those other movies, Crewe turns his back on the warden's promises and joins his team-mates in beating, and beating-up, the guards.

Shot in Georgia state prison and with real life prison warden Joe S. Hopper as technical adviser, *The Longest Yard* managed to bridge the awkward gap between sports and prison.

Less successful have been a number of movies which have tried to link prison with boxing, even though the one-on-one confrontation of the square ring seems more appropriate than the freer ranging escapism of team sports.

Prison Shadows (1932) tells the tale of Eddie Nugent (Gene Harris), a boxer who comes out of the joint after serving three years of a five-stretch for manslaughter in the ring. He kills again but then discovers that he is an unwitting pawn of a gambling ring who are administering an untraceable drug to his opponents. (Now there's a plot Charlie Chan could have got his teeth into.)

Among the movies that have more recently taken the rocky road of boxing is *Penitentiary* (1979), set in a prison housing mostly black inmates. Nothing that happens on-screen bears much relation to real life and barely gets away with being defined as entertainment although the movie does have an engaging if occasionally repellent dynamism. Sent down in *Penitentiary* is Too Sweet (Leon Isaac Kennedy) who stamps his potential upon the prison scene by beating up his animalistic cellmate in self defence against homosexual rape. Sent on his way by this encounter, Too Sweet sees boxing as a means of rehabilitation and early parole.

The simplistic nature of the movie did not inhibit its remarkable success (mostly in the video market) which led to sequels entitled (you've guessed it) *Penitentiary II* and *Penitentiary III*, the last named also sprouting, heaven help us, a record album.

Rehabilitation in these movies bears no signs of being afflicted by anything altruistic and it is hard to believe that they come from the same

Kristoffer Tabori about to take a flier from the third level; a sure but lethal way out of The Glasshouse **(1972).**

industry that irregularly does its damnedest to demonstrate a measure of awareness and social conscience.

The same criticism cannot be levelled at *The Glasshouse* (1972) which was also shot inside a real state prison, this time in Utah and with not a sportsman in sight. This is another occasion when prisoners were used as actors and in an advisory capacity, adding flavour to the dialogue and on one occasion showing how a 'real' knife fight would take place after disapprovingly watching the shooting of the movie makers' version. The 'real' fight is the one seen in the movie.

The main concern of *The Glasshouse* is the corruption possible within prisons and how it can affect everyone, whichever side of the bars they are on.

The storyline follows the induction into prison life of three new arrivals, two prisoners and a guard. The prisoners are Allan Campbell (Kristoffer Tabori), a young man terrified of what lies ahead of him, and Jonathan Paige (Alan Alda), a college professor convicted of manslaughter for killing a motorist who killed his wife (and is thus rather obviously the man which whom the audience is supposed to identify). The new guard is Brian Courtland (Clu Gulager), fresh out of the Marines and eagerly looking forward to a socially useful career. None of the new arrivals is prepared for what greets him in the prison which is controlled as if it were his own personal fiefdom by top con Hugo Slocum (Vic Morrow). Slocum's control is aided by corrupt officers like Brown (Roy Jenson) and is unhampered by the disinterest of Warden Auerbach (Dean Jagger).

Both new prisoners fall foul of Slocum. Paige is given a job in the prison pharmacy replacing one of Slocum's men who has used his post as a means of supplying Slocum with drugs; Campbell is approached by Slocum who wants him as his sexual partner but he rejects the con's advances. Officer Courtland knows that trouble is brewing but the warden ignores his reports. After Allan is gang-raped he takes a fatal flier from the third floor landing. A con under sentence of death by Slocum gives Paige a book containing evidence against the villainous con but when the former college professor tries to hide he is trapped in the pharmacy by Slocum's men. Handed a home-made gun by Lennox Beach (Billy Dee Wiliams), the leader of the black cons, Paige shoots Slocum then runs through a door only to be shot down by Officer Courtland who takes the book intent on telling the truth to the outside world. The warden doesn't agree; as far as he is concerned, the matter is closed.

Wisely, given such a complex situation as exists in this fictitious prison (the screenplay is based upon a story by Truman Capote and

Wyatt Cooper) and which in many respects replicates the complexity of real prison life, the movie offers no hint that the problems will be resolved or that solutions are possible in a growingly impossible prison climate. The makers of this movie are wise enough to know that theirs is not the task of making things right and that happy or up-beat endings serve no purpose other than to send audiences home in the belief that social problems will reach a satisfactory conclusion if left alone or to the 'experts'. No one in the audience of *The Glasshouse* is expected to accept the validity of Warden Auerbach's statement, 'I'm not in love with this system, but it's the only one we've got, and it's better than no system at all.'

In 1967 Thomas O. Murton, a real life prison officer who was definitely not in love with the system, was appointed by Governor Winthrop Rockefeller as superintendent of Arkansas State prison with instructions to clean up the corrupt prison farm system. Among such practices as the use of convict labour gangs for private gain, by hiring them out to local farmers, Murton also discovered the iniquitous use of the 'Tucker telephone' – an old-fashioned crank telephone complete with battery which was used to send electric shocks through a prisoner's genitals. He also investigated rumours that at one farm more than 200 convicts had died and were buried in fields all across the surrounding countryside.

Without waiting for such niceties as an official authorization, Murton ordered certain fields to be dug up and promptly unearthed three headless skeletons. At this point Governor Rockefeller relieved the assidous investigator of his duties, later claiming that he did so because his objective – the stirring up of the system – had been achieved. Not surprisingly, the governor's sanguine view was not widely regarded as having much validity.

Murton's story appeared in a book co-written with Joe Hyams and eventually became the basis of *Brubaker* (1980), a movie on which he was technical adviser. In *Brubaker* a new prisoner, 'Stan Collins' (Robert Redford), arrives at Wakefield Prison Farm. Even before the bus

Robert Redford will need more than a brush if he's to make the sweeping changes needed to root out the corruption running rife in Brubaker **(1980).**

carrying 'Collins' and other new prisoners arrives at the farm they see a badly wounded con who has been shot by an armed trusty, but worse awaits them. For two weeks 'Collins' endures squalid living conditions, inadequate and barely edible food, he observes trusties using electric shock treatment on other inmates to say nothing of witnessing frequent beatings with leather straps. Medicines and medical services are sold, homosexual assaults are rife, convicts are hired out to the local business community. 'Collins' also sees the Hole, a series of

cells so small that anyone placed in them must remain upright and where men are isolated for months at a time. It is at this point that 'Collins' decides he has seen enough and reveals his real identity: he is Henry Brubaker, the new warden of Wakefield Prison.

Brubaker succeeds in ending the misuse of medical resources and he also improves the inmates' food after uncovering the systematic theft of supplies which are being sold to local storekeepers. But his hopes of cleaning up the prison soon meet with stiff opposition. The crunch comes when Abraham (Richard Ward), an old man who should have been released long ago, tells Brubaker about bodies buried in the fields. Abraham is killed by the trusties who see their days of power fading. Brubaker uncovers four bodies but now loses the support of Governor Deach (Murray Hamilton), who appointed him, and encounters the active opposition of state Senator Hite (John McMartin). The well-meaning co-operation of the Governor's aide, Lillian Grey (Jane Alexander), doesn't help Brubaker very much in his stand against higher officials who want him to compromise, a stand which he refuses to temper even though he knows it will lead in the end to his dismissal.

Although obviously well-meaning, the movie fails to convince in its portrayal of a man whose eyes are so set on an ultimate goal that he misses most of what is happening around every corner. For example, Brubaker makes no apparent attempt to counter the rampant homosexuality which is shown at the beginning but then vanishes from the screen; the only benefit he grants to the prisoners in the Hole is that once a day they will be allowed out for one hour. Not exactly a great step forward for humanity. On the other hand, his refusal to punish the trusties is more in keeping with a man of strong liberal inclinations; he is aware that if he puts them back into the prison community they will surely suffer at the hands of the men they have been tyrannizing.

For all its commendable moral outrage *Brubaker* lacks conviction and does insufficient justice to Thomas Murton whose real life struggles to root out corruption in Arkansas in 1967 meant that even by the time this movie was made he was still unable to land a job in the prison service.

A measure of the problems Murton was up against emerged in 1971 at the 101st Congress of the American Correctional Association. Delegates were invited to vote for an official investigation into the rumours of wholesale deaths in Arkansas. Walter Dunbar, the Chairman of the Association's Resolutions Committee, stated that this was a matter for the police and not for prison officers and urged delegates to deliver a 'no-vote'. After some behind-the-scenes haggling the motion was debated but was defeated.

A few weeks later Chairman Dunbar appeared at a press conference during the riot at Attica prison in New York state where he gave details of the deaths and mutilation of guards, thus clearing the way for the subsequent Attica bloodbath. In fact, there had been no deaths, no mutilation; Walter Dunbar, it seems, was as sparing with the truth in New York as he was anxious to avoid inquiries into corruption and mass murder in Arkansas.

The story of Thomas Murton which prompted the making of *Brubaker*, like the story of Robert E. Burns which was the inspiration behind *I Am a Fugitive from a Chain Gang*, are two socially conscious examples of numerous prison movies that took true stories as the basis for their screenplays.

Sometimes these other true life tales also had social consciences, other times movie-makers used them because they saw them as a way to exploit the public's apparently insatiable desire for vicarious suffering. Sometimes true stories were brought to the screen simply because they contained all the ingredients for an exciting and entertaining movie. The way of the movie-making world being what it is, this last group, of morally bankrupt tales, was frequently the source of the best movies.

3

Factual Fiction: True Prison Movies

'If we cannot live as people, we will at least
try to die like men.'
(unnamed Attica inmate)

Some prison movies based on true stories, and which also displayed a social conscience, took their impulse from the nature of the case. They might, perhaps, contain a plea for improved conditions, maybe a demand for a change in the methods of the justice department, occasionally they highlighted the potential for irreversible miscarriages of justice inherent in a system that condoned capital punishment. Often, it is hard to avoid the assumption that a true life story was used simply to give movie audiences an added thrill. The knowledge that this was a tale which had really happened to a fellow citizen could enhance a movie's box-office potential.

The manner in which many Americans on the outside personalized the plight of a character imprisoned in a movie is easy to understand. Statistics published in the early 1970s revealed that 1 in every 370 adults in America was in either a state or federal prison, a city or county jail. Even if due acknowledgement is made to the fact that this included people awaiting trial, the figures are still alarming. Another 1970s statistic, from the President's Crime Commission Survey of 10,000 households, concluded that 91 per cent of the people interviewed had committed crimes punishable by imprisonment but which were as yet unde-

tected by law enforcement agencies. With figures like these many outwardly law-abiding citizens nervously considered the odds against their own chances of going to jail. Joe Public was also understandably wary of falling foul of a system which, if the movies are to be believed, is as careless and indifferent towards ordinary members of the public as it is towards criminals.

Real life tales, of course, have one strike against them in Holywood. Acting against the intentions of film-makers who drew their inspiration from biographical accounts or newspaper reports was the film community's general inability to tell a true story without a great deal of inaccurate embroidery. It is justifiable to paint a true story with a thin layer of fictionalization in order to improve its dramatic structure, but there is no excuse for the frequent appearance of movies so changed from reality as to make one wonder why they pretended to be true stories – unless, perish the thought, the makers of the movies concerned were motivated by just plain greed.

Although most of the true prison stories that became movies were contemporary, or at least took place in the recent past, one frightening account of State persecution took movie-goers back to the nineteenth century and a black moment in American history.

On 14 April 1865 the President of the United States, Abraham Lincoln, accompanied by his wife and two younger acquaintance, attended a performance of *Our American Cousin* at Ford's Theatre in Washington, D. C. Although the war between the states was nearing its close there was still tension in the capital (after all, Washington is in the South) and the President asked the War Department to provide his party with a guard. Strange though it may seem to us in these days of armour-plated limousines and squads of heavily-armed presidential minders, the request was refused and the only person standing between the President and anyone who might wish him harm was a local police officer who, after the play began, left the theatre to bend a convivial elbow in a nearby bar.

Later that evening, with the performance still in progress, John Wilkes Booth, a member of a noted family of actors, who as a youngster had whiled away dull afternoons shooting dogs and cats, entered the President's box and shot him in the head.

The actor, who had been drinking heavily, then leapt from the President's box to the stage and in so doing fractured his left leg. Despite this injury there was so much confusion that Booth managed to escape into the street, mounted his horse and galloped to a rendez-vous with a comrade who had failed to carry out the intended simultaneous assassination of Secretary of State William Seward. The two fugitives called at the home of a certain Dr Samuel Mudd who set the injured actor's leg. Twelve days later Booth and his companion, David Herold, were cornered in a barn; Herold surrendered but Booth was shot and fatally wounded.

Between early May and the end of June, seven 'conspirators', including Herold and Dr Mudd, were arraigned in a show trial. Herold and three of his co-defendants, one of them a woman, were sentenced to death and were hanged on 7 July. One man was sentenced to six years imprisonment, three received life sentences. A seventh man, husband of the hanged woman, fled the country before he could be arrested. (He was brought back two years later by which time passions had cooled and he was freed when the jury failed to agree their verdict.)

One of the three men given life sentences was Samuel Mudd. The 'evidence' against Mudd was non-existent. There was no reason for the assassins to expect they would need a doctor and if, as Mudd claimed, he was not a conspirator then he could not even be accused of aiding a criminal because, at the time, he did not know that the President had been shot. Mudd's standing in his community was above reproach and he was a dedicated and caring physician. As for his stance on the burning political issues of the day, even the most casual investigation would have revealed that upon secession he had freed the slaves on his plantation and could therefore have scarce grounds for complaint at President Lincoln's intentions for the nation.

However, few are so deaf and blind as a panicky establishment in hot pursuit of a scapegoat. The doctor's record was disregarded and he soon found that he had become one of the most hated men in the country. But Samuel Mudd had more to worry about than the fact that his family's name would become the origin of a derisive phrase which eventually evolved into the misspelled, 'Your name is mud'. A more pressing concern to him was the fact that his life sentence was to be served at one of the country's most notorious prisons, Dry Tortugas.

In 1846 the military had built a fort on a tiny coral isle off the south-west coast of Florida in the Gulf of Mexico. When the fort was ready for action it was discovered that the surrounding water was so shallow no enemy ship could come within range of the fort's guns. So, Fort Jefferson became a prison, taking its popular (or, rather, very unpopular) name from the little island on which it stood. Unfortunately for the prisoners and for the guards and their families, the island was a breeding ground for mosquitoes. At the time medical science had yet to associate the mosquito with disease and the repeated bouts of yellow fever which swept the prison community were regarded as an unrelated problem. The severity of conditions on Dry Tortugas was such that only prisoners the government felt deserved particularly harsh treatment were sent there.

When Samuel Mudd arrived at Dry Tortugas he found that if the local conditions and the habitual brutality of the guards were not bad enough, he had been singled out as a man who deserved even worse treatment than any common murderer.

Just how many years Samuel Mudd might have served on Dry Tortugas is a matter for speculation because the appalling conditions proved to be his salvation. A particularly virulent outbreak of yellow fever swept through the prison, felling prisoners and guards alike. As the death rate climbed it soon became apparent that only one man stood between the isolated community and total extinction; that man was Dr Mudd.

Samuel Mudd's work in saving lives with selfless dedication eventually came to the ears of the public and in 1869 he was pardoned. With public attention now focused on the assassination's aftermath the other surviving victims of the administration's rush to hysterical judgement also received pardons.

The first film version of Dr Mudd's story came in 1936 with *The Prisoner of Shark Island*, written by Nunnally Johnson, directed by John Ford, and starring Warner Baxter as the doctor. The story is told with a powerful sense of indignation even if the doctor's nobility is unnecessarily highlighted by making almost everyone else in the movie an intellectual and moral midget. By present day standards there is also an uncomfortable use of racial and social stereotypes. The manner in which the white characters, particularly Samuel Mudd, speak to blacks can be seen as an indication of how little about race relations even the more liberal of 1930s Hollywood residents understood. Of course, another eminently reasonable view is that this represented a measure of verisimilitude as even an 'enlightened' Southerner like Samuel Mudd would still have regarded blacks as his inferiors. After all, even Abraham Lincoln was

not especially concerned with stamping out racism and abolishing slavery, but directed his energies, via these means, to holding together a nation that was in danger of fragmentation. Nevertheless, when seen today, the implicit racism in much of the movie's dialogue diminishes what is otherwise an impassioned plea for justice.

For all its imperfections, however, the movie has great authority and its indignation at least has the merit of appearing to be righteous. There are many impressive moments, among them Samuel Mudd's plea to his judges:

> And till the day you die, ask yourselves in your heart three questions: Does an assassin confide his plans to anyone? Was I, a physician, in the plot because it was part of John Wilkes Booth's plan to break his leg and need me? Does a man whose first devotion is no longer to a lost cause, or to any flag that flies, but to his wife and child, risk any act that could only bring misery and heartbreak on their innocent lives? In the sight of the holy God I worship, I am innocent.

When the story of Samuel Mudd was retold in 1980 in *The Ordeal of Dr Mudd* the racism that damaged the earlier version was removed. The doctor was also changed from being the epitome of white Southern aristocracy (which the real man was) to a down-to-earth, hard-working, small-town physician. Dennis Weaver was well-suited to the role of this more bourgeois character but the deliberately middle-of-the-road liberal stance the movie adopts causes it to fall behind the emphatic stature of the earlier version.

A 1952 western, *Hellgate*, took as its basis the broad principles of Dr Mudd's tale but removed the assassination connection, settling instead for the less inflammatory crime (because hardly anyone knows what it means) of sedition.

Another island that featured in American prison history is Blackwell's Island, which briefly housed Edward Z. C. Judson when he fell foul of the law during the 1849 riots in New York. Judson, better known by his pen-name, Ned Buntline, wrote an account of his days in prison but the book had none of the impact of his later tales of derring-do featuring Buffalo Bill Cody, which made an international star of this previously obscure plainsman, to say nothing of making the author rich and famous.

Blackwell's Island was in the news again in 1914 when 700 inmates rioted, demanding the release from solitary confinement of 40 of their comrades. By the 1930s the prison was a hotbed of corruption involving local politicians, many of whom were taking kickbacks from prison officials and inmates who ran the place as though it were their own.

It is this tale which runs raggedly through *Blackwell's Island* (1939), which stars John Garfield as Tim Hayden, one of Hollywood's typically fearless newspaper reporters. Hayden contrives to be sentenced to the prison in order to discover at first hand the facts that will expose the ringleaders. While there, Hayden is almost killed by a gangster whose imprisonment resulted from an earlier investigation by the journalist.

On the island, the gang lord, Bull Branson (Stanley Fields), controls the prison from his cell, running a gambling joint and doling out favours, good jobs, and edible food only to those who can pay for such little luxuries.

Once Hayden has amassed enough evidence he escapes (amazing, isn't it, how easily Hollywood's newspapermen can get out of prison at the drop of a typewriter?) and tells his story to the district attorney, who organizes a raid on the island. This part, at least, has a ring of authenticity as it parallels the raid led on the real prison by DA Austin MacCormick in 1934. The rest of the movie neither rings true nor is especially well made, suffering as it does from the studio's discovery part way through filming that in Garfield they had a new star on their

Complaints about the food are the least of the problems for inmates in the corruption-ridden prison on Blackwell's Island **(1939).**

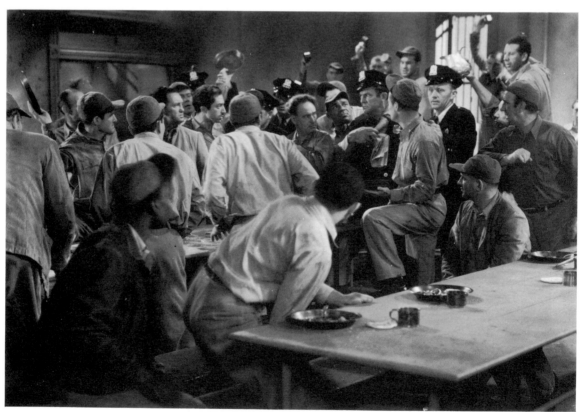

hands. The movie was hastily rewritten as they went along to build up Garfield's part and their haste shows in the movie's awkward pacing and style, although the actor's rugged honesty shines through.

Much stronger in its construction is *Unchained* (1955), which traces the attempts by Kenyon J. Scudder to establish an open prison system on a 2,600 acre site at Chino in California. The movie, which was shot on location at Chino, benefits from intelligent writing by producer-director Hall Bartlett (based upon Scudder's book, *Prisoners Are People*) and strong playing of the two central roles: Elroy Hirsch as Steve Davitt, an impulsive and murderously inclined young prisoner transferred from San Quentin, and Todd Duncan as Bill Howard, an old lag determined to give the new ideas a chance. The main thrust of the story, which fictionalizes real incidents from Scudder's case histories, is the gradual reformation of Steve. He succumbs to the benefits of the open system and is eventually prepared to serve out his time secure in the knowledge that his wife, Mary (Barbara Hale), will be waiting for him when he gets out. The appearance of Chester Morris as Scudder introduces an interesting iconographic reference, for his role in *Unchained* is quite different to that in *The Big House* back in 1930.

Open prisons such as that at Chino were not designed for the hardcore criminal, or for those that the system regarded as incorrigible, and the story of a prisoner held in Folsom and San Quentin many years before Kenyon Scudder experimented with open prisons at Chino seems to have escaped the attention of moviemakers. Towards the end of the nineteenth century Ed Morrell became, at 20, the youngest member of the California Outlaws, a band formed for the sole purpose of robbing the Southern Pacific Railroad, a company which itself robbed, swindled and killed anyone who stood in its way.

Morrell became a double agent and was urged by the SPR to participate in the killing of a captured Outlaw. Instead, he helped his comrade escape and for this was sent to Folsom prison in 1891 for life with hard labour. Bad as

such a sentence would have been anywhere, it was particularly unfortunate that he should be incarcerated at Folsom which was then little more than the railroad's private prison. But Morrell was a hard man and he stoically withstood both the hard labour and the brutal punishments. Among his mistreatments were the 'lime cell' and time spent on the 'derrick'. These punishments were meted out for little or no reason. There was to be no relief when Morrell was eventually transferred to San Quentin. Here he was subjected to the 'San Quentin overcoat', on one occasion for four and a half days. Eventually placed in solitary, in the infamous San Quentin dungeon, Morrell displayed his unbroken spirit when, together with another occupant of the dungeon, Jake Oppenheimer, he developed the means of communicating by rapping on the wall of his cell with his fist. This coded 'knuckle talk' eventually became a method of communicating in prisons throughout the world, and features in just about every prison movie ever made.

Following the efforts of reforming wardens at San Quentin, Morrell was released in 1908 whereafter his autobiography and work for prison reform made him a national hero.

A San Quentin inmate who didn't get out but did become the subject of a movie was Erwin Walker. In the movie *He Walked By Night* (1948), the killer of a highway patrolman is hunted down by the police and killed attempting to evade arrest. In real life, and in real death, things were a little different. Walker was captured, tried and sentenced to death for the murder. When he went to the gas chamber the movie was playing at cinemas just down the road from San Quentin.

More amenable to rehabilitation than Erwin Walker was John Resko who was sent to prison in 1931 for the killing of a storekeeper. While inside, Resko took up painting and thus escaped into a world he had never imagined possible while 'free' on the outside. *Convicts Four* (1962) traces the story of Resko (Ben Gazzara) as he lives through the regime of a tough warden of the old school (Broderick Crawford) and into the enlightened days of a new regime under a principal keeper (Stuart Whitman) who seeks to rehabilitate the men in his care.

Among real life prisoners who have found their way onto the screen thanks to their escapes are the Frenchman Henri Charriere, Englishman John McVicar, and the black American singer Huddie Ledbetter.

Charriere was a smalltime Paris gangster whose persistent brushes with the law eventu-

Steve McQueen looking very much in need of a rest after spending years in solitary in Papillon **(1973).**

ally earned him a sentence to Devil's Island. The feared prison settlement of St Laurent du Maroni actually comprised three islands, the Iles du Diable, Royale and St Joseph. Conditions were so bad that du Diable is the name by which the whole complex became known. Charriere, whose nickname was 'Papillon' (French for butterfly) was not only one of few to escape, he was one of few to get away alive by any means. In the 100 years the prison was in operation up until its closure in 1954, only 2,000 out of the overall total of 70,000 ever returned to France.

Steve McQueen takes the title role in *Papillon* (1973), a despairing and slow-moving tale which suffers from having as its central character an individual who is not especially likeable. Persistent attempts to gain the sympathy of the audience therefore depends heavily upon the personality of the actor and his acting ability. Much better suited to more dynamic roles, McQueen manages to overcome most of the holes in the script that undermine an already essentially unlikeable individual. Papillon claims he is there only because he has been framed, a claim that does not ring true, partly because there is only his word for it but also because he is clearly a Parisian lowlife, the type all good moviegoers are conditioned to mistrust. Of course, whether Pappy's claim is or is not true, there is no justification for mistreatment of prisoners. Yet the progressively deadening effect of his lengthy spells (two years, then five) in solitary, wreak almost as much damage on the audience as they do on the hapless convict.

Papillon eventually escapes at the third attempt (he has previously fallen in with Indians and lepers, who help him, and nuns who do not) and floats away from Devil's Island borne along by favourable currents.

Although the long-drawn out style of the movie is an effective way of imparting the numbing sense of despair that must afflict prisoners serving life sentences, the overall result in *Papillon* comes dangerously close to being merely boring. Audiences stumbling out of movie theatres after this particular moviegoing experience were probably as relieved as if they'd just completed hard time them-selves. This is a fate none of the participants, not even Papillon himself, really deserves.

The same prison colony (and several Holly-wood lookalikes) has turned up in many other movies. *Devil's Island* (1939) takes the Dreyfus case as its jumping-off point and even says so in the credits but then spoils things by assert-ing, in the same credits, that the movie is not based on fact (a case of having one's cake and not eating it) apparently in order that the French were not so upset they wouldn't go to see the movie.

Alfred Dreyfus was a soldier, a French Jew in the War Ministry who was accused in 1894 of betraying military secrets to Germany. Court-martialled, he was sent to Devil's Island protest-ing his innocence. Two years later it was discovered that he was not guilty, a Major Esterhazy was the spy, but the French High Command attempted to suppress the truth even to the extent of forging documents. Retried in 1899 Dreyfus was found guilty with extenuating circumstances; in 1905 he was declared inno-cent and reinstated.

In *Devil's Island* a French doctor, Charles Gaudet (Boris Karloff), is convicted of treason and sent to the colony. While there he performs brain surgery on the daughter of the comman-dant who then reneges on his promise to help Gaudet regain his freedom. The commandant's wife steps in and helps Gaudet to escape but he is recaptured and sentenced to death. The arrival of a government minister with promises of a wholesale clean-up of the colony hints that the future might not be so bleak. There is very little here to suggest the Dreyfus case; perhaps the movie's disclaimer was right after all. By 1958 more accuracy was possible (maybe no one cared by then if they upset the French) but a re-evaluation of the Dreyfus case, *I Accuse!*, was gloomily well-meaning and the end result was star-studded boredom.

The post-prison life of British criminal John McVicar shows that full rehabilitation to a useful and exemplary life is possible, but during the period covered by *McVicar* (1980) he is anything but a reassuring individual. McVicar

McVicar **(1980) traces the life of a man who eventually made it to full rehabilitation but at this moment in the movie Roger Daltrey is all tied up with no place to go.**

(Roger Daltrey) is bright enough to realize that he is a thoroughly mixed-up individual and he graduates from being a fundamentally unpleasant character to one in whom the seeds of a future responsible citizen are already taking root.

Alongside pop singer (and co-producer of the movie) Daltrey is another former singer turned actor, Adam Faith, who plays the role of Walter Probyn, a hard-nosed but humorous and likeable villain while Steven Berkoff plays 'Ronnie Harrison' a notorious and somewhat chilling gang leader. (Unlike McVicar and Pro-byn, 'Harrison' is not the real name of the prisoner concerned; presumably a case of protecting the not-so-innocent.)

A mixture of names litters the life and career of classic blues singer Huddie Ledbetter, known as Leadbelly, who used a string of aliases to conceal some of his singing and criminal activities. The story of the singer came to the screen in *Leadbelly* (1976). With Roger E. Mosley in the title role, the movie is well-directed (by Gordon Parks Sr) but failed to gain popular success, partly due to the general difficulty in promoting black movies outside the black community.

Leadbelly was born in 1889 on a Louisiana plantation and left home at 16 in pursuit of a career as a musician. Afflicted with a violent temper he served time in Texas in 1916 for assault but escaped only to be nailed again two years later, this time for murder. He served seven years at Shaw State Prison Farm, Huntsville, Texas, then worked outside music for a while before being put away again, for attempted murder, in 1930. During this spell in prison he was found by blues researcher John A. Lomax Sr and recorded for the Library of Congress. Released in 1934, Leadbelly managed to stay out of trouble, or at least out of prison, until 1939 when he served a year at Rykers Island, NY, for assault.

Throughout the 1940s Leadbelly worked extensively on radio in New York City and Los Angeles, dying in 1949 of lateral sclerosis.

Leadbelly thus had a rich musical life, a fascinating criminal career, and with three wives a potentially interesting private life too. The movie thus had a lot going for it and generally made good use of this material. But the limitations of the market for movies about blacks, added to a grimly determined liberal approach, helped sabotage it. Most damaging to its success, however, was its realistic depiction of violence inflicted by whites on blacks during the 1920s and 1930s. It must also be conceded that Leadbelly was far from being a homely individual who automatically drew sympathy from an audience, white or black – he was decidedly unpleasant. As movie heroes go, Leadbelly was a non-starter.

Of special merit in the movie are the prison farm sequences which are satisfactorily realized. The everpresent threat to life is conveyed by one of Leadbelly's chain gang comrades, Dicklikker (Albert P. Hall), when he observes: 'When they're out to kill you, living is winning.'

The uneasy place of blacks in prison movies such as *Leadbelly* was nothing new, even if the starring roles were. Most movies that used black actors suffered from similar problems, and to a great extent still do even when made by the most liberal whites or by blacks themselves. Indeed, both groups sometimes make the worst attempts at integrating blacks into their movies by falling over backward in their attempts to avoid falling flat on their faces.

In fact, it should not have been too hard to incorporate blacks into American prison movies with rather more integration than seems to have been possible; if only because, being a part of the poorer classes in the community, there are rather a lot of them in prison. If some of the statistics quoted earlier are adjusted according to the colour of a man's skin they create some alarming impressions. In the early 1970s in the age group 25 to 34, one white man in every 163 was in prison; for blacks it was one in 26. (British statistics of 1988 make even more disturbing reading; blacks, who represent 5 per cent of the general population, provide 14 per cent of the prison population. Anyone who thinks that this merely confirms prejudices that blacks are more criminally inclined has an uneasy grasp of the depths to which racism has permeated the judicial system.)

Only rarely do prison movies convey the black:white ratio with any degree of accuracy. A rare early example is *Hell's Highway* (1932) in which the chain gang is predominantly black although, naturally for the period, the stars are all white. Tipping the balance well and truly

Singing the blues may have helped Roger E. Mosley, as Leadbelly **(1976), pass the time and eventually reach international fame, but it didn't improve his temper.**

the other way is *Brothers* (1977), a movie based loosely on the imprisonment of black activist George Jackson. Depicted in the movie as David Thomas (Bernie Casey), the movie traces a period in the life of a militant black man sent to San Quentin following a shoot-out in a Marin County courthouse during which a judge and the activist's younger brother, Joshua (Owen Pace), are killed. (George Jackson's real-life brother was named Jonathan.) Although essentially well-meaning, the movie's polemical thrust is somewhat blunted thanks to the one-sided viewpoint of the screenplay. The white guards are uniformly malevolent, the white prisoners persecute their black co-inmates, the black convicts, meanwhile, are all good guys and the only reason any of them are in the joint is because it's Whitey's world outside. Despite some good performances from the leads (Vonetta McGee plays Paula Jones, a thinly-disguised screen character substituting for Angela Davis, the black militant writer and teacher) the movie's potential power for generating a change in attitude is dissipated by its imbalance.

A realistic balance of black and white in keeping with reality appears in the movie based upon the riot at Attica prison, NY, in 1971.

The Attica prisoners rioted, took hostages, and gathered in D-Yard where they demanded better working conditions, more religious and political freedom, and amnesty for those taking part in the riot. Negotiations between the prisoners and the state commissioner for prisons, Russell G. Oswald, were protracted. A spokesman for the prisoners was Jerry Rosenberg, a convicted murderer who had escaped the death penalty through legal means, an exercise which resulted in his becoming the first jailhouse lawyer and the subject of a 1986 TV movie, *Doing Life*. State governor Nelson Rockefeller was involved in the background, but public opinion was inflamed following claims made by Walter Dunbar (who, as Chairman of the 101st Congress of the American Correctional Association, had tried to stop Thomas Murton's call for investigations into the Arkansas massacres). Dunbar alleged that several guards had already had their throats cut and some had been badly mutilated, thus precipitating a violent assault on the prison.

In the ensuing battle guards poured hundreds of rounds of shotgun pellets and bullets into the massed prisoners. Many of the bullets were 'Silvertips', a nifty little example of man's ingenuity. They do not mushroom immediately but only when the round has penetrated far enough into the body to do real harm. At the time the prisoners were gathered in the prison yard and none had attempted to escape through the wire. As a result of this fusillade, 29 prisoners and 10 of their hostages were killed and scores more were wounded.

In fact, despite Dunbar's claims, up to that point none of the hostages had been killed or injured and the only hostages who died did so as a result of their comrades' haphazard fire. Furthermore, although the tally of weapons gathered afterwards was huge, there were no guns. The state's firepower had been turned on sitting targets armed with baseball bats, knives, scissors, clubs and the like. While there is no doubt that 1200 men so armed could have wreaked a great deal of harm, and killed many, at the time of the assault they were not trying to escape and had not killed or wounded anyone. On top of all this mayhem, no wounded inmate was treated until a few hours after the shooting stopped. One way or another, New York state officials did not come out of the Attica incident smelling of roses and neither of the two movies which resulted spared the authorities.

Attica (1974), a documentary by Cinda Firestone, is unashamedly slanted in favour of the prisoners, while *Attica* (1980), a TV movie starring Charles Durning, Roger E. Mosley, Anthony Zerbe and Henry Darrow has George Grizzard in the role of New York journalist Tom Wicker upon whose account the movie is based. Generally faithful to the facts, the screenplay for this TV movie was subjected to changes forced upon the writers until it was much more moderate in its criticism of Governor Rockefeller. What it must be like to have friends in high places.

According to *Time* magazine, one of the prisoners at Attica summarized the events at the prison with a line that might have come from a script for a prison movie (and possibly did): 'If we cannot live as people, we will at least try to die like men.'

There was little chance for any of the inmates of the prison in Istanbul, Turkey, to live like people, or even die like men. This was where Billy Hayes was sent following his arrest when trying to smuggle drugs out of the country.

Midnight Express (1978) traces the events which follow Hayes's arrest with a not-so dispassionate eye. Although a touchy subject today, a measure of cold detachment suggests that the reality of the world-wide drugs trade is akin to that of the Prohibition years in America. Nevertheless, drug smuggling is against the law and many people regard it as one of the most heinous of crimes. Even with this latter point only in mind it is hard not to feel some sympathy for Billy Hayes (played in the movie by Brad Davis) as he is sucked into the bestial world of the prison in Istanbul.

Sentenced to three and a half years, Hayes is within two months of release when he is returned to court to learn that his sentence has been reviewed: now he must serve a minimum of 30 years.

Menaced by a sadistic head guard, Hamidou (played by Paul Smith), Hayes and two of his

Mike Kellin (l) says goodbye to his son, Brad Davis, who is about to start a harrowing sentence, not helped by the menacing guard, Paul Smith (c, back). It was a long time before he was able to take the Midnight Express **(1978) out of prison.**

fellow prisoners, an Englishman named Max (John Hurt) and Jimmy Booth (Randy Quaid), an American, dig through the crumbling walls of their cells and succed in breaking into the sewerage tunnels beneath the prison.

Their attempt to cover the entry to the tunnel is ineffective and is spotted by another prisoner, Rifki (Pauolo Bonacelli), who is also an informer. Max is taken away for interrogation, which in this prison means torture and beating. In a violent rage, Hayes attacks Rifki, gouging out an eye (he only has one) and biting out his tongue. For this sickening assault, Hayes is thrown into the prison's dreaded psychiatric wing. Filled with zombie-like shadows of men, the wing has all the appearance of a hell on earth and Hayes' mind begins to give way. When his girlfriend, Irene (Miracle Sarons), visits him, she smuggles in some money and Hayes summons up a vestige of willpower and tries to buy a favour from Hamidou who responds by dragging Hayes to a room where he prepares to sodomize him. In a desperate attack, Billy takes the huge guard by surprise, smashing him into the wall where a clothes hook is driven into the back of his neck.

Hastily dressing in a guard's uniform Hayes heads shakily for the way out. Another guard spots him and casually tosses a key to the door. Moments later Hayes is outside the prison walls and the movie ends with him walking unsteadily but hurriedly towards freedom.

Tightly constructed (directed by Alan Parker from an Oliver Stone screenplay) and well acted, *Midnight Express* portrays a world which, while very different from that of the American, or British, penal systems, is still filled with the smell of slowly rotting humanity.

Anyone who suspects that the prison system in Turkey is not as bad as that painted here might well heed a statement reportedly made by a Turkish police officer to two sisters who

were systematically abused while in prison. In a TV documentary shown in Britain on Channel 4 in the *Dispatches* series, they recalled this particular guardian of law and order as declaring, 'I'm such a fascist that even if my own daughter were brought in here I'd rape her.'

The main weakness of *Midnight Express*, and given the nature of the tale it is a fairly significant one, is that Billy Hayes appears not to have had many regrets over committing the crime that put him inside. His only mistake, so the impression is given, is that he was caught.

A similarly salutory tale, of a young American caught smuggling drugs in a foreign country, appears in *Escape* (1980), a TV movie, which stars Timothy Bottoms as Dwight Worker who was imprisoned in Mexico's Lecumberri prison for trying to smuggle cocaine out through Mexico City airport. Beaten up by warders and fellow inmates who demand money as a means of ensuring he has 'better' treatment, Worker plans an escape with a visiting American, Barbara Chilcoate (Kay Lenz), who later becomes his wife, and Lily Levinson (Colleen Dewhirst). Worker is eventually successful, thus becoming, or so it is claimed, the first man to escape from Lecumberri prison since Pancho Villa did it in 1913.

Like Billy Hayes, the sense of outrage at the treatment to which the prisoner is subjected comes over rather more strongly than any sense of remorse. Although the film's director, Robert Lewis, is less assured than Alan Parker and the movie is slightly toned down for its TV origins there is still a powerful message: Don't smuggle drugs!

Given what has happened in recent years to British and American visitors to some Middle-Eastern, Latin American, and Far-Eastern countries the best way to stay out of trouble would be an even more circumscribing message: Don't get off the plane!

4

Alcatraz:
The Movie

'...I always think of this place as the
final port of wasted lives.'
(Robert F. Stroud)

Although it has already been touched upon, mainly in connection with Al Capone, there is one American prison deserving of special attention. Or, at least, that is what Hollywood would have us think.

When, in 1868, the United States War Department sought a suitable place for the incarceration of prisoners (whether enemies or their own deserters), a tiny island in San Francisco Bay seemed eminently suitable. A bleak and hostile chunk of rock, Alcatraz was accessible only by boat; while fast and dangerous tides and undertows made escape by swimming next to impossible. After 60-odd years the army had no further use for the Rock and the Department of Justice took it over. In 1934 a new federal prison was opened there and hailed as a place which could safely house America's most dangerous criminals. The impregnability of the Rock was underlined to public and convicts alike with special attention being given to those dangerous currents and water-borne dangers. (One highly unlikely tale which gained remarkable credence among inmates was of an injured shark which had a fin missing on one side of its body and hence could no longer swim in a straight line and was doomed to endlessly circle the island feeding on anything carelessly, or foolishly, entering the water.)

The use of a silent regimen, long hours banged-up in their cells, and the frequent use of solitary confinement, helped the guards impose severe if usually non-violent restraints upon their charges. Most feared of all restraining methods at Alcatraz (after the legendary one-finned fish in the bay) was the Hole.

Most American prisons had a 'hole'; at Alcatraz it was in Cell Block 'D'; which was designated as segregation quarters. All cells in D Block were for solitary confinement but cells 9 to 14 had solid doors, not bars, and the only light was from an electric bulb controlled from outside. Prisoners in these six cells, which together constituted the Hole, could thus be deprived of light and all human contact.

This non-scientific sensory deprivation gave the warden and guards at the prison a powerful weapon even if they did not understand its potential for creating severe psychological damage as thoroughly as did many later regimes in police states around the world.

Alcatraz became home to some of America's most hardened criminals and if Al Capone was the best-known during the 1930s he was superseded in the public mind in the 1950s by a man whose crimes were much less serious than those of the brutal booze baron of Prohibition. This was Robert Franklin Stroud, a man who became known – erroneously as it happens – as the Birdman of Alcatraz.

Robert Stroud was born in 1890 and had his first brush with the law in Alaska in 1909 when he shot and killed a man who had beaten up his girlfriend, a prostitute twice Stroud's age. After some plea-bargaining Stroud pleaded guilty to manslaughter but a new 'hanging' judge sentenced him to the maximum term in prison, 12 years in the McNeil Island penitentiary.

At first Stroud was a model prisoner but a fight with another inmate lost him any chance of parole. In 1912 he was transferred to the new prison at Leavenworth, Kansas, where, by studying mathematics and engineering, he began to develop a natural ability with figures.

Four years later, Stroud's brother, Marcus, travelled all the way from Alaska to see him but was refused admission because he arrived on a no-visiting day. Stroud became angry and argued with a malevolent guard who put him on report for speaking during a meal, thus making it impossible for his brother to see him at all before his return to Alaska. A few days later Stroud and the guard had another argument in the prison dining hall; the guard made a move to beat Stroud with his club and Stroud stabbed him to death.

This killing took place in 1916 and Stroud was soon plunged into a series of legal complexities resulting initially from certain peculiarities of Kansas state law and later as a result of mistakes, poor communication, and general apathy towards his plight. Eventually, he was sentenced to death for the murder of the guard, sentence being finally affirmed early in 1920.

In April of that same year Stroud's mother, Elizabeth, a determined woman, met with Edith Wilson, wife of the President of the United States, at the White House. Many people thought Mrs Wilson was running the presidency on behalf of her gravely ill husband and although she would not let Elizabeth Stroud see the President she took from her the documents that stipulated the sentence of death. A few minutes later Mrs Wilson returned with the papers across which the President had scrawled his signature. Robert Stroud's sen-

tence had been commuted to life imprisonment.

A condition of the commutation was deemed to declare that Stroud should be placed into permanent isolation. Uncomplainingly, he returned to his studies and also took up painting. One day, in the summer of 1920, during his exercise period, Stroud saw four fledgling sparrows in a nest that had been blown from a tree. He took the little creatures back into his cell and as a result of this small caring gesture the course of Robert F. Stroud's enclosed life was changed.

So far Bob Stroud's life had all the ingredients for movie melodrama: a bar room brawl over a golden-hearted floozy ending in a shooting, a tough uneducated young man growing up in prison, confrontation with a brutal guard, another killing, court room dramatics, a last-minute stay of execution from a stroke-crippled President of the United States. There was more here than the most desperate Hollywood hack dare crowd into a screenplay. And yet, when Stroud's story was eventually brought to the screen it was none of this which was the principal motivation; it was what happened in the years after the 30-year old prisoner found those tiny fledglings.

In the movie, *Birdman of Alcatraz* (1962), starring Burt Lancaster as Stroud, the long, wearying years of solitary in the claustrophobic confines of a tiny cell were potentially hazardous for a film-maker. Fortunately, direction was in the hands of John Frankenheimer, here at one of the high points of his roller-coaster career.

The movie made some adjustments to truth for the sake of dramatic effects. For example, although it was Marcus Stroud who had been turned away from the prison in 1916 after travelling many miles to see Robert, the movie decided the scene would carry more impact if this happened to Bob's mother, Elizabeth Stroud (Thelma Ritter).

As Stroud learns to care for his tiny birds he also develops an ability to form human relationships and begins a cautious, edgy friendship with a prison guard, Bull Ransom (Neville Brand, who was by this time a familiar minor

Cages within cages; bars behind bars. Burt Lancaster studies his captive canaries in Birdman of Alcatraz **(1962).**

prison movie icon although usually on the other side of the bars).

A prize-winning article Stroud writes for a magazine leads to friendship with Stella Johnson (Betty Field) with whom he enters into a business relationship: she supervises the marketing of patent bird medicines he has developed. The real Stroud began a necessarily distant relationship with Della May Jones, a widow in Indiana who kept canaries. Della Jones (who was renamed for the movie) began writing to Stroud, then visited and they eventually formed a business partnership as the prisoner's fame spread through the international world of bird fanciers.

When, in 1931, an attempt was made to deprive Stroud of his birds and to prohibit any further work of the kind which had occupied him now for more than ten years, he smuggled a long letter out through Della Jones and soon the bird lovers who used his medicines and methods, who wrote to him seeking advice (a dozen letters a day), learned to their astonishment that the man they so admired was a two-time killer serving life in an American penitentiary.

To put it mildly, fur and feathers flew as angry bird fanciers wrote thousands of letters to Leavenworth, to the federal authorities, and to their congressmen and senators. Stroud was allowed to keep his canaries, he was given better facilities for his research, and it was even hinted that he might be paroled when his next review came up in 1937. Most valuable of all the concessions made to Stroud was that a hole was knocked through into the adjoining cell so that he could have more space for his bird cages. But the prison authorities did not like the fact that they had been beaten by a con. Imperceptibly at first, they began to tighten up on Stroud's activities and soon he heard rumblings that he was on a short list of prisoners being considered for transfer to a new prison being made ready on an island in San Francisco Bay.

Telly Savalas plays Feto Gomez, a fellow prisoner in solitary to whom Stroud gives one of the four sparrows as he begins to learn about birds and their way of life. When Stroud later obtains some canaries he begins breeding and selling the birds. The activities of Stroud and Gomez, which includes pre-masticating food for their tiny charges, is viewed with amazement and a curious pride by prisoners and prison guards alike. Maybe these two tough murderers were a little crazy but as birdsong fills the bleak building everyone admits that they are actually achieving something with their closely-watched lives.

Stroud reads everything the prison library can obtain on the care and treatment of birds. He also builds cages for his tiny charges, using scraps of wood surreptitiously passed to him by other prisoners and even the guards who recognize the fact that the atmosphere in the isolation wing of the prison benefits from the behaviour of Stroud and Gomez. When disaster strikes and a newly arrived canary brings with it a serious disease which begins to kill off his birds, Stroud enters a more intense and dedicated phase of his new life. His intensive, practical study of what is happening to his birds helps him devise a cure for a lethal sickness known loosely as 'septic fever'.

Working 18 hours a day, disregarding his own health, Stroud observes, studies and learns and eventually confides his knowledge to other breeders by way of articles to the *Canary Journal.*

Late in 1933, using an obscure, and slightly dubious, piece of old Kansas legislation Robert Stroud and Della May Jones announced to the newspapers that they had entered into a contract of marriage. The prison authorities were outraged but they were also cautious. If they wanted to get even, and they certainly did, they had to bide their time. Of unexpected help to the authorities was Stroud's mother. Although Elizabeth Stroud had stood by her son for almost 20 years her son's marriage angered her and she bitterly told a reporter that she no longer believed that her son should be released from prison, that he was better off where he was. The movie's implication, that Stroud was an emotional prisoner of his mother, barely stands up to scrutiny; he spent too little time in her company for that.

To add to the growing pressure on Stroud, his 'wife' was not allowed to visit him nor were they allowed to exchange letters. Later in the movie, Stroud instigates a 'separation' from his wife, realistically pointing out the futility of their relationship.

The birdman of Leavenworth continued his researches, aided by a microscope given to him by members of the public who had benefited from his work. He was visited regularly by officials interested in seeing this already legendary figure. Even J. Edgar Hoover, the head of the Federal Bureau of Investigation, bought one of Stroud's canaries during a visit to the prison.

In 1937 Stroud's request for parole was turned down. He was now 48 years old, he had spent the last 29 of those years in prison.

Part of his time was now being spent in writing a comprehensive study on bird diseases (an earlier, hastily-written volume on canary care had already appeared in print). His brother reappeared in his life and when he discovered that the typescript of Stroud's new book lay in Washington, Marcus attempted to have the work published. He was met with official disinterest. (Marcus Stroud added a curious footnote to his brother's story: he went into vaudeville as, of all things, an escape artist and even appeared in some silent movies.)

Stroud's health was deteriorating and his circumstances became steadily more proscribed by officialdom. Then, early on the morning of 15 December 1942, Stroud was given only ten minutes in which to make himself ready for a journey. His birds and his research equipment left behind, the birdman of Leavenworth was on his way to Alcatraz.

The only immediate bright spot on Robert Stroud's horizon was the release to his brother of the typescript of his book. When the book, *Stroud's Digest of the Diseases of Birds*, appeared in 1943 it was a sensation in the narrow but still extensive world of bird fanciers.

Isolated in D Block on Alcatraz, Robert Stroud now turned his still acquisitive mind to further study and began scouring the prison library. This time he studied law, determined to find a legal way off the Rock. When his efforts failed he began working on another book, this time about men in prison.

In 1946 a group of prisoners in D Block attempted to escape. The ensuing storming of the cell block by guards and a detachment of US Marines brought much bloodshed but Robert Stroud, who was released into the main cell block during the fracas, did not take part in the escape attempt nor in the orgy of violence. Indeed, he actively tried to avert unnecessary killing by assuring the authorities that none of the prisoners with him in the block was armed and hence there was no need to persist with their panic-stricken bombing of the block. When order was restored Stroud was returned to solitary.

The year 1948 brought a change in Stroud's circumstances and he no longer enjoyed the privileges of communicating with either his publisher or the many people who wrote to him. Further denials of privileges occurred. When his publisher wanted to reissue the *Digest* and asked that the author should be allowed to update it, the request was refused. Despite this, he finished work on his new book in 1951, entitled *Rehabilitation*, and handed it to the prison authorities. He then returned to his own case and prepared yet another appeal. The appeal was rejected and Stroud, sick and

in pain with gall bladder trouble, took what was for him a most uncharacteristic step, he tried to commit suicide.

When Thomas E. Gaddis's book *Birdman of Alcatraz*, appeared in 1956, public attention was once again focused upon the case of Robert F. Stroud. This time, Hollywood was also attracted.

Gaddis's book and the Lancaster-Frankenheimer movie (in which Edmond O'Brien plays the role of the writer) made the misnamed Birdman of Alcatraz a national celebrity but this fame did nothing to persuade the authorities to change their intransigent stance. They refused to co-operate in the making of the movie, and they did not accede to requests that Stroud be paroled. However, in 1959, after Gaddis's book had appeared, Stroud's health had deteriorated to the point where he was transferred from Alcatraz to a prison hospital at Springfield, Illinois, where he remained for the rest of his life. A new attempt to obtain parole failed but he did hear a judge declare that the order sending him to solitary confinement back in the early 1920s had been illegal.

In 1963 Robert Stroud was aged 73, he had been in prison since 1909, had had a clean record since 1916 and he was internationally famous as a specialist in bird diseases. This work alone should have been enough to prove that he had lived up to the title of his second major book. But Stroud was deemed not to have been rehabilitated, or was at best so badly institutionalized that he could not be expected to cope with life outside. His book *Rehabilitation* remains unpublished to this day.

Robert Stroud, who had gone to prison during the term of office of William Taft, the 27th President of the United States, died in his sleep on 21 November 1963. The event might have made world headlines had it not been the following day that John F. Kennedy, the 35th President, was assassinated.

The fact that Robert Stroud was not really the Birdman of Alcatraz (Birdman of Leavenworth would have been a more apt but much less resonant description) was, nevertheless, a source of some misplaced pride to the prison service. As late as 1980 a guide book on sale at the prison featured him and declared, inaccurately, 'Stroud died in isolated confinement in Cell Block D.'

The film industry can also take some pride in its treatment of the story of Robert Stroud. Studiously unsensational, reasonably accurate and even-handed in its balanced approach to its subject, *Birdman of Alcatraz* does not shirk the need to show the dull routine of prison life. Nor does it overplay the potentially overt symbolism of a caged man caring for caged birds. By assiduously avoiding the creation of a false impression of reality the film acquired stature and remains one of the best of all prison movies.

Long as they doubtless seemed to him, Robert Stroud's 54 years in prison do not qualify him for top place in this roll of dishonour. Among other long-term prisoners in American penitentiaries are Paul Geidel and Richard Honeck.

In 1911, when he was 17 years old, Geidel was sentenced to 20 years-to-life for murder. He was released from prison in 1980, having served just short of 69 years. Richard Honeck was sentenced to life imprisonment in 1899 and was released a month after Stroud's death at the age of 84.

Alcatraz Island (1937) improbably and ineffectually combines the world of Robert Stroud with that of Al Capone in depicting a mobster named Gat Brady (John Litel) sent to Leavenworth on a tax rap. Later transferred to Alcatraz, Gat (where *do* they get these names?) is befriended by District Attorney George Drake (Gordon Oliver) who sent him down in the first place. George's change of heart might have something to do with the fact that he has fallen in love with Gat's daughter, Ann (Mary Maguire). Unremarkable in the extreme, *Alcatraz Island* displays an endearingly schoolboyish touch with a dining-room sign that reads:

CLEAN YOUR PLATE
OR GO WITHOUT THIS
MEAL THE NEXT DAY

A famous name who served real time at Alcatraz was George 'Machine Gun' Kelly who was generally conceded to be a fairly harmless cove but unfortunately fell foul of J. Edgar Hoover's empire-building campaign.

Early in a career that culminated in his holding national government, even the presidency, in thrall, Hoover realized that to build an empire he needed vast amounts of tax-payers' money; to persuade Congress to give him his millions he had to have real need. What better need could there be than if he had to defeat an army of gun-toting villains? Recognizing that organized and white-collar crime, however rich the pickings for the perpetrators, simply wasn't very glamorous, Hoover set about exaggerating the danger of gun-toting latterday cowboys like Kelly and John Dillinger, who thus became all-American heroes, the subjects of scores of movies, and ended up in prison or dead. The FBI should really have been grateful to George Kelly because he provided them with a public relations coup one day in 1933 when they learned from his lips the special name by which the underworld referred to government agents. Surrounded by heavily-armed men he yelled: 'Don't shoot, G-men.'

Just before he died in Leavenworth in 1954, Kelly summed up his years in prison in a letter to Charles Urschel, the man whose kidnapping had ended with Kelly's capture and imprisonment two decades before: 'Nothing can be worth this.'

The events surrounding the trouble in Alcatraz in 1946 in which Robert Stroud was peripherally involved provided the basis for a 1980 TV movie, the somewhat inaccurate title of which is *Alcatraz: the Whole Shocking Story*. With technical guidance from Clarence Carnes, who had participated in the real life events, the movie dwells upon the unpleasant aftermath of a failed attempt at a breakout.

Heading the plot to escape is Bernie Coy (played in the movie by Ronny Cox), a hillbilly bandit who had noted the fact that a determined man could overpower a guard during the regulation inspection of D Block. Aiding Coy are Crazy Sam Shockley, a man whose record, intellectual level and state of mind should have earned him a place in a hospital for the criminally insane rather than isolation in Alcatraz; one-time Public Enemy No 4 Joseph Paul 'Dutch' Cretzer (Telly Savalas); Marvin Hubbard, a friend of Coy's; Miran Edgar 'Buddy' Thompson, a vicious killer; and Clarence Carnes (Michael Beck), a Native American serving time for kidnapping and murder.

Coy's plan is put into operation but everything grinds to a halt when a key which should have been on its regular hook is missing. A guard had forgotten to replace it, a neglect that saved an embarrassing escape but led to much bloody violence.

With the escape bid stalled, but having already taken several guards hostage, Coy tries to improvise an alternative escape plan. Cretzer, who has already killed one of the guards, wants to settle for killing them all on the shaky grounds that this would eliminate eyewitnesses and hence keep them out of the gas chamber. Thompson and Crazy Sam agree with Cretzer but Hubbard and Carnes do not. When Cretzer fires a fusillade of bullets into the cell where the guards are held he hopes to kill them all. Carnes is horrified at this act and when he is sent in to see how many are dead he reports that all have perished when in fact five are wounded and three completely unharmed.

Coy and Hubbard set out to kill Cretzer, not out of malice but because he is trying to kill them. While this is happening the US Marines arrive and, under a hail of grenades and bullets, storm the building driving most of the convicts back to their cells and in their enthusiasm place many more than the would-be escapers at risk. It is at this point that Robert Stroud (here played by Art Carney), steps in to avert unnecessary bloodshed. The ringleaders' crazed anger is turned upon one another and Cretzer kills Coy before being killed by the guards who also kill Hubbard.

After order was restored the cleaning up took place, part of which saw the trials of Thompson, Shockley and Carnes. Thompson and the obviously insane Shockley went to the gas chamber at San Quentin. Thanks to his action which undoubtedly saved the lives of

eight hostages, Carnes escaped the death penalty and received a life sentence to add to the time he was already serving.

Clarence Carnes, who had been the youngest prisoner to go to Alcatraz, was eventually paroled in 1973 and in July 1980 he was back on the Rock, this time as technical adviser on the movie that told the tale of this failed attempt to escape from Alcatraz.

This tale was too good for movie-makers to let it go. *Six Against the Rock* (1987) was made without the benefit of Carnes's insight (onscreen a character named Dan Durando appears in his stead) but is generally a much better movie, crisper and suspensefully played in its first half. Bernie Coy (David Carradine) and Hubbard (David Morse) are much more sympathetic and even Dutch Cretzer (Howard Hesseman) has a touch of normality, being driven into gunning down the guards by the quietly malevolent Thompson (Jan-Michael Vincent) and the psychotic Crazy Sam (played with staring-eyed, slobbering intensity by Charles Haid). Almost as manic, in his insistence on destroying the rioting cons, is Warden Johnston (Richard Dysart) who declares at one point, 'Hit hard and hit fast. If we have to we'll blast 'em all to hell.'

For all its marginal shift in balance, the tale, however well told, is much the same as before and, of course, the escape bid is just as unsuccessful.

Much more successful, or so it seems, was an escape attempt in 1962 when Frank Lee Morris and the brothers John and Clarence Anglin vanished from their cells, never to be seen again.

The fact that Morris and the Anglins made good their escape meant that their story was potentially much more adventurous, although still restricted, than that of Robert Stroud. It was, however, much less dramatically bullet-strewn than that of Coy, Cretzer, Carnes and company. The movie that tells Morris's story, *Escape from Alcatraz* (1979), was therefore a very different affair to the stories of either Stroud or Carnes and one that appealed to Clint Eastwood, who stars as Morris, with Patrick McGoohan in the role of Warden Olin G. Blackwell.

Earnestly concerned with prison life, *Escape from Alcatraz* offers no hint that rehabilitation is possible or even encouraged by the authorities. One convict, Chester 'Doc' Dalton (Roberts Blossom), paints to while away the monotonous hours but his privileges are taken away when he produces an unflattering portrait of the warden. In despair at this action, Doc deliberately cuts off some fingers. Frank Morris is a tougher customer than this; when asked what kind of childhood he had, he has a cryptic answer: 'Short.'

Morris fends off violence from Wolf (Bruce M. Fischer), and with Charley Butts (Larry Hankin) joins forces with the Anglins in an escape bid. They cull a useful idea from *Popular Mechanics* which they hope will get them safely across the

water outside but first they have to break out of their cells.

Morris, Butts and the Anglins (Fred Ward and Jack Thibeau), make dummies with *papier-mâché* heads, complete with hair filched from the barber shop, to fool guards into thinking they are sleeping quietly in their beds during the time they are using spoons to dig their way out of their cells and into the service ducts and chambers that criss-cross the prison.

At the last moment Butts changes his mind but the others make their bid for freedom on 13 June 1962, slipping into the waters of San Francisco Bay using a raft improvised from scraps of driftwood and inflated raincoats (the idea from the magazine), and vanish.

The movie, and popular assumptions, takes a slightly optimistic view of what happened to Morris and the Anglins and has the authorities find a chrysanthemum, a flower associated with Doc's paintings, on nearby Angel Island. How-

Clint Eastwood (third from l) is not anticipating blue riband cuisine and plans instead to make his Escape from Alcatraz **(1979).**

ever, the fact that the three men were habitual criminals and yet never afterwards appear to have committed another crime lends credence to the assumption that in reality they didn't make it across the short but difficult stretch of water to the mainland.

Similar assumptions were made about the fate of the only other men to disappear from Alcatraz, Ralph Roe and Theodore Cole, who vanished in 1937.

More successful, as far as he got, was John Paul Scott, who escaped a few months after Morris's disappearance. Scott swam the two and a half miles to the mainland where guards awaited his arrival and took him back, cold, wet and exhausted. Scott didn't escape but did prove that the water barrier was not impassable.

The prison on Alcatraz was closed in 1963 but the impact it had made upon the consciousness of the nation, and on people all around the world, is such that more than a quarter of a century later it is a major tourist attraction, drawing 800,000 visitors every year.

Despite the existence of such famous prisons as those at Leavenworth, San Quentin, Folsom and Sing Sing, the name of Alcatraz is capable of instantly evoking memories of real and imaginary prisoners, of true and fictitious events, and of images that mingle the prison of fact with the prison of imagination.

Although the prisoners who served their time on the Rock would certainly disagree, it is probably as well that Alcatraz existed – otherwise Hollywood would have had to invent it.

Women in Prison

'This is a prison, not a finishing school.'
(The Concrete Jungle)

In early years, stereotypical movie women were either bad girls men would do well to avoid, or goody-good ones no red-blooded male in his right mind would want to tangle with. Of course, these movies were made by men with only rare incursions by women into such important behind-the-scenes roles as screenwriter and, even less frequently, as director. Those stars who had enough weight to persuade the studio bosses that they might be allowed to portray women with enough intelligence and determination to successfully run their own lives were few. After listing Joan Crawford, Bette Davis, Ida Lupino and Barbara Stanwyck it becomes increasingly difficult to conjure up names until the 1970s and the start of a gradual, but still inadequate, shift in the sexual power base.

It is not surprising, therefore, that in most prison movies women had to settle for a place fairly well down the supporting cast list, usually appearing as devoted wives or mothers or girlfriends on visiting day, or in the regulation flashback sequence. In these sequences, audiences learned why the hero was doing time and, were shown that he wasn't really to blame for his incarceration – it was the actions of a heartless woman that had put him in the slammer. But the popularity of movies about men in prison led some studio bosses to think that there might be some mileage in women's prison movies. There was, but on the whole women didn't come out of this sub-genre too well.

A precursor of the first crop of such movies was a strange little film entitled *Prisoners* (1929), actually a murder mystery, which used a Hungarian setting, perhaps to distance it from America and any implication that American women could do anything bad enough to deserve a spell in the joint. (Or maybe it was merely a device to accommodate villain Bela Lugosi's mittel-European appearance.) Interestingly, the film ends with waitress Riza Riga (played by Corinne Griffith who was billed by her studio, First National, as 'the world's most beautiful woman'), starting a seven-month prison sentence for stealing money to buy a dress while the bad guy goes free.

In 1931, hard on the heels of *The Big House* (1930) came *Ladies of the Big House*, which doubled the usual innocent-in-jeopardy plot by having a young married couple sent down for a murder they did not commit.

Kathleen Storm (Sylvia Sidney) is framed when she elbows a gangster on the make and her new husband, Standish McNeil (Gene Raymond), finds himself in the frame too. With her husband's execution imminent, Kathleen joins a desperate escape bid. It all comes out predictably enough with its seemingly compulsory happy ending, but the movie's chief merits lie in its unflinching (for its day) look at conditions in a penitentiary for women. Even the prison stereotypes: a blowzy gangster's moll, an upper-class dame, the hard-faced muscular matron, are done with panâche. One soon-to-be-stereotype of women's prison movies who has no counterpart in the male world is the pregnant girl whose chief concern is that her baby will not be born in prison. Over the years there would be better women's prison movies than *Ladies of the Big House*, but there would also be many that were a whole lot worse.

Speaking of which, *Women in Prison* (1938) was a cheapo production with not much going for it except a new if improbable twist which found Martha Wilson (Sarah Padden) as a prison warden whose own daughter, Ann (Wynne Gibson), is one of the cons in her care.

Convicted Woman (1940) had the usual stock characters: Hazel the hard case (Lola Lane), Duchess the stool-pigeon (June Lang), and Betty the railroaded innocent (Rochelle Hudson), but had an interesting plot development which brought the convicts a measure of self-govern-ment within the prison system following the termination of a brutal regime thanks to the intervention of newspaperman Jim Brent (Glenn Ford) and crusading lawyer Mary Ellis (Frieda Inescort).

Prison Girl (1942) used the prison farm as the setting for a tale of a doctor, Rosemary Walsh (Rose Hobart), convicted of a mercy killing, a subject only rarely touched upon by movie-makers.

While some movie-makers appeared to think that a woman in prison was an awkward subject, others saw the possibilities for high drama and rampant exploitation.

Only mildly exploitative and greatly rede-emed from possible disaster by two excellent central performances is *Caged* (1950). The movie traces the changes in character forced upon a young woman, Marie Allen (played by Eleanor Parker), from when she first enters prison to the point where, out of the need for self-preservation, she becomes as hard as the toughest inmate. Part of the imperative that forces the change in her character stems from the actions of a sadistic matron, Evelyn Harper (Hope Emerson), while the ineffectual but well-meaning warden, Ruth Benton (Agnes Moor-head), looks on. To a great extent this is the mixture very much as before, but thanks to the

Eleanor Parker discovering what it means to be Caged **(1950) as Hope Emerson towers menacingly in the shadows.**

acting of Parker and Emerson, and masterly direction by John Cromwell, a routine prison melodrama becomes a powerful movie without too much moralizing.

The movie's impact is helped by the fact that, although one of life's innocents, Marie Allen is guilty of the crime for which she is punished, a petty robbery. A strong case is made for society to seek the rehabilitation of offenders or, if that cannot be achieved, to determine a form of punishment which fits the crime.

The fate of Marie Allen is uncompromising. After witnessing the killing of the matron by one of the prisoners and the sight of another inmate going insane, Marie is desperate to get out but she knows that she has no chance of parole unless she co-operates with one of the prisoners, Elvira Powell (Lee Patrick), who runs a string of prostitutes on the outside. Marie agrees to become a hooker and is released.

The basic plot of *Caged* was reused in 1962 for *House of Women* but the bite of the original and its powerful acting were missing. It also took some swallowing to accept the premise of a pregnant woman, Elvira (Shirley Knight), who so melts the heart of gruff Warden Cole (Andrew Duggan) that he resists her parole because he can't bear to lose her.

A strong cast graced *Women's Prison* (1955), which touches, cautiously, on the disturbance prison can wreak upon the sexuality of inmates and custodians alike.

Warden Amelia Van Zant (Ida Lupino), described in the movie as a 'border-line psychopath', is unable to form an attachment with any man. Arising out of this, she takes retributive steps against those women in her charge who have done better in their relations with men. Amelia's underlying motivation is not adequately pursued and the audience is left a little in the dark as to why she feels the way she does. If it is sexual the movie doesn't say so (but, then, lesbianism was hardly movie material in 1955). Nevertheless, this vague hint of some deeper side to Amelia lends the film a quality the later exploitation movies lack.

A prime failing of *Women's Prison* is that Amelia Van Zant is so thoroughly black that the convicts all look like angels in comparison (now where have we heard that before?). The cons are the usual mixed bunch: Brenda Martin (Jan Sterling), a tough forging floozy, Helene Jensen (Phyllis Thaxter), a careless driver who has killed and is going through severe guilt problems, Dottie (Vivian Marshall), a stripper on the downhill slope to nowhere.

The exploitation of women in prison was given its head in a cycle of movies emerging from New World Pictures' studios in the early 1970s. Among the movies, most of which were made (quickly) in the Philippines and released in 1971–2, were *The Big Doll House* (there is worse to come), *Women in Cages*, *Caged Heat*,

The Hot Box and *The Big Bird Cage* (you were warned).

The Big Doll House (1971) is set 'somewhere in a banana republic' (and you can bet your life the innuendo is intentional) and features a sadistic matron and lots of shapely gals bursting out of their prison uniforms, or when they're not bursting forth they are pulled out to be searched 'inside and out'. Lesbianism is rife and while there are no sexually explicit acts (these are not, of course, hardcore films and, indeed, these days barely rate as softcore) there is none of the pussyfooting around the subject that was imposed upon earlier moviemakers. All the stereotypes are here including the tough (in this context 'butch' might be a better word) cons, Helen Grear and Karen Alcott (Pam Grier and Roberta Collins), who lord (lady?) it over a collection of junkies, weaklings and other assorted misfits.

Appalling conditions, torture and a bloody escape are featured with, in the end, a gun-battle in which, as William Wolf observed in *Cue* magazine, the women 'break out with guns blazing, and die like James Cagneys with breasts . . .'.

The Hot Box blends, a little uneasily, New World's women in prison cycle with their earlier successful nurses series. Here, the prisoners are a batch of American nurses captured by a gang of revolutionaries some of whose fighting men are in need of medical attention. The women learn the hard way that the world outside the antiseptic cleanliness of a hospital ward is a grubbily unpleasant place.

The Big Bird Cage (1972) is pretty much the mixture as before: women prisoners with a minimum of clothing sweating it out in the tropics, indulging in a great deal of physical violence and using lots of words their mothers never taught them. They escape, of course, thus justifying in part the movie's marketing slogan: 'Women so hot with desire they melt the chains that enslave them.'

For all their cheapskate production values and undoubted harm they do to the image of women, these New World adventures do have the merit of being made tongue-in-cheek.

The studio's reputation, however, is such that many people condemn its products out of hand; a fact which gave another film an unwarranted hard time before common sense prevailed and it was seen to be really rather good.

Jackson County Jail (1976) tells the harrowing tale of Dinah Hunter (Yvette Mimieux), a Los Angeles advertising executive, who quits her job and her faithless lover and sets out for New York City and a new life. Unfortunately, she decides to drive across country and very quickly finds that the real world outside her own, partly self-induced, life of image-conscious unreality is very different indeed.

When Dinah picks up a couple of seedy hitchhikers in the middle of redneck country she appears to be asking for trouble. She certainly gets it. This unsavoury pair, Bobby Ray and Cassie Ann (Robert Carradine and Patrice Rohmer), beat her up, take her money and all means of identification and her car. Finding her way to a bar, Dinah is assaulted by the owner and when the police arrive she is busted on a vagrancy rap and jailed.

Also in the county jail is Coley Blake (Tommy Lee Jones), a murderer awaiting extradition to another state, but Dinah's next problem comes not from her fellow prisoner but from Hobie the jailer (Frederick Cook) who savagely rapes her. Driven to violent self-defence, Dinah clubs her attacker to death with a wooden stool.

Coley Blake convinces her that no one will believe her story and the two of them make a break for freedom. The fugitives are hotly pursued by the fatherly sheriff (Severn Darden) and their problems increase when he dies, albeit accidentally. With two dead lawmen to account for they are certain losers whatever happens. Ambushed in a small town during the Bicentennial parade, Coley is shot dead, breathing his last on an American flag which is in turn draped across a 'Stop' sign. The movie ends with Dinah under arrest and facing a future which can only get worse.

Very well made and acted, *Jackson County Jail* is a film which deserves attention; even its explicit rape scene has the notable, and

unusual, merit of being depicted from the viewpoint of the victim. Dinah Hunter's terror at the attack, her outrage and disgust at the aftermath, and her desperate attempts to cleanse herself, sharply convey, as much as any movie can, the true horror of this particular crime.

Nightmare in Badham County (1976) starts off in a similar way to *Jackson County Jail* as two young college girls (Deborah Raffin and Lynne Moody) drive through the Deep South only to fall foul of corruption in low places. The movie's origins as a TV movie limit it rather badly but the plight of the two girls, as they are arrested and handed over to a local prison farm that needs a docile labour force, hints at the wider context in which American society exploits women.

For all their often shoestring production values, the New World movies of the 1970s were way ahead of such cheapo productions as *The Concrete Jungle* (1982), a movie of staggering ineptitude whose worst failing is that it takes itself seriously (a mistake New World never made). Once again the story is of a young woman, Elizabeth Demming (Tracy Bregman), who is innocent of any crime but ends up in prison. Once the iron door has slammed behind her, Elizabeth is immediately surrounded by a collection of social misfits most of whom are under the spell of Cat (Barbara Luna), who controls drugs and other forbidden delights in the prison. Although Cat periodically darts suggestive glances at Elizabeth's body, sex appears overtly only in heterosexual form when one of the male guards rapes Elizabeth. When a friend she has made is given a forcible overdose of drugs by Cat and her kittens and dies, Elizabeth improbably becomes a tough nut, goes after Cat and kills her. All ends predictably happily for Elizabeth and the movie lurches to its end leaving the makers to go on to produce a movie about men in prison billed as, 'More brutal than *The Concrete Jungle*. The ultimate film of life behind bars.' True or not, you can bet your life it didn't have as many wet T-shirts.

Women, subjected to forms of imprisonment

other than a concrete cell, have appeared on the screen many times, mostly in ways not relevant to a prison theme. A variation worth pausing over is *The Collector* (1965) in which Miranda Grey (Samantha Eggar) is imprisoned in an attic by Freddie Chess (Terence Stamp). Freddie's hope is that Miranda will fall in love with him, a hope that remains unrealized as the tragedy unfolds. Indeed, in psychological terms, Freddie is more a prisoner than Miranda. Seemingly freed from dependency upon others when he wins a large sum of money on the football pools, Freddie's emotional immaturity and intellectual limitations have combined to render him helpless.

Diana Dors facing death with help from a sympathetic Joan Miller (r), in Yield to the Night **(1956), a film which disturbed consciences in Britain.**

As for his suffocating obsession with the girl; this has made him as much her prisoner as she is his.

The central premise of *The Collector*, of a man holding a woman captive out of sexual motivation, was ineptly countered in *Three in the Attic* (1969), which tells of three young women who have unwittingly been the concurrent lovers of the same man. They hold him captive in their attic in order to extract sexual favours from his progressively wilting person.

Women in prison and as victims of a male-dominated society were much more soberly treated in films that drew upon two real life cases of the 1950s, one in England, the other in America.

A case which did much to rouse public opinion in Britain against capital punishment was that of Ruth Ellis executed for the murder of her faithless lover. Ruth Ellis's story provided the basis for the fictionalized *Yield to the Night* (1956) and was used again in 1984 for *Dance with a Stranger*.

Although it suffers from the social and sexual attitudes of the times in which it was made, *Yield to the Night* retains much of the grip of the true story as it traces the fall of a pleasure-seeking, overtly sensual woman from the glossy high life to a squalid ritualized death at the hands of the State. The central character's lifestyle may not be one with which many women in Britain at that time were familiar through personal experience but it was one they had read about in lip-smacking sensationalized accounts in the mass circulation press of the day. For all the sensationalism, however, enough was understood about Ruth Ellis's circumstances to force many people to question a society that had double standards in so many areas, not least in that of crime and punishment.

In *Yield to the Night* Mary Hilton (Diana Dors) murders the woman who has driven her lover to suicide thus shifting the motivation and with it diverting audience sympathies towards a blanket condemnation of capital punishment. This response was largely achieved through the central performance which is excellent (unexpectedly so at the time because Diana

Miranda Richardson living life her way in
Dance With a Stranger **(1984) before retribution
destroys her for not conforming to society's
cosily unreal image.**

many improvements they were still second-class citizens. *Dance with a Stranger* came at a time when sex attacks on women were increasing and the courts were handing down sentences on rapists which would have been laughable were the cases themselves not so appalling. Women, and men, were beginning to question the imbalance of justice's scales in cases involving women as victims. It followed naturally that a different attitude was also evident in cases involving women as perpetrators.

Dance with a Stranger does not take a revisionist view of the Ruth Ellis case but the manner in which the central character's private life is displayed certainly restores the balance in favour of a woman who, while not the victim of a miscarriage of justice, was certainly a victim of male-dominated society with its correspondingly male-orientated judicial system.

Ruth Ellis's life, simultaneously hedonistic yet bound by a desperate need to bring up her children as normally as possible, is traced without any overt plea for sympathy and with a clear understanding of the class barriers surrounding her love affair with David Blakely (played by Rupert Everett). Ruth Ellis (Miranda Richardson) may have known that her hopes of marrying above her social class were doomed and this might well have precipitated the emotional storm under the clouds of which she shot her violent, possessive and unfaithful lover; it certainly seems likely and the screenplay of *Dance with a Stranger*, by Shelagh Delaney, has no hesitation in adopting this view.

Unlike *Yield to the Night*, which follows this hapless victim of society and the State into the death cell, *Dance with a Stranger* ends as Ruth Ellis stands silently beside the body of her dead lover outside The Magdala public house in Hampstead. For this reason *Dance with a Stranger* does not qualify as a prison movie; yet it is one that touches indirectly and with feeling and compassion upon more aspects of that world than many movies which are set entirely behind iron bars and grey concrete walls. Ruth Ellis's prison, *Dance with a Stranger* tells us, is one inside which countless women are permanently confined.

Dors was then regarded only as a blonde pin-up, a fact that might explain the unforgivable American retitling of this movie as *Blonde Sinner*).

By the 1980s attitudes had changed, particularly towards the role of women, but despite

In striking contrast with the Ruth Ellis case is that of Barbara Graham, a California prostitute who was arrested in 1953 following a series of brutal kidnappings, in which victims were tortured, robbed, and sometimes killed. These crimes were the work of a gang led by Jack Santos and at least six men, women and children died before the police made their arrests. Barbara's chief role with the gang appears to have been to give them a seemingly innocent front, someone who could persuade intended victims to open their doors. However, after the gang's arrest one member gave the police evidence that one of the killings was the direct work of Barbara Graham. This was the pistol-whipping to death of an elderly cripple, Mabel Monahan, in Burbank, Los Angeles.

With the only direct evidence against Barbara that of another gang member and the introduction by the prosecution of facts about her past unsavoury life, doubts were raised about the fairness of her trial.

Pre-trial publicity in articles by journalist Ed Montgomery destroyed any chance that she might be treated leniently, or even fairly. One comment exemplifies his attack on Barbara: 'It's her tough luck to be young, attractive, belligerent, immoral, and as guilty as hell.'

Later, Montgomery decided that he had gone too far and wrote more articles, this time in Barbara's favour. But he'd done his hatchet job too well. Barbara Graham was a scarlet woman and American society in the 1950s was no more responsive to the needs of women than was British society, which condemned Ruth Ellis for her lifestyle. As in the Ellis case, once the wheels of justice had begun to grind it took more than a few doubts to stop them crushing anyone tossed into the mill.

During her trial Barbara posed for dramatic pictures with the youngest of her three children but neither these nor a string of desperate attempts to establish alibis helped her.

Barbara went to the gas chamber at San Quentin on 3 June 1955, along with Santos and Emmett Perkins, another member of the gang.

Where the circumstances of the Ruth Ellis case understandably gave rise to compassion-ate movies, the case of Barbara Graham led to a movie that aimed not at compassion for a woman as a victim of society but simply sought to bring an end to capital punishment.

The movie is *I Want to Live* (1958) starring Susan Hayward. Under the direction of Robert Wise she builds an impressive performance that ranks among the best of her career. However, despite the fact that Barbara Graham's guilt was open to some question (unlike Ruth Ellis's which was never in doubt), the movie conveys a measure of uneasiness as if its deliberate manipulation of the audience is somehow inappropriate. Despite the fact that this manipulation is in a worthy cause, the abolition of capital punishment, the movie falls well short of the empathy displayed in *Dance With a Stranger* and is sometimes a lesser movie than *Yield to the Night*. For all its flaws, however, *I Want to Live* is always interesting and its closing seq-

The words of the priest, John Marley, bring little comfort to Susan Hayward as she prepares to go to the gas chamber after her 'trial by newspaper' in I Want to Live **(1958).**

ences, as the central character is taken to the gas chamber, are among the most powerful and harrowing ever filmed. For her performance in *I Want to Live* Susan Hayward won the Academy Award as Best Actress of 1958.

The case of Barbara Graham notwithstanding, Hollywood, and film-makers in general, rarely came to terms with women in prison movies. For the most part they either dumped them on the sidelines or simply exploited them.

Few, if any, film-makers brought to their stories of women in prison a fraction of the sym-

pathy and understanding displayed in the penultimate stanza of Pat Arrowsmith's poem *Stone Womb*, a work that stemmed from her own experiences in prison:

> Here to be punished, cured, deterred,
> turned into well-adjusted citizens,
> these women simply cling and huddle together,
> seethe, explode with spurious laughter,
> dreading the moment of expulsion into
> the dangerous cold outside.

Kids' Stuff:
Reform School Movies

'The delinquent has become the demon of
the twentieth century.'
(Masud Hoghughi)

If Hollywood usually treated women rather badly, in or out of prison movies, they often didn't treat delinquent kids badly enough, erring, instead, on the side of a quite appalling cuteness.

As juvenile delinquency becomes increasingly a matter for concern, especially in the light of a recent tendency towards extremes of mindless violence, the children's prison movie takes on added interest. As some recent movies have shown, there is a tough fate in store for young offenders (if they ever get caught), which is perhaps what society really wants. Certainly, many sections of contemporary society in Western Europe and America appear to believe that children have become a race apart, to be feared and avoided at all costs.

Things were rather different in Hollywood in the 1930s and there is very little in that decade's movies to placate those who seek tougher retribution for Clockwork Orange thugs. In those days, Hollywood must have been filled with an unnaturally high proportion of film-makers who looked on the world of juvenile crime through eyes attuned to the principle of 'there but for the grace of God and Pat O'Brien go I.'

In a string of 1930s' movies tough but lovable teenagers grew steadily less tough and more lovable as each movie wore on. In *Mayor of*

Hell (1933) the kids in the reformatory are very hard done by, thanks to malfeasance in office by Warden Thompson (Dudley Digges). As a mother observes, 'They sent my last boy there and he came out a murderer.' All is not lost, however, for along comes gangster Patsy Gargan (James Cagney) who has been given an official post as a reward for helping fix an election. When poor mistreated little Jimmy (Frankie Darro) tries to escape and ends up tangled in the barbed wire fence, Patsy changes sides and cleans up the reformatory.

The movie's ending is considerably tougher than many which followed; Patsy goes on the lam, the old warden comes back and imposes even harsher discipline, the boys rebel, the warden falls onto the barbed fence and dies. Patsy then returns and the movie ends with him reinstating enlightened methods of rehabilitation.

Warner Brothers' *Dead End* (1937) is not concerned directly with the reformatory, although the threat of this and adult prison hangs over the deliberately artificial studio set. The juveniles in *Dead End* are played by a group of teenage actors, including Huntz Hall, Billy Halop and Leo Gorcey, known collectively as The Dead End Kids. The Kids appear again in *Crime School* (1938), a remake of *Mayor of Hell*, which stars Humphrey Bogart and depicts a regime of corporal punishment, bad food, and an environment guaranteed to depress even the jauntiest kid. The plot was used again as *Hell's Kitchen* in 1939, this time with an ex-racketeer, Buck Caesar (Stanley Fields), putting a reform school to rights with the aid of Jim and Beth (Ronald Reagan and Margaret Lindsay), a pair of amiably inept social workers.

1938 saw one of the best of this group of movies, *Angels with Dirty Faces*, in which delinquent youngsters are given lessons in life by gangster Rocky Sullivan (James Cagney) and Father Jerry Connelly (Pat O'Brien, Hollywood's priest-in-residence) who grew up together but went their separate ways when Rocky was caught by the cops after a joint escapade. As Father Pat never tires of explaining, had he not been able to run as fast as he did he

might well have ended up alongside his pal Rocky in the gangs. This plea for the environment as the sole shaper of men's destinies lays the delinquent movie philosophy squarely on the line.

Cagney's aggressive, twitchy, pants-pulling performance, and his catch-phrase, 'Whaddya hear? Whaddya say?', caught the imagination of millions of fans (and almost that number of impressionists). Cagney claimed he based his characterization on the behaviour of a hophead pimp he saw hanging around street corners near his childhood home in Yorkville, New York City.

The ending of *Angels With Dirty Faces* still

Priest or not, Spencer Tracy (l) is about to teach young punk Mickey Rooney some table manners in Boys' Town **(1938).**

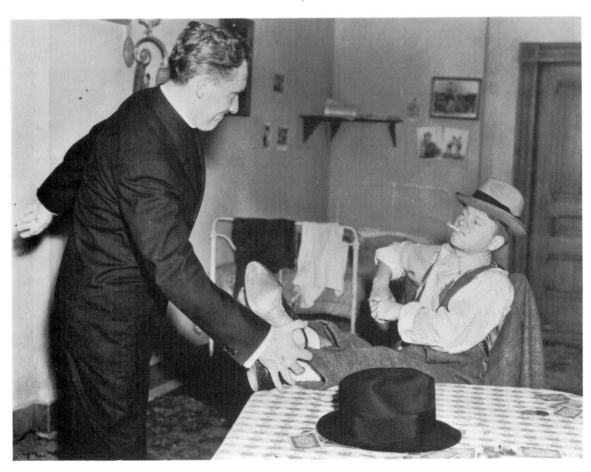

causes arguments: Father Jerry asks tough-guy Rocky, whom the kids emulate, not to go easily to the chair. Rocky refuses, 'Crawl on my belly? Nothin' doin'!', and walks out of shot as tough and bantam-cocky as ever. But then he starts to yell and scream for mercy; the kids are shaken into the straight life when the press asserts: ROCKY DIES YELLOW. The argument revolves, of course, around the reason for Rocky's change. Was he really yellow or did he do it all for God, Father Jerry, and the immortal souls of the Dead End Kids? No one will ever know for sure.

The popularity of the delinquent movie saw variations on limited themes from most of the studios with MGM, which loved sentimentality, trying a predictably softer variation on *Dead End* with *The Devil is a Sissy* (1936) with lovable, wouldn't-harm-a-fly rascals Mickey Rooney and Jackie Cooper. Monogram took a fling with *Boys of the Street* in 1937 while 1938 saw Columbia's *Reformatory* with ex-Dead End Kid Bobby Jordan. In the same year MGM tried again with *Boys' Town*, based upon the efforts of real life Father Edward J. Flanagan (Spencer Tracy) to solve the environmental problem by taking the delinquent kids, led by Whitey (played by the still rascally if not quite so lovable Mickey Rooney), out of the corrupting city to the clean air of the countryside (the movie does not dwell upon what the country-dwellers think of this invasion).

Father Flanagan's motivation comes from a condemned murderer he meets on a prison visit, who tells him that if he had been helped as a child he wouldn't be where he is now.

The improbable ending has Father Flanagan and his boys tracking down the recently escaped Whitey to the headquarters of an (adult) gang of outlaws, rounding them up, and claiming the reward money, which is desperately needed to keep Boys' Town in existence. Well, it's more exciting than holding a flag day.

Other 1938 juve-movies included *Beloved Brats*, in which the delinquents are girls driven to bad ways by curiously fascistic parents, and *Delinquent Parents*, the title of which left no one in any doubt who was to blame for junior's ills.

1939 saw RKO's *Boy Slaves*, which takes the action out of the city and onto a prison farm where hoboing kids are picked up on vagrancy raps and used as a sub-contract labour force at a privately-operated turpentine camp. Two of the boys, Tim and Jesse (James McCallion and Roger Daniel), escape and are eventually befriended and freed by a kindly judge. Essentially a welfare-orientated polemic against forced labour, *Boy Slaves* has its moments but has failed to withstand the passage of time.

As their titles suggest, *Angels Wash Their Faces* (1939) and *Men of Boys' Town* (1941) were hedging their bets as the cycle wound to a close. The Dead End Kids were not merely growing older, they were also being steadily more influenced by the MGM-Mickey Rooney syndrome. Despite changes of personnel and name (they became the Little Tough Guys, the East Side Kids and the Bowery Boys), they were also losing popularity.

Curiously enough, few of these films were as tough-minded as the much earlier *Are These Our Children?* (1931), which allowed its teenage hero to go to the electric chair. Even in later, harder times such an event was a rarity.

A later juvenile movie capitalized upon the youthful appearance of much-decorated war hero Audie Murphy but *Bad Boy* (1949) finds nothing new to say. Made under the auspices of Variety Clubs International as a means of boosting their Boys' Club ranch at Coppers Cove, Texas, *Bad Boy* centres upon disturbed Danny Lester (Murphy) whose case is investigated by Marshall Brown (Lloyd Nolan). After a fair amount of psychiatric soul searching all is resolved; Danny thinks he caused his mother's death and has been making everyone else's life miserable ever since.

Riot in Juvenile Prison (1959) features the problems encountered when Dr Paul Thurman (Jerome Thor) tries to amalgamate a reform school for boys with one for girls. As the male school includes a handful of convicted rapists Thurman's notion is viewed somewhat suspiciously but it all ends happily, after Stu Killion (Dick Tyler) has unsuccessfully tried to rape Kitty (Virginia Aldridge).

The Bad Boys **(1983) go on the rampage proving that decades of 'correctional' establishments have failed to achieve their aims.**

By 1971 and Stanley Kramer's *Bless the Beasts and Children*, times were changing. This well-meaning movie strove to be up-to-date in its philosophy – a group of delinquent kids try to save a herd of buffalo imprisoned as prospective gun fodder for hunters. However, it has about it a slightly old-fashioned air as it equates socio-political problems with society's disinterested attitude towards the environment.

Just as backward-looking in its theme is *Bad Boys* (1983) in which a tough, street-wise punk, Mick O'Brien (Sean Penn) is sent to Rainford Juvenile Correctional Facility where he finds himself caught up in internecine conflict and interracial battles between other juvenile offenders. Out of the heated confrontations that develop, O'Brien (and the prison movie echoes that that name brings with it cannot be entirely coincidental) builds a resolve to serve his time and later attempt to go straight.

Throughout the 1930s, and the subsequent juvenile delinquent movies, the prevailing theme was that which Eddie Smith (Frankie Darro) declaimed in the courtroom scene in *Wild Boys of the Road* (1933):

You're sending us to jail because you don't want to see us. Well you can't do it because I'm not the only one! There's thousands just like me and out there's more hitting the road every day. Go ahead! Put me in jail! Lock me up! I'm sick of being hungry and cold. I'm sick of freight trains. Jail can't be any worse than the street, so give it to me.

The problem for this movie and most of the others lies in their conflict with reality. By the 1960s, and most certainly thereafter, delinquent kids on the outside were no longer little rascals, they were frequently villainous thugs who could and did maim, murder and rape at random and regarded property as something to take or destroy upon a passing whim. The vicious Clockwork Orange world of Anthony Burgess had arrived with a vengeance.

The violence inside a British institution for young offenders was shown to grim effect in *Scum* (1978), a movie made originally for the BBC who then decided it was not for them. Starring Ray Winstone, Mick Ford and Phil Daniels, and directed by Alan Clarke from Roy Minton's script, the movie looks unflinchingly at the life led by juvenile offenders in detention and relentlessly drives home to the audience that the only possible outcome for anyone sent here is that they will return to society as better, tougher, more ruthless criminals. Accurate or not, *Scum* helped reinforce the public's imagination of how degrading and frightening such establishments can be and helped underline the futility of expecting anything good to come out of them. Although young offenders are sent to such institutions as a punishment, such places appeared to inflict punishment, which is by no means the same thing.

Another unintentional effect of many juvenile prisons is to provide young offenders with a first-class criminal education. Interviewed by Ian Williamson for the *Independent* in December 1988, Fred Crowe, governor of Huntercombe Young Offenders Institution in Oxfordshire, England, observed, 'If your son came here, if he didn't know before, by the time he left he would know how to start a car without a key, how to open a Yale lock, where to get drugs – all the information needed to survive on the streets.'

A grim threat to young offenders in reform schools, and especially if they were placed in adult prisons, is that of homosexual attack. This

was rarely if ever hinted at in early movies but today homosexuality in many walks of life is an acceptable movie subject and latterday prison movies thus have an element their predecessors could barely hint at.

While homosexuality appears as an element in many post 1960s prison movies, including *Riot*, it was the *raison d'être* for *Fortune and Men's Eyes* (1971), which was based upon ex-convict John Herbert's stage play. This disturbing and frequently harrowing tale had at least one genuinely beneficial effect upon society at large. During the play's off-Broadway run in 1967 audiences were invited to attend regular seminars to learn more about prison life and to meet ex-convicts and discover at first hand what life behind bars is really like. Out of these seminars grew the Fortune Society, which became one of the most important rehabilitation organizations in America and one of the few that use ex-convicts as counsellors.

To some extent the movie, which was shot in Quebec prison, does less than justice to the problem of homosexuality in prisons, descending as it occasionally does to a soap-opera superficiality. The storyline follows the misfortunes of Smitty (Wendell Burton), a naïve collegian who is canned for possession of pot. Smitty's cellmates are Rocky (Zooey Hall), whose outward toughness hides a sensitive bookworm, Mona (Danny Freedman) and Queenie (Michael Greer). Smitty is given an unstraight choice: he can either be the victim of a weekly gang rape in the dining hall, or he can appoint Rocky as his protector and be sodomized nightly, but solitarily, in the showers. Smitty settles for the latter and is unsurprisingly hardened by his experience.

For all its failings in comparison with the original play, the movie is a couple of jumps ahead of a sensational revival for the stage which starred Sal Mineo and featured on-stage nudity and simulated sex.

An American documentary film from the late 1970s, *Scared Straight!*, follows a group of teenage criminals who are sent on a visit to prison in lieu of punishment in order to be shown what life there was really like with the admonition that they could take the warning seriously or suffer the consequences. Surrounded by some of the biggest, most frightening-looking cons in captivity the kids swore they would never put a foot wrong. At the time they probably meant what they said; whether their obvious fear of the big cons lasted afterwards is another matter. A dramatized documentary follow-up, *Scared Straight! Another Story* (1980) used some actors as kids and cons but still conveyed a powerful message.

Short Eyes (1971), shot on location in Tombs prison on the corner of Centre and Franklin Streets, New York City, also looks at an aspect of sexuality in its tale of Clark Davis (Bruce Davison), a child molester. He is plunged into danger when he is imprisoned with assorted robbers, rapists and murderers. According to the dubious code of honour which exists in the joint, his is deemed an unforgivable crime and one for which the other cons seek summary justice.

Homosexuality is one of the prompts to the downfall of a juvenile in a 1982 movie which is rather more concerned with the potential dangers of the short, sharp shock principle of punishment. *In the Custody of Strangers* traces the descent of the Caldwells, a blue-collar American family into a kind of contemporary hell.

When one of the kids, Danny (Emilio Estevez), steps out of line his well-meaning father tries an old-fashioned remedy. The youth is not bad but merely restless. His parents are ordinary people, the father is out of work and trying desperately to find a job and is filled with 'old-fashioned' ideas about how people, especially children, should behave. The mother tries to keep the family well-balanced, sharing her affection equally between her husband and her three children. (The parents are played by Martin Sheen, Estevez's real-life father, and Jane Alexander.)

When Danny gets drunk and drives a car into the back of a police car his father takes a predictable but fateful step. He tells the police officer who has telephoned to ask him to come and collect Danny, that a night in the cells will do him a world of good.

This home-made short sharp shock treatment backfires alarmingly when Danny is approached in the police lock-up by a man in the adjoining cell who tries to molest him through the bars. Danny fights the man off, injuring him badly and the next day, when his father arrives to take him home, he finds that his son faces further, more serious charges, and release is impossible.

In the weeks that follow Danny is bounced around between judges, lawyers and social workers, and becomes steadily more desperate as a widening gulf separates him from his bewildered parents. Locked in an isolation cell Danny becomes briefly catatonic and it is at this point that the police chief, Caruso (Kenneth MacMillan), takes a hand. Caruso has no axe to grind for Danny, he dislikes him in the same way that he dislikes all lawbreakers. But while the lawyers and social workers bicker and prevaricate, Caruso can see that the youth is being turned into a criminal psychopath.

Eventually, after months of legal wrangling, Danny is released. His father has finally found a job in another town and the family is reunited. But the closing image of Danny, as he stands in his impersonal room in the new home in which he is a stranger, with barred shadows falling across his face, is a clear message that the shock, however well-intentioned, has served only to alienate him from a society guilty of imposing these traumatic events upon him. The future for Danny Caldwell looks bleak indeed.

If what befell Danny Caldwell sounds like the overheated imaginings of a screenwriter (the unemotional script is by Jennifer Miller), it might be salutory to look briefly at two real life cases, one which began in the 1920s, the other in the 1960s.

In 1925 Stephen Dennison, then aged 16, stole a $5 box of sweets and was sent to a reformatory in New York. As a result of his treatment there he rebelled and was transferred to the state prison. As he continued kicking against authority, more and more time was added to his original sentence. He was finally released in 1959. By any stretch of the imagination, 34 years in the slammer is a high price to pay for stealing candy. Even Jean Valjean in Victor Hugo's *Les Misérables* didn't have it that bad.

In 1966 Edward Lee McNeil, a brilliant 19-year-old black student, was convicted (without a jury trial) of an assault on a police officer and assault with intent to rape and was sent to Patuxent Institution, Maryland. The sentence was for not more than five years and McNeil could have expected release in 15 months. Unfortunately for McNeil, he decided that if he co-operated by agreeing to be evaluated and treated he would, in effect, be admitting his guilt, which might jeopardize his appeal. He therefore refused such co-operation and was put on the 'receiving tier' of the prison (the other tiers leading inmates towards their eventual release). It was six years before McNeil's case came before the US Supreme Court and he heard Justice Douglas angrily expound upon the Catch-22 situation in which the young prisoner had found himself:

> First the staff refuses to diagnose him . . . unless he talks . . . Second, if there is no report on him [because he refused to talk] he remains on the receiving tier indefinitely and receives no treatment. Third, if he talks and a report is made and he is committed as a 'defective delinquent', he is no longer confined for any portion of the original sentence [but then is liable to be held in prison indefinitely] . . .

Unfortuntely for the Edward McNeils and Stephen Dennisons of this world, or even those represented by the Danny Caldwells of the movies, what a US Supreme Court Justice thinks and what happens in the real world of reformatories and prisons for juvenile offenders is a very different matter indeed.

One thing that becomes apparent from many cases brought before the courts is that the prevalent attitude unpleasantly resembles that of Jean Valjean's nemesis, Javert, in *Les Misérables* who observed, 'I administer the law; good, bad and indifferent.'

The men behind the administrators are no more flexible in their thinking and, indeed, offer a remarkably high level of support for their appointees in the prison service. Not many years ago a prison warden in Washington, DC, was given the city's highest award for public service just two weeks after eight violent criminals, four of them murderers, had broken out of the prison he commanded, a prison which, 56 years earlier, had been condemned as inadequate.

Maybe there's a moral in such events; on the other hand, maybe a moral is what's missing.

Out of Our Sight and Out of Their Minds

'...in this Godless crypt of the damned,
I somehow managed to survive.'
(Frances Farmer)

Neither Hollywood nor, to be fair, feature film-makers elsewhere ever felt wholly at ease with mental illness. Nevertheless, on some occasions the incarceration of individuals in the largely unknown, and hence greatly feared, world of psychiatric hospitals has offered movie-makers opportunities for serious drama. Predictably, some have churned out wildly exploitative movies.

The range of institutions depicted on the screen has included those for the criminally insane in which inmates played their eye-rolling parts by way of introduction to murder stories, horror flicks, or even comedies. Other times, movies focused upon psychiatric units, of all grades, complete with portrayals of patients whose cases afforded opportunities to examine America's curious love affair with Freud, an affair in which misunderstanding played a greater role than film-makers might have realized. Time and time again audiences have been regaled with half-baked ideas on psychology and psychiatry, presented to them as if they were Holy Writ.

The ideas of many early movie-makers were coloured by the German Expressionist classic *The Cabinet of Dr Caligari* (1919). The film was not shown in America until two years after its completion by which time it was already hugely successful in Germany and in other countries where it had been screened covertly. (The secrecy stemmed from an embargo of sorts placed upon German films following the end of World War I.) The impact of the film on audiences and on other film-makers was emphatic. Powerful cinematic images abound throughout this strange tale whose protagonist claims to have been the powerless tool of an insane doctor, Caligari (Werner Krauss). The man, Cesare (played by Conrad Veidt), claims to have been hypnotized into committing dreadful acts including the attempted rape of a beautiful woman (Lil Dagover) and the murder of her lover. Cesare insists that as a result of these acts the woman has been placed in a lunatic asylum where she sits blank-faced and uncommunicative. At the film's conclusion, the entire tale turns out to have been the crazed imaginings of Cesare who is himself a patient in an asylum where he is under the benign care of the doctor he claims to be his manipulator.

Despite the impact *The Cabinet of Dr Caligari* had on American film-makers, the visual morbidity of the Expressionist art movement, which lent Gothic imagery to the German film industry in the 1920s, was generally avoided by Hollywood. There were exceptions, notably

The surreal dream world of psychotic patient Conrad Veidt as he kidnaps Lil Dagover in The Cabinet of Dr Caligari **(1919).**

where it suited a special kind of non-naturalistic film of which Universal's horror cycle of the early 1930s offers two excellent examples in *Frankenstein* and *Dracula* (both 1931).

As for the subject matter of *Caligari* – insanity – this was something which needed careful handling if it was to be the core of a movie and not just audience titillation. All too often, careful handlers were in short supply.

Although essentially a romantic melodrama of love among the doctors, the setting for *Private Worlds* (1935) is a mental hospital, which is used to generally good effect.

Tentatively skirting the edges of insanity, the film's main concern is with three psychiatrists, Jane Everest, Charles Monet and Alex Mac-Gregor (Claudette Colbert, Charles Boyer and Joel McCrea), each of whom has a 'private world' which influences his or her behaviour.

Jane nurses her love for a boyfriend killed in the war, Charles hides the fact that his sister, Claire (Helen Vinson), is an insane murderer, Alex neglects his wife, Sally (Joan Bennett), for his work in which Claire provides an intriguing facet.

The problems of the patients provide anecdotal opportunities for simplistic remedies while the effect the doctors' shenanigans have upon them is an area studiously ignored by the screenplay (which comes not from life but is based upon Phyllis Bottome's novel).

Perhaps surprisingly, considering the way in which it was received by the British censors, there is an absence of sensationalism in *Bedlam* (1946), a horror film from the Val Lewton stable. Like all of Lewton's films the technical quality is very high, with excellent photography from Nicholas Musuraca and workmanlike direction by Mark Robson. *Bedlam* was originally denied a release in Britain for reasons which, today, are difficult to understand. Perhaps just the thought of Boris Karloff as the master of an eighteenth-century London lunatic asylum was enough to give British censors sleepless nights.

Set in St Mary's of Bethlehem, the London asylum immortalized in Hogarth's paintings, *Bedlam* takes a dark look at the good old days when such establishments were part of show-biz. Members of London's high society paid to visit such places, there to view the crazed antics of fellow human beings as they suffered in anything but silence.

The movie is not, of course, a high-minded tract. It sets out to tell a yarn and commendably fulfils its brief. Nell Bowen (Anna Lee) is an actress who tries to help the inmates of Bedlam but rouses the antagonism of the asylum master, Sims (Karloff), and winds up there herself when he pulls a few well-connected strings.

Once inside, Nell makes friends but, being a thriller, the film's denouement centres upon Sims who is captured by the inmates and put on 'trial'. Sims's intellectual gifts are such that

he is judged sane but that doesn't prevent summary justice for past mistreatments. He is stabbed and bricked up in a chamber within the asylum.

It was a fate the heads of a few real life institutions in some countries might well have deserved, even up to the present day.

Darryl F. Zanuck's decision in 1948 to put the weight of his studio, Twentieth Century-Fox, behind a major feature set in an insane asylum was quite remarkable for the day. The director of *The Snake Pit*, Anatole Litvak, had bought the rights to Mary Jane Ward's novel and came to Zanuck after he had failed to persuade more cautious Hollywood moneymen to back him. Astutely, Zanuck homed in on the central theme, the plight of a young woman who suffers

A horrifying nightmare becomes reality as Olivia de Havilland awakens to find herself in *The Snake Pit* (1948).

a mental breakdown and is incarcerated in an asylum for the severely ill, and believed that a strong and successful movie might result if correctly handled. For the most part Zanuck was proved right and a strong script, by Frank Partos and Millen Brand with contributions by Zanuck, allied to a superb performance from Olivia de Havilland as the patient, made the movie a massive box-office success.

Virginia Cunningham (de Havilland) awakes in a mental hospital and to her growing horror realizes that this has been her home for the past five months, a period of which she is only hazily aware. Virginia's distress is effectively conveyed and so too is her gradual recovery aided by the careful and sympathetic treatment of Dr Kik (Leo Genn) who traces the cause of her breakdown.

Dramatic tension is maintained as Virginia's recovery is impaired but everything comes to the conventional happy ending of *The Snake Pit*'s era with her reunion with husband Robert (Mark Stevens).

If the manner in which the psychiarist cures his patient by explaining the causes of her breakdown seems a trifle pat, the movie's heart was certainly in the right place. *The Snake Pit* was a critical and financial success earning five Academy Award nominations, although failing in all categories.

Seen today, the movie's principal weakness is its casual acceptance of now suspect, if not actually dishonoured, assumptions about the treatment of the mentally ill. As countless thousands have found to their cost, despite the medical world's almost universal advocacy of electroconvulsive therapy, this was not a panacea that would solve the problem of how to deal with psychiatric disorders at the flick of a button.

Although few feature film-makers chose to set their tales exclusively in the world of mental illness, many used short scenes set in mental hospitals without proper justification. Fortunately, a handful used such scenes in ways that were not merely dramatically effective but were also appropriate and sensitive.

The Secret Fury (1950) centres upon a plot in which someone is trying to drive Ellen (Claudette Colbert), a concert pianist, crazy. Her wedding to David (Robert Ryan) is stopped with allegations that she is already married and when her 'husband' Lucien (Dave Barbour, real life guitarist and husband at the time of singer Peggy Lee) is murdered Ellen is arrested and put on trial. A subsequent mental blackout is followed by incarceration in hospital where only music helps her keep a grip on her sanity.

The meaning of the title emerges when a doctor refers to the erratic peaks on an encephalograph reading as 'the hills of secret fury'. As the movie is really a dramatic thriller, the plot against Ellen is eventually unwound by David, who discovers that her attorney, Kent (Philip Ober), himself more than a little unstrung, wants to drive her insane by way of revenging himself over an injustice her father committed many years ago.

Music is also a factor in the life of fading nightclub singer Rose Hopkins (Peggy Lee) in *Pete Kelly's Blues* (1955) but her case is precipitated by a beating she receives at the hands of her hoodlum lover Fran McCarg (Edmond O'Brien). Rose is doomed to spend her days in confinement and the scene in which she is interviewed by Pete Kelly (Jack Webb, who also directed) is treated with great restraint and sympathy.

Little restraint is shown during Elizabeth Taylor's visit to a mental hospital in the desperately uneven *Suddenly, Last Summer* (1959), a film which also touches on another of medical science's most drastic treatments for mental illness, the frontal lobotomy.

Simple-minded psychology and psychiatry enjoyed a brief vogue in the early 1960s with such films as *Psycho* (1960), *Pressure Point* (1962), which also doubles as a tract for liberal attitudes on race, and a remake of *The Cabinet of Dr Caligari* (1962) which, despite a script by Robert Bloch who had also written the novel on which *Psycho* is based, fails to get to grips with the theme of psychiatric disorder. The movie's title is about all the resemblance it bears to the 1919 classic.

Pressure Point explores racism and bigotry in a study of an attempt by a black psychiatrist

(Sidney Poitier) to cure a severely disturbed German-American Bundist (Bobby Darin) who is serving time for sedition. The film, which is based upon Dr Robert Lindner's book, *The 50-Minute Hour*, condenses several factual case histories into one. The Jew of the original becomes black here, thus patching into the rising tide of black consciousness, which even Hollywood couldn't ignore for ever.

Behind Locked Doors (1948) had used the ploy of sending private investigator Ross Stewart (Richard Carlson) into a sanitarium where he believes a missing judge is being held against his will. A similar idea initiates the plot of *Shock Corridor* (1963) in which Johnny (Peter Breck), a journalist, has himself committed to an asylum for the insane in order to track down a killer he believes is sheltering there. Directed with his usual quirkily dramatic style by Samuel Fuller, and brilliantly photographed by Stanley Cortez, the movie contains many genuinely gripping and even scary moments despite the fact that Fuller occasionally unlooses his inclination to shock for the sake of shocking.

In the asylum Johnny encounters a world he cannot begin to comprehend, surrounded by such individuals as Stuart (James Best), an ex-POW who has been brain-washed by the Koreans, Trent (Hari Rhodes), who has cracked under the pressure of being the first black to attend an all-white university in the deep South, and Boden (Gene Evans), a nuclear physicist who has reverted to childhood.

Johnny finds himself becoming entangled in the insanities of his new world, fantasizing about his girlfriend, Cathy (Constance Towers), a stripper who had warned him: 'Their sickness is bound to rub off on you.' Later, the sexual balance is reversed and Johnny is subjected to mass rape (or its 1960s' cinematic equivalent) by a gang of female patients.

The slow slide Johnny takes to becoming genuinely schizophrenic is effected with frightening verisimilitude. The movie's messages, and there are several, flit through his crumbling mind: the brainwashed POW thinks himself to be a Civil War hero; the black student

believes he is white and a member of the Ku Klux Klan; the physicist prefers the uncomplicated world of childhood to the terrifying world of mass destruction he has helped to create. Johnny, too, disappears into a mirror-image world wherein he obsessively pursues his inquiries until nothing else matters.

The movie leaves him as a hopeless, catatonic schizophrenic and the final line, from Euripides, comes as a warning to all: 'Whom God would destroy, he first sends mad.'

Very much an odd film out in the 1960s was Robert Rossen's *Lilith* (1964), which dismayed critics and audiences at the time of its release. In part this was due to the sometimes disorientating style Rossen chose to give his compelling tale of a young schizophrenic, Lilith Arthur (Jean Seberg). Without a clearly defined character with whom to identify, audiences were unsure of their own place in the complex,

Jean Seberg plays her alluring tune in Lilith **(1964).**

shifting patterns as Lilith unwittingly weaves an alluring web for her fellow patients and staff at Poplar Lodge, a psychiatric hospital. Rossen's style also made it difficult for audiences to take a detached view, forcing them into involvement with first one, then another of the characters until their judgement was impaired. In this way the audience became as helpless to shifting compulsions of diseased minds as were those individuals whose story was unfolding on the screen. It was not customary for audiences of commercial films, even those with a psychiatric basis, to be obliged to face up to the difficulties encountered in real life by patients and staff of such establishments.

Another factor that made the movie rather hard to swallow was that the prime mover in the eventual disaster which overtakes Lilith and Stephen Evshevsky (Peter Fonda), a young patient who is in love with her, is a well-meaning member of the hospital staff. In other movies of the day decisions were made by competent staff sure of the validity of the treatment they prescribed for their patients. The actions of Vincent Bruce (Warren Beatty), a trainee therapist, disturbed audiences who were unwilling to concede that the professionals were frequently very much in the dark about the vagaries of the human mind.

When Vincent also falls in love with Lilith the way is open for a tragic ending as he jealously pretends to Stephen that the girl has rejected him. Stephen kills himself and Lilith, who confuses Stephen with her dead brother, falls into a catatonic trance. The closing line of dialogue in the movie, delivered by Vincent who has first tried to run away from the disaster he has precipitated, further unnerved American audiences accustomed to regarding psychiatrists with blind faith. How could they any longer trust a profession whose representative on the screen turns to appeal directly to the camera with the words: 'Help me.'

A decade later the wheel had spun so that a psychiatric movie which did *not* question the care and treatment of the mentally ill was the exception. Indeed, the white coats worn by members of staff at movieland's psychiatric hospitals became the latterday counterpart of the black hats worn by villains in silent westerns.

Consequently, audiences had no difficulty in deciding whose side they were on when Randle P. McMurphy, an intermittently violent itinerant worker the police can no longer handle, is sent to a psychiatric hospital for assessment in *One Flew Over the Cuckoo's Nest* (1975).

Although the movie, which won five Oscars including Best Picture and Best Director, completely misses the rampant paranoia of the remarkable Ken Kesey novel on which it is based, there is still much to enjoy as McMurphy (Jack Nicholson, who won an Oscar as Best Actor) stomps his way through the hospital, rousing the patients from their drug-induced apathy until they reach the point of revolution. McMurphy, however, is not content with jolting the patients out of their stupor, he must also confront and defeat the white-coated representative of authority, Nurse Ratched (Louise Fletcher, another Oscar winner).

The main flaw in a film which deserved pretty well all the plaudits it received is that it disregards the allegorical nature of the novel. For author Ken Kesey, the patients, depicted as victims of the all-powerful Combine, are representatives of all ordinary men and women who have come up against authority in any form. In the movie, they are sympathetic characters but there is never any suggestion that they should not be where they are, merely that their treatment should be different. Another failing is that the film takes McMurphy's point of view; although McMurphy, the self-declared 'bull-goose looney', is central to the novel he is seen through other eyes. The novel is narrated by the supposedly deaf and dumb Native American Chief Bromden, another patient who drifts in and out of a drug-induced fog thus giving his narrative moments of hallucinatory confusion which sharpen and clear as his medicine wears off and he nears the moment of his next dosage.

The total war waged by McMurphy in the novel descends in the movie to a series of set pieces, each of which gives McMurphy a small victory: a wildly enjoyable outing on board a boat; a basketball game in which McMurphy mounts the shoulders of the giant Chief Bromden (Will Sampson) to score basket after basket; the electroconvulsive therapy sessions, before one of which the Chief reveals to McMurphy that he is neither deaf nor dumb.

Ultimately, the movie becomes a personal confrontation with Big Nurse, one which she knows she will win in the end. When McMurphy brings a hooker into the hospital, partly in order to allow young Billy Bibbit (Brad Dourif) to lose his cherry, Big Nurse moves in for the kill, even though it means sacrificing Billy who kills himself after she mercilessly harangues him. Driven inexorably to attack Big Nurse, McMurphy is taken away and lobotomized.

Jack Nicholson having fun before he realizes that the Big Combine is out to destroy him in One Flew Over the Cuckoo's Nest **(1975).**

Having centred upon McMurphy throughout, the closing sequences are perhaps the movie's weakest whereas they are among the novel's strongest as the narrator, Chief Bromden, repays McMurphy's rejuvenating friendship by placing a pillow over his head and suffocating him. With his friend free from the Combine at last, the Chief too breaks out, smashing through windows and bars, just as McMurphy had earlier suggested to him, and heads for the hills of his untroubled youth.

Against all expectations *One Flew Over the Cuckoo's Nest* was a massive commercial and critical success and the clutch of Oscars it earned ensured that it continued its money-earning ability into a successful video release.

Although the intended target of Ken Kesey's novel was not the world of psychiatric medicine, the movie version homed in on this area and its success confirmed that audiences no longer held the profession in unquestioning awe. While this might well be regarded as an

important step forward the film could, and
sometimes does, go too far. Psychiatrists, the
men and women in the white coats, are not a
suitable replacement for black-hatted cowboys
as movie villains; but the movies love stereotypes and for a while they were in danger of
becoming the new cardboard cut-out all-purpose baddies.

Whether or not the white-coats were bad,
good or in between, psychiatry was no longer a
box-office risk and a string of movies appeared
which were, like their characters, good, bad
and sometimes neither.

Among these grim cinematic worlds was one
that appeared in a tale of life in a hospital for
the criminally insane wherein patients are not
treated for their illness but are merely subju-
gated by sadistic, bullying guards. This seems

an unusual entry among movies made
especially for American TV but this is what
appeared in *The Other Side of Hell* (1978),
which stars Alan Arkin and Roger E. Mosley.
Directed by Jan Kadar, the movie conveys a
disturbing sense of the helpless and hopeless
despair of inmates unable to speak or even
think clearly for themselves.

A lighter and more optimistic world appears
in *I Never Promised You a Rose Garden* (1977),
a low-key account of the tribulations of Deborah
Blake (Kathleen Quinlan), a schizophrenic teen-
ager, and a surprisingly thoughtful product of
Roger Corman's New World stable.

Deborah's story starts with her parents (Ben Piazza and Lorraine Gary) placing her into the care of Dr Fried (Bibi Andersson) who digs into the girl's past and succeeds in exorcising a few demons. The fact that the audience is privy to a physical manifestation of these demons weakens the account.

Deborah's eventual cure is never really in doubt and neither is that of the female protagonist of *The Cracker Factory* (1979), a TVM directed by Burt Brinkerhoff and starring Natalie Wood as a disturbed young woman with severe drink and attitude problems.

David Cronenberg's *The Brood* (1979) gives warning of the director's penchant for powerful horror flicks with imaginative special effects. Here patients at a psychiatric hospital manifest their mental illnesses in a succession of physical ways, each more hideous than the last. That no one is supposed to take any of this seriously is signposted by the casting of Oliver Reed as Hal Raglan, the chief psychiatrist.

The psychiatrist is the outsider in *Birdy* (1984), which traces the struggle of one Vietnam vet to aid the recovery of another. Al Columbato (Nicolas Cage) is in a psychiatric hospital recovering from what was once called battle fatigue and is now named combat trauma (but is, apparently, no more understood now than it ever was). In the hospital he finds his childhood friend Birdy (Matthew Modine) who is wholly withdrawn and lives in a fantasy world in which he believes he is a bird with all the qualities of such creatures, including that of flight.

Al applies his knowledge of Birdy's background, his love of birds, his over-dominant parents, his diffidence with girls, and his gradual immersion into a world in which he can relate only to the little creatures to which he has devoted his life, and slowly makes progress. In so doing he not only improves upon the performance of army psychiatrist Dr Weiss (John Harkins), but also succeeds in unwrapping the cause of his own psychosis. This 'gifted amateur' approach may not be especially believable but the movie, directed by Alan Parker, carries over any inherent problems by giving wing to Birdy's fantasies.

The hospital in *Birdy* is a grim, dark place from which flight, metaphorical or in this case literal, is seen as the only true release and if the authority figures are not considered to be corrupt they are at least inept.

As suggested, the authority figures in many present-day movies set in institutions for the mentally ill, be they psychiatric hospitals or asylums for the criminally insane, rarely come out well. Instead, they are shown to be inept, incompetent, corrupt, brutal; at best they are well-meaning muddlers. Quite clearly such stereotyping is inaccurate and unfair but patient care in some psychiatric hospitals in America and Britain, to say nothing of less enlightened countries where such establishments are used as a form of state prison, still leaves much

Nicolas Cage takes care of Matthew Modine while the baseballs take care of themselves in Birdy **(1984).**

to be desired. Film-makers do right to point to flaws in the system, even if they are sometimes guilty of overstating their case. The manner in which many authorities react to criticism by film-makers is exemplified by the actions of the state authorities in Massachusetts who banned the showing of Frederick Wiseman's harrowingly depressing, yet impressively honest documentary, *Titicut Follies* (1967), which was shot in one of the state's mental institutions. Massachusetts is not alone in believing that if you close your eyes such things will go away.

Feature films made about such places could do more to change public attitudes if only movie-makers would learn to treat their subject matter with a little more insight and sympathetic understanding. The greatest failing of almost every movie made about psychiatric illnesses is that the makers only rarely get to grips with one of the central issues of psychiatric care. This is the manner in which patients are not given the care their individual cases demand. Rather, they are too-often assessed, and their fate determined, by the manner in which they respond to the circumstances and conditions of the institutions in which they are kept. Most outsiders would agree that kicking and fighting, literally if necessary, against unwarranted incarceration in a mental hospital, is a sign of razor-sharp sanity. Yet such behaviour is often regarded by the authorities as proof positive of the validity of their previous decision to commit an individual who may be not insane but merely different. As a result it has become alarmingly common to read in the popular press or see television exposés about men and women who have become embroiled in a frighteningly unbreakable predicament resembling a world which combines the bureaucractic hopelessness of *Catch-22* with the nameless dread of Kafka.

Whether or not the individual concerned is sane is, to some extent, immaterial. Obviously, if a sane person is placed into psychiatric care, benevolent or not, the effect would be traumatic, possibly causing irreparable damage.

But is it any less terrifying for someone who is psychologically disturbed to be thrown into such a place? The sane do not have exclusive rights to feelings of fear, distress, helplessness, hopelessness, and the terrifying knowledge that they have been imprisoned in a place from which there may well be no release but death.

One particularly frightening example of the State's ability to take away the freedom of an individual and subject that person to enforced imprisonment in a psychiatric hospital and hideous treatment skirts uneasily close to the artificial world of the movies. The individual who suffered many years of despair, humiliation and brutality was not a criminal but a member of the most highly visible branch of America's aristocracy – a Hollywood star.

The popular view of Frances Farmer is that she was a movie star who went mad. Beneath that surface impression lies a murky truth – the story of a beautiful, talented and spirited young woman who was destroyed by a dangerous combination of quasi-legal psychiatric malpractice and her own inability to compromise.

After being a non-person in Hollywood for almost 40 years a sudden burst of interest occurred in the early 1980s when three movies were announced: *Committed*, a low-budget independent, *Will There Really Be a Morning?*, a TVM, and a fully-fledged feature, *Frances*.

The difficulty for all the intending makers of these movies is that no one, least of all Frances herself, ever seems to have been sure what drove her to behave the way she did. In *Frances* (1982) the title role is played by Jessica Lange (an actress with a remarkable physical resemblance to Frances Farmer) and follows her real life traumas with reasonable accuracy. Among changes made is the introduction of a narrator-figure, Harry York (Sam Shepard). This would have been an acceptable detraction from the truth were it not for the fact that the character also becomes involved with Frances, thus dislocating anyone with knowledge of her case. There are also one or two altered names including 'Dick Steele' (Christopher Pennock) who substitutes for Frances's real first husband, actor Wycliffe Anderson, who later changed his name to Leif Erickson.

Such alterations to reality as those made in

Frances are, however, generally unimportant and for the most part a serious attempt is made to build a framework for the persecution that followed Frances's occasional and often incoherent outbursts of radicalism.

Frances's childhood was spent in and around Seattle, Washington, a strange corner of the United States where radicalism flourished alongside reactionary extremism. This dichotomy was even present in the Farmer household: her father was a lawyer who often defended radicals, her mother was a demented right-winger who once displayed her patriot-

ism by attempting to breed a red, white and blue chicken.

Frances upset the local community when she won a national school essay-writing competition with a piece entitled, 'God Dies'. Later, she became locally prominent as an actress and attracted much favourable publicity, which rebounded on her when she became involved with pro-Communist agitators in Seattle. Then, two students sold subscriptions to a Seattle-based Communist newspaper in her name and did so well that she won a contest. Her prize was a trip to Moscow from which she returned outspoken in her praise for Communism.

Soon after the trip to Russia she was in Hollywood, being groomed by Paramount, and when she married Wycliffe Anderson it looked

Jessica Lange, as Frances **(1982), starts to make the enemies who will eventually destroy her.**

as though she had grown out of her youthful flirtation with the left. She hadn't, and she shocked the narrow film world, and her mother (played in the movie by Kim Stanley), by going to New York where she became a member of Group Theater, the home base of such radical minds as Elia Kazan, John Garfield and Clifford Odets.

Frances fell in love with Odets (played by Jeffrey DeMunn) but their relationship was traumatic for her and after he rejected her she returned to Hollywood and began drinking heavily. She was also taking amphetamines, drugs with then unknown side effects.

Her drinking and drug-taking brought confrontations with the police, who took unkindly to the language she used to describe them. Calling a cop a 'cocksucker' is no way to handle a drunk driving rap.

By now Frances's behaviour had antagonized three groups of people who, if they did not hate her, were certainly unfriendly towards her: the right-wing American Vigilantes of Washington State in her hometown, who had previously threatened to 'get even' with her; the capitalistic film community, which frowned on her links with Communism and, for that matter, with the left-wing theatrical groups in New York; and the local law enforcement agencies. To these can be added her mother who disapproved of her daughter's rejection of Hollywood. Frances's marriage was on the rocks but even if things between her and her husband had been better it is doubtful if he would have been much help. For one thing, as he would later assert, he never really knew her. For another, his political views were quite different. In the mid-1950s, Erickson made a statement on the Hollywood blacklist to *American Mercury* in which he indicates his attitude towards radicalism. Among his comments is the declaration that no 'loyal producer or director has any business hiring an actor who for ten years has fronted for subversion . . . If this type of actor doesn't know the score by now, let him starve to death . . .' Quite clearly, Frances Farmer could have expected little aid and comfort from that quarter at a crucial moment in her life.

Frances was dropped from a movie being made on location in Mexico when she was taken ill with dysentery but as this was an undignified illness for a movie star the studio announced that she had suffered a nervous breakdown. They couldn't have picked a worse substitute illness if they'd tried.

Arrested by the police after a fracas with a studio hairdresser, Frances was dragged from her hotel. The carefully alerted press eagerly took pictures of the drunken, half-naked actress being hauled into a police car on her way to jail. Her studio, who could and frequently did get their actors off much more serious charges than this, did nothing. Maybe they thought their unruly star should be taught a lesson.

The next day Frances abused a judge and was committed to a private sanitorium and from there was sent to the psychiatric ward of the Los Angeles General Hospital where she was subjected to insulin shock treatment. Although this was done without her consent it was not unlawful. California law in 1943 not only permitted this but also allowed any practising psychiatrist who showed an interest to have free access to any patient. Not surprisingly, several chose to dabble with the case of an already notorious film star.

Released into the care of her mentally unstable and now divorced mother, Frances went back to Seattle. She refused a film role because the treatment she had received made learning lines difficult; her mother was incensed by this perfectly reasonable decision and applied for a committal order. The application was heard by Judge Frater (also renamed in the movie) who was a leading member of the American Vigilantes of Washington State. Judge Frater did not believe in half-measures; he sent Frances to the mental hospital at Steilacoom.

In 1944 Steilacoom was dark, overcrowded and greatly resembled the worst imaginings of those visitors who had heard about Nazi concentration camps in Europe. Wards had floors of packed earth mixed with human excrement; hygiene was non-existent, treatment was brutal. Frances was subjected to electroconvulsive therapy and hydrotherapy (for which patients are plunged naked into a bath of ice-cold water and held there for hours on end).

Sexual degradation at Steilacoom was rife. Trusties permitted soldiers from a nearby army base to use the female wards as a brothel and eye-witnesses reported Frances being held down and repeatedly raped by gangs of drunken soldiers. Somehow, Frances hung on to her sanity but in 1948 came the final abrogation of her human rights.

Walter Freeman (unnamed in the movie) was America's foremost psycho-surgeon. While visiting Steilacoom he eagerly demonstrated his newest surgical technique in which he inserted a needle-like instrument through a patient's eye-socket thus enabling him to perform a lobotomy without leaving the usual telltale scars on the patient's temples. Another advantage was that Freeman's method took only seconds to perform.

Frances, who had been rendered unconscious with electric shock, was seen by Freeman. No one actually saw him operate on her although he certainly did operate on numerous patients that day. But he was alone with her and shortly after his departure, from being declared incurable, Frances Farmer became docile and obedient and within two more years was deemed fit to return to the outside world. Depressing though the thought may be, the lobotomy had granted her a form of release from the torture she had endured with such spirited determination.

Frances drifted around for the next few years, even married again, and suffered the ultimate show-business accolade of an appearance on *This Is Your Life* (which thus demonstrated what a numbingly offensive sham this TV institution really is).

The movie ends here with closing captions recounting the rest of Frances's life. She made a movie, hosted a TV show in Indianapolis, drank heavily, was diagnosed as having cancer, and in 1970 she died after a long and painful illness. She was 56.

The screenplay of *Frances*, by Eric Bergren, Christopher DeVore and Nicolas Kazan is not especially sensational. Given the nature of

Fallen star. Frances Farmer made many mistakes in her tragic life but none was so great that she deserved the appalling punishment meted out by a vengeful society.

Frances's story this is commendable although it is unfortunate that the screenplay was based largely upon Frances's autobiography, *Will There Really Be a Morning?*, published after her death with some obvious tinkering by Jean Ratcliffe, an acquaintance of her last years. For a variety of reasons the scriptwriters were unable to use *Shadowland*, the meticulously researched and powerfully moving account of Frances's life written by William Arnold and published in 1978. *Shadowland* evokes the grim tragedy of this beautiful actress who was destroyed because she did not, or could not, conform.

If, as some critics complained, the film fails

to focus on precisely what Frances Farmer rebelled against, or to determine whether or not there truly was a conspiracy against her, this is understandable given the circumstances of her life. Rebels in any country in any age do not always have a cause; a slow, choking build up of unfocused anger, of unarticulated protest, can be enough to cause them to kick over society's traces.

As for the conspiracy theory; there probably wasn't one because one wasn't necessary. Enough areas of American life and, increasingly, life in Britain are fraught with perils for noncomformists. Frances Farmer made enemies and once she was vulnerable to attack they closed in with ultimate effects more damaging than any formal conspiracy could have been.

Frances Farmer's case throws a disturbing sidelight on American (and other 'free world') societies not examined by the movie of her life. It is becoming steadily more difficult for the land of the free to also be the home of the brave. In the eyes of the American establish-

ment the two are increasingly incompatible. When brave men and women speak out, their mouths are closed by calumny, by imprisonment, by misuse of psychiatric medicine, even by death.

There are signs of improvement in attitudes in some places. A 1975 US Supreme Court ruling in the case of Kenneth Donaldson, who was detained in a Florida mental hospital for 15 years, held that, 'A finding of mental illness alone cannot justify a state's locking a person up against his will and keeping him indefinitely in simple custodial confinement.'

But such judgements came too late for Frances Farmer and there has been no similar shift in judicial opinion in Britain where cases are periodically unearthed of individuals confined for absurd periods of time.

The case of Frances Farmer might well be taken as a warning. She had a mind of her own and because her enemies could not control it they chose instead to destroy it and through their actions destroyed her.

8

Laughing at Lifers:
Prison Comedies

'Everyone in the world is bent.'
(The Italian Job)

In real life not many citizens, respectable or otherwise, will think a spell in the slammer is something to smile about. Yet some movie-makers have found in the subject of prison the source of light relief and a fair number of belly laughs.

Up the River (1930) was already on the studio floor when its producers became aware of some similarities to *The Big House*. Suffering a sharp attack of cold feet, the producers made some last-minute changes which turned *Up the River* into a quasi-comedy. Given the talent they had on hand, both experienced and untried (the film was directed by John Ford and marked the feature film debuts of Spencer Tracy and Humphrey Bogart), their panic at the potential competition from *The Big House* may have been a shade unnecessary.

What emerged was a casually engaging tale of a pair of con men, Saint Louis and Dannemora Dan (Tracy and Warren Hymer), who meet up in prison with Steve (Bogart) while doing time. Steve's girlfriend, Judy (Claire Luce), is across the way in the women's pen. The young couple are soon released only to be blackmailed into helping out in a scam. Judy asks Louis and Dan to help and they obligingly break out of prison, put the blackmailer in his place, and break back in again.

The same title appeared a few years later

when *Up the River* (1938) featured not only jokes but also a handful of songs. This time a pair of cardsharps, Chipper Martin and Darby Randall (Preston Foster and Arthur Treacher), are serving time in Rockwell penitentiary where the football team is making use of them. These two enterprising heroes break out of the joint, dressed as women, to help their pal, Tommy Grant (Tony Martin), save his mother from the attentions of a swindler. Then what do you suppose happens? Why, they break back into prison to help win the big football game. This amiable hokum is enlivened by a splendid dance routine with a line-up of cons dressed as chorines backing the superb tap dancing of Bill 'Bojangles' Robinson contributing their services.

Stan Laurel and Oliver Hardy were among life's losers for whom prison was an ever-present threat, if only by reason of the fact that they were permanently hovering on the edge of vagrancy, a state which, in their world, was an open invitation to a spell in the slammer.

Stan and Ollie bumbled their way into prison in *The Second Hundred Years* (1927), *The Hoose-Gow* (1929), and were there again two years later in *Pardon Us*.

In *The Second Hundred Years* the Boys (as they are still known to their loving fans) are doing more time than even the most hardened Big House denizen was likely to face. Doleful

Stan, on learning that a fellow con still has another 40 years to serve, promptly hands him a letter to mail when he gets out. The Boys decide to tunnel their way out but, being Stan and Ollie and not Bogart and Cagney, they promptly tunnel their way into the warden's office. Next, they slip through the main gates disguised as painters. Replacing a pair of Frenchmen whose car they hijack, the Boys have to return to the prison as distinguished guests of the prison governor (played by manic Jimmy Finlayson) and lay waste to a dinner party thrown in their honour before ending up back where they belong, in the cells.

In *The Hoose-Gow* Stan and Ollie wreak innocent mayhem all around them. Stan, put to work chopping down trees, fells the long pole atop which a guard dozes peacefully. When the Boys make a break for freedom, they try to escape in the governor's car, which they have already tried to repair by plugging its burst radiator with rice. When they hit a paint truck everything, and everyone, is covered in painted rice.

Like so many other good Americans (well, actually, Stan remained a British citizen to the end of his life) the Boys fell foul of the law during Prohibition. By this stage in their careers they had become endearing dunderheads and their films generally eschewed most forms of lawlessness. However, the climate of public opinion allowed them to become bootleggers in *Pardon Us* without losing their homely status.

Sent to prison when they botch their attempts to sneak around an unreasonable law, Stan and Ollie are soon up to their necks in bother thanks to Stan's bad tooth which causes him to emit a loud raspberry at usually inconvenient moments. The governor (Wilfred Lucas) declaims a stern warning, issued to countless cons in serious prison movies (and maybe in real life too): 'If you break the rules it will be just plain hell on earth.' This moment, and many others, effectively burlesques *The Big House* which was currently doing good business at the nation's box-offices.

The Boys share a cell with the prison's toughest con, Tiger (Walter Long), who is charmed by Stan's inadvertent raspberrying defiance of his authority (but when Ollie tries the same trick he swiftly learns that the Tiger's tail can't be tweaked twice). Soon involved in various escape bids, the unwilling duo also runs foul of the prison educational officer (James Finlayson, in mortar board and gown). After an orgy of ink-pellet flicking and a few other misdemeanours they are sent to the Hole. 'Have you got the time?' Stan asks the guard just before the door slams on him.

During an escape bid Stan finds himself with a machine-gun in his hands. Predictably enough, for someone whose film career was beset by inanimate objects that rear up and attack him at every conceivable moment, the gun keeps going off. The other prisoners are cowed into submission as bullets ricochet all over the place and a grateful warden pardons them – but not before Stan's raspberrying tooth almost undoes all their efforts.

For decades comedy duos have been likened to Laurel and Hardy, never with complete justification and often with none whatsoever. *They Went That-a-Way and That-a-Way* (1978) features Tim Conway and Chuck McCann as a pair of dumb cops who go into the joint to discover the whereabouts of some stolen loot. Later, they race off in hot pursuit of escaped convicts but it is a mostly hit-and-miss affair. The movie's publicity suggested kinship with Stan and Ollie; nothing else did.

A slightly creaky British comedy, *Convict 99* (1938), stars Will Hay as Dr Benjamin Twist, an academically inept schoolmaster (what else), who is accidentally appointed as governor of Blackdown Prison. Another case of mistaken identity puts Twist into a cell but he eventually sets about reforming the prison before being exposed as an unwitting imposter. Given Twist's characteristics of staggering ineptitude and academic ignorance, coupled with more low cunning than the most hardened criminal could ever hope to possess (attributes that Hay portrayed to perfection in all his films), he triumphs in the end. An entertaining twist to Twist's problems is created by Blackdown's longest-serving inmate (played with toothless glee by Hay's old sparring partner, Moore Marriott) who has spent his years of confinement burrowing through every level of the prison like a demented Abbe Faria until the building teeters above a honeycomb of incompleted tunnels.

In an unusual change of pace, Edward G. Robinson tried a comedy role in *Brother Orchid* (1940) some time before he moved into the long succession of excellent character roles that graced the second half of his film career. Robinson was wearying of gangster roles but had agreed to make one more for Warner Brothers in return for being allowed to make a medical drama about the search for a cure for syphilis, *Dr Ehrlich's Magic Bullet*, in the same year. In *Brother Orchid* Robinson plays Little John Sarto, an ageing gang boss who returns from an overseas trip to find that his rackets have been taken over by an underling, Jack Buck (Humphrey Bogart). With his solitary loyal aide, Willie the Knife Carson (Allen Jenkins), taking refuge in a psychiatric hospital Sarto also decides to hide out. He enters a monastery where he finds unexpected kinship with the reclusive monks and develops a flower business which attracts the attention of Jack Buck who tries to muscle in on this racket too. Sarto deals with Buck but has found his unexpected niche in life and opts to stay within the confines of a 'prison' of his own choosing, the monks having won him over to their gentle ways.

Thanks to Robinson's toughly sensitive playing, which never sinks into the cloying sentimentality that lay in wait for unwary actors in similar about-face roles, *Brother Orchid*

Peter Sellers (l) and Bernard Cribbins are up to no good behind Lionel Jeffries' back as he discusses the finer points of dynamite with David Lodge in Two Way Stretch **(1960).**

remains an entertaining movie and a diverting variation on the theme of isolating gangsters from society in prisons of concrete and iron bars.

An uneasy mixture of gentle, if occasionally lethal, comedy and a philosophical plea for tolerance, *We're No Angels* (1955) stars Humphrey Bogart, Aldo Ray and Peter Ustinov as three escapees from Devil's Island who halt their flight in order to assist a storekeeper and his daughter who are threatened by an individual far more villainous than anyone they knew inside. Only intermittently amusing, the movie strains for effect and most of the blame lies with Bogart and Ray, neither of whom was really suitable for this kind of role.

Psychology, prison and light comedy are blended together with a measure of success in *My Six Convicts* (1952), which stars Millard Mitchell and Gilbert Roland as convicts James

Connie and Punch Pinero who are test cases for a psychiatrist attempting to develop new ideas about rehabilitation of offenders. Based upon the real life experiences of Donald P. Wilson (played in the film by John Beal), this account centres primarily upon the need for the psychiatrist to engage the confidence of the prisoners with whom he works. Told with unnecessary oversimplification, but with commendable easygoing charm, the film also manages to combine some high drama with the jocularity. An escape bid by one of the six guinea-pigs turns nasty when the con, played by Henry Morgan, uses Wilson as a hostage. The other five cons realize that the psychiatrist has kept up his end of their unwritten bargain and not relayed their secrets to the governor even though this placed him at risk. In an appropriately upbeat ending they rally round and rescue him. Way down among the bit part players, appearing as an unnamed con, is a certain Charles Buschinsky; a couple of name changes later this actor, as Charles Bronson, became rather more prominent but was still occasionally behind bars.

The British comedy *Two Way Stretch* (1960), which owes a passing nod to *Convict 99*, features a parade of well-known comedy and character actors who use the prison in which they are doing time as a law-proof base for their light-hearted larceny. Occupying a 'luxury' cell are Dodger Lane, Jelly Knight and Lennie Price (Peter Sellers, David Lodge and Bernard Cribbins) who plan to give themselves an alibi for their next blag. They will surreptitiously break out of prison, pull the job, and slip back before anyone knows they've been naughty. Unfortunately, a new hot-shot governor throws them off their stride and opens the way to a sustained string of comic antics. The principals are well supported by Maurice Denham as the first dim governor and Lionel Jeffries as a sneering, vicious warder.

Among a number of other British comedies with prison content is *Ooh, You Are Awful* (1972), starring Dick Emery as con man Charlie Tully who whiles away a brief spell in the pokey by reading *Papillon*, surely a banned book if ever there was one. *The Prisoner of Zenda* (1979), stars Peter Sellers in a rather desperate attempt to send up a classic *Boys' Own Paper* adventure tale which had already been made at least four times before (once, in 1937, to non-comic cinematic perfection).

In *The Italian Job* (1969) the stereotype of the master criminal as Supercon takes its ultimate form. Mr Bridger (Noël Coward) controls the prison and his outside activities from a comfortable, pink-lampshaded cell complete with leather armchair. Even Mr Bridger's visits to the lavatory have a special flavour as he is escorted there by two fawning warders, one of whom carries Supercon's toilet roll. As Mr Bridger has discovered, everyone is bent.

Towards the end of the film, when the job he has sanctioned is successfully carried out, Mr Bridger, a rampant royalist, takes the plaudits of the admiring prisoners and staff with all the *élan* of a conquering hero.

By far the best use of prison as a setting for a British comedy was on television which, as usually happens, made a not-so successful transition to the big screen in 1979. *Porridge* stars Ronnie Barker as old lag Norman Fletcher dispensing wit and wisdom to the delight of cellmate Godber (Richard Beckinsale) and the stiffnecked frustration of Chief Prison Officer Mackay (Fulton Mackay). Superb scripts by Ian La Frenais and Dick Clement and excellent characterizations deservedly made the TV series a major success. If the movie version has its faults it is still much better than many more grandly conceived but ultimately lesser efforts.

A fairly successful American attempt at parodying serious-minded prison movies came

Surely Papillon **is a banned book in all self-respecting prisons, but Dick Emery (r) seems to have persuaded Norman Bird to let him have a copy in** Ooh, You Are Awful **(1972).**

with *Stir Crazy* (1980), which stars Gene Wilder and Richard Pryor as Skip Donahue and Harry Monroe, two innocents who are wrongfully arrested. Dressed as chickens, the pair are working on a sales promotion unaware that a pair of bank robbers have adopted a similar disguise for their more nefarious exploits. Not surprisingly, the court doesn't believe there could be *four* big chickens in town at the same time and into the can they go, facing 120 years apiece.

Like Laurel and Hardy before them, Skip and Harry are housed with the joint's toughest con, a giant looney named Grossberger (Erland Van Lidth De Jeude) whom Skip manages to dominate. Unlike Stan and Ollie, who had unlimited charm, neither Wilder nor Pryor has much to spare. Instead, both actors possess a great deal of frenetic energy and many of the gags work as a result of the impetus they build up with a manic display of typical Wilder-hysteria and Pryor-mugging.

Given his well-known love for old movies it is not at all surprising that Woody Allen is highly skilled when it comes to parodying the classics. Even if he was still learning his trade in 1969 when, directing for the first time, he made *Take the Money and Run*. The movie has several very funny moments.

Allen plays the leading role, that of the inept and hopelessly timid lawbreaker Virgil Starkwell, whose life is a succession of failed crimes (he carefully cuts a hole in the window of a jewellery store and runs off with the piece of glass) and spells in prison. Allen reprises, in his own anarchic image, several familiar movie scenes including the shuffling lock-step of the chain gang from *Hell's Highway* and *I Am a Fugitive from a Chain Gang*. He also uses the chain-breaking scene from *Fugitive* and even summons up the nerve to parody the same movie's whipping sequence.

When Virgil and some of his chain gang pals make a break for freedom, still chained together, he pokes fun at *The Defiant Ones*. He also upends stereotypical Hollywood when five men, four white and one black, race for freedom on four bicycles; it is not the black man but Virgil who trots alongside like a well-trained dog.

Among other delights of *Take the Money and Run* is the moment when Virgil is visited by his loyal but dumb girlfriend, Louise (Janet Margolin), who tries to push a hard-boiled egg through the screen that separates them in the interview room; a spell in the sweatbox becomes purgatory because Virgil is locked in there with an insurance salesman. Another scene has Virgil participating in a prison break which, unknown to him, has been called off so that he's the only one in the yard demanding, 'Where is everybody?'

There is also a moment, during another of Virgil's attempts to break out of prison which might have been drawn not from an old movie but from real life. Late in 1934, shortly after John Dillinger's death, two members of his gang, Harry Pierpont and Charles Makley, attempted to break out of Death Row at Ohio state prison. They had made imitation pistols, carved out of soap, with which they fooled one guard before they were fired on by others. Makley died but Pierpont survived to go to the electric chair.

In Woody Allen's version, Virgil Starkwell makes a gun out of soap but with typically bad timing makes his escape bid during a rainstorm. As he threatens two of the prison guards, Virgil's gun dissolves into a mass of inoffensive bubbles.

Although for most people prison is a very serious business indeed, it may be fortunate that a few, admittedly outsiders, saw the potential for humour. From Laurel and Hardy to Woody Allen, with several lesser lights in between, prison briefly proved to be a laughing matter.

9

Prisoners of Colour,
Conscience and Creed

'We do not merely destroy our enemies,
we change them.'
(Nineteen Eighty-Four)

Hollywood never did very well by racial and religious minorities, perhaps a surprising fact given that many of the film capital's moguls were themselves members of the same minority groups.

For many years the least well-served of these groups were the blacks (although Native Americans, who bit the dust in countless horse-operas might well challenge this statement). Unlike the moguls who did pretty well in their off-screen lives, blacks were kept in lowly positions behind the scenes. In this respect it might be argued with some justification, but little justice, that the appearance of blacks on-screen in such menial roles as janitors, housemaids, railway porters and the like was merely reflecting reality.

A few early prison movies had an occasional black face far down the cast list but only *Hell's Highway* allowed a touch of realism to intrude by displaying substantial numbers of blacks among the chain gang prisoners. Sometimes small but key roles were granted, as in *I Am a Fugitive from a Chain Gang* where it is a black prisoner who helps free James Allen from his chains. In *The Prisoner of Shark Island* the much put-upon Dr Samuel Mudd lays down the law to the blacks he meets at Dry Tortugas, causing one cowed black to observed, 'Dat am no

Yankee talkin' jus' to hear himself talk. Dat's a Southern man an' he means it!'

Ladies of the Big House had a black prisoner (played by Louise Beavers), while the first version of *The Last Mile* included a black denizen of Death Row.

It was not until the changing times of *The Defiant Ones* that a leading role went to a black actor.

But hardly any of these movies so much as brushed against the greatest imprisonment suffered by blacks – slavery – and certainly none dealt with it head-on. Of course, slaves popped up in a great many movies that dealt with the South but even in *Gone With the Wind* (1939) they formed a muted chorus against which the drama was played out. In the earlier *Birth of a Nation* (1919), a true classic of the cinema but also a viciously racist tract, it was taken for granted that slavery was the rightful place of blacks in America.

By the 1970s blacks had begun to take a much more prominent place in the movies (at least in front of the cameras) and it might have been hoped that someone would tackle the admittedly thorny subject of slavery in a feature film. Well, someone did but the result, perhaps predictably, was not serious drama but mere exploitation.

Mandingo (1975) is based upon the steamily sensational novel by Kyle Onstott and features a parade of highly improbable characters including ageing plantation owner Hammond Maxwell (James Mason) who cannot satisfy his sexy young wife, Blanche (Susan George), whose earlier dalliances with her brother Charles (Ben Masters) have left her lusting after more than marriage will allow. The fact that among her husband's slaves is tall, powerfully-muscled Mede (Ken Norton) opens the way for all manner of naughty goings-on in the hot Southern nights.

The fact that sexual violation during the centuries of slavery was a cruel fact of life for countless black women makes the events depicted in *Mandingo* particularly distasteful.

The movie met with sufficient success to prompt a sequel. Having already dealt with miscegenation and incest, other forms of titillation had to be found and *Drum* (1976) offers a lesbian relationship between slaves Marianna and Rachel (Isela Vega and Paula Kelly). Hammond Maxwell (Warren Oates) has a hot-hipped teenage daughter, Sophie (Ranbeaux Smith), who gets her kicks, and more, from hanging around the slave-quarters wherein resides (you guessed it) the tall, powerfully-muscled Drum (Ken Norton).

As has happened too often to give movie-makers pleasure, it was left to television to tackle an important subject in an adult and open manner. *Roots* (1977) is a 12-hour saga which traces the story of a black family during a 250-year period from when young men and women were wrenched from their African homes and brought to the Americas and sold into bondage. Based upon the book by Alex Haley, whose family tree sprang from these tragic roots, the series captured the public's imagination and garnered great critical praise and massive, record-breaking audiences. Just how much it did for race relations is debatable, certainly it did little to enhance the status of blacks in American television (hardly any blacks were involved in the behind-the-scenes production). But there can be no doubt that it did a whole lot more to force white Americans to face up to

what generations of their forefathers had done before emancipation than all the products of Hollywood strung together. The 14-hour sequel, *Roots: The Next Generations* (1979), brought the story up to the present and if slavery was no longer central to the tale, it was still implicit in interracial relationships and the attitudes of blacks towards a white society that persistently refused to grant them anything better than second-class citizenship.

Unfortunately for the world we live in, colour of skin is not the only factor that determines the level of their society to which men and women might aspire.

For any citizen fortunate enough to live in a democracy the thought of being put into prison or held *and* treated in a psychiatric hospital for nothing more serious than disagreeing with the current political authorities is the stuff of nightmares.

Terrifyingly, such nightmares show an alarming propensity for coming true. Figures published by Amnesty International in 1988 show that in half the countries of the world people are imprisoned for simply expressing disagreement with their government. But it is not only in countries governed by extremists of the left, the right, the military or the church that such things happen. Ordinary law-abiding citizens of Great Britain and the USA, hitherto major bastions of democratic principles, have recently become increasingly subject to curtailment as their governments drift to the right. Prison looms for dissenters and critics when they speak up against racism, disarmament, censorship and numerous other restrictions on civil liberties previously taken for granted. Freedom of speech, through the medium of newspapers, books, radio and television, and the movies is no longer an inalienable right. Basic freedom is fast becoming what government decrees it to be.

The American Freedom of Information Act is an important bright spot in the midst of pervading gloom but the adamant refusal of the British government to agree to a similar enactment inevitably brings fears that the society portrayed in shades of grey by George Orwell in his novel *Nineteen Eighty-Four* may well become more than a satirical vision of out-of-control State interference in personal liberties. It might well be a foretaste of reality – if it isn't a picture of a state that already exists.

Until fairly recent times politics was not a particularly favourite topic for film-makers. Hollywood risked a handful of bio-pics about presidents and other leading statesmen but these movies were frequently unpopular. Indeed, before the outbreak of political radicalism in America, politics meant almost certain death at the box office. From the 1960s onwards dissent among teenagers, at the time the mainstay of cinema audiences, suggested that the subject might be worth risking, but only rarely did the resulting movies concern themselves with imprisonment. Protest was the thing in which the youth of America was involved and this was the way the movie-makers went, doubtless comforted by the thought that protest was often dynamic and visually exciting. Trials could be satisfyingly dynamic, but the harsh aftermath of a political trial, the prison sentence, was a risky business for the big studios and on the few occasions when film-makers took the risk it was usually left to the independents.

Orwell's modern classic novel has appeared twice as a feature film, the result on both occasions being rather uneven.

Nineteen Eighty-Four (1955) was made in England during the period when it was commonplace to import minor American stars for the leading roles. For this film the quality of the actors concerned was rather better than was often the case in such deals, with Edmond O'Brien playing the role of Winston Smith and Jan Sterling as Julia.

Cut to the bones, Orwell's novel is a discussion of the effects of a world divided into zones of influence and through parody he examined the implications of totalitarianism.

Even a casual glance at Orwell's book clearly shows that the writer was as much, if not more, concerned with the dangers from an out-of-control right as from the left. To a great extent public reaction took the opposite view, seeing *Nineteen Eighty-Four* as a portent of a world dominated by Communism. Britain in 1955 was not as fearful of Communism as were the Americans, at the time still wrestling with red-baiters and anti-Russian hysteria. But there is nothing in the movie to allay fears that the grim threat of an Orwellian future came not from the capitalist West but from the Communist East.

In Orwell's world there are three great powers, Oceania, Eurasia and Eastasia and each is perpetually at war with the others. The setting for the novel is London, the capital of Airstrip One, which is itself the third most populous province of Oceania. The 'Party' rules Oceania through four ministries each of which has absolute powers. The Ministry of Peace deals with war, the Ministry of Love with law and order and includes the dreaded Thought Police, the Ministry of Plenty deals with scarcities, and the Ministry of Truth is concerned with propaganda. It is the last of these ministries that employs Winston Smith whose job is the endless revision of official records to accommodate shifting political needs.

Smith's desperate attempts to create a private world inside the regimented, controlled society in which he exists, to have a true love affair with Julia, and to attempt, however feebly, to plot against the State is eventually uncovered by the Thought Police. This brings him into the orbit of O'Brien (played by Michael Redgrave), a member of the Inner Party, who confuses Smith with his apparent kindness and consideration, which in fact conceals an implacable and ruthless individual dedicated to the supremacy of the State and the State's unseen but venerated leader, Big Brother.

Smith's imprisonment in the Ministry of Love heralds a period of physical and mental torture the object of which is Smith's reintegration into society (a near cousin of the rehabilitation aimed at by all penologists). Under the Party this reintegration is in three stages: learning, understanding and acceptance. The culmination of Smith's treatment takes place in Room 101 of the Ministry of Love, the room in which even the strongest can be broken.

The special torture of Room 101 is that here to each individual is given that which he most hates. In Winston Smith's case it is the threat of being eaten alive by rats. When he cries, 'Do it to Julia! Not me!' he has finally capitulated to Big Brother. It is with this ultimate capitulation that Orwell's novel ends; Winston Smith has won the victory over himself and now loves Big Brother.

Movie audiences in 1955 were not ready for such despair, or so movie-makers thought, and this version of *Nineteen Eighty-Four*, scripted by William P. Templeton and Ralph Bettinson and directed by Michael Anderson, ends on an upbeat note of defiance.

On the surface of the world immediately outside the cinemas of the 1980s there might have been a patina of consumer society glitz mingling uncomfortably with a new wave of clockwork orangery but beneath that surface there was much that resembled Orwell's fantasy. By and large he'd got it right; and it was the right that was in power not the left of earlier popular suppositions and fears.

When *Nineteen Eighty-Four* was remade in 1984 those changes that had occurred in society were accommodated and the original defeated ending returns. Although there is no overt shift in the shading of the ideological content of the movie, perhaps a rather higher percentage of the film's audience in Britain realized that they were looking at a mirror image of the world in which they were already living. In 1984 *Nineteen Eighty-Four* was no longer a version of life in some distant land in a far off time; it was here and it was now. Audiences, accustomed to a recent plethora of films and TV plays which railed against the existence of a State-manipulated conspiracy of secrecy and censorship, saw themselves in the same plight as Winston and Julia.

Nineteen Eighty-Four (1984), written and directed by Michael Radford, stars John Hurt as Smith, Suzanna Hamilton as Julia and Richard Burton as O'Brien. The setting is intelligently realized as a blend of the familiar and the unexpected. This is no super-tech state in which the computer has replaced man but rather a creaking, broken-down society held together by a combination of apathy and mistrust.

If the political inclination of *Nineteen Eighty-Four* is equivocal according to the leanings of the audience, *The Prisoner* (1955) is more readily defined as a Church versus atheistic State polemic, and is accordingly angled against left-wing totalitarianism. Although a powerful work, and a showcase for the two principal actors, Alec Guinness as the Cardinal and Jack Hawkins as his Interrogator, the theatrical origins of *The Prisoner* in Bridget Boland's play are too evident and her screenplay takes too few of the liberties necessary to make it work satisfactorily on the screen.

The Prisoner is loosely based upon the case of Cardinal József Mindszenty, the Hungarian archbishop sentenced in 1949 to life imprisonment for treason against the Communist government but released in 1956 to the American embassy in Budapest where he remained until 1971.

Following his arrest Mindszenty was held at the notorious Andrássy Street interrogation centre where he was questioned by Police Colonel Gyula Décsi and, according to his memoirs, subjected to relentless psychological pressure and severe physical torture designed to produce a confession of sins real and imagined. A frequent statement by the Cardinal's interrogators carries echoes of George Orwell's Room 101 in the Ministry of Love: 'Here the police decide what is confessed, not the defendant.'

In the movie, the Cardinal attempts to undermine the outcome of his arrest by declaring that any 'confession' will be either a lie or a sign of human frailty. As his interrogation proceeds, the Cardinal's self-image deteriorates as he realizes his own inadequacy and that he not only hates himself but bears no love for his fellow men. Worse, in his own eyes, he no longer finds pleasure in his belief in God.

At his show trial the Cardinal confesses to having betrayed the people to the Nazis during the recent war, that his entire public life has been a worthless sham, and that he has even been guilty of petty theft and blackmail. The confession proves good for the Cardinal's soul and he enjoys brief peace of mind. But then his

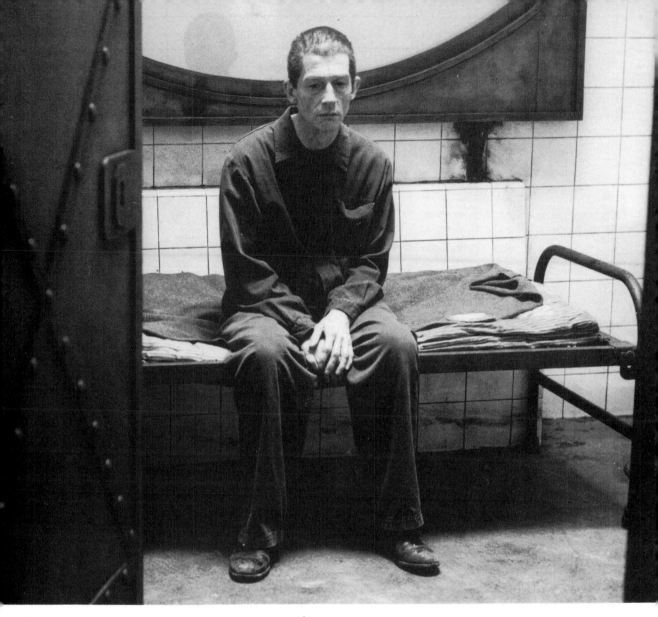

John Hurt discovers that the Ministry of Love is not what it seems in Nineteen Eighty-Four **(1984).**

death sentence is commuted and his release ordered. Now he will have to face the people, potentially an even greater punishment. As for his Interrogator, the long hours with his prisoner have taken their toll. He can no longer sustain his own beliefs in what he is doing and must resign his post; his last official act is to sign the Cardinal's medical discharge.

The powerful acting of the two principals, who are almost upstaged by Wilfrid Lawson as the Cell Warden, carries this wordy movie along and it still has an impact today. (Coincidental or not, 18 months after completing work on the movie, Alec Guiness was admitted to the Catholic Church.)

Events in several South American countries in recent years have shown the dangers of making simplistic assumptions about right or left, Church or State. In Argentina and Chile in particular there have been countless examples of imprisonment without trial, of execution without sentence. Some of the movies which have touched upon the subject have done so with care and sympathy. Notable among these is *Missing* (1982), written and directed by Constantin Costa-Gavras and starring Jack Lemmon. The 'prison' here, in Chile, is a football stadium and the use of such a place – one normally associated with pleasure – for holding and executing individuals suspected of political intrigue or dissidence adds to the threatening atmosphere. The fact that *Missing*'s message is sometimes undercut by the director's plainly one-sided view of American attitudes towards and involvement in South and Central America is easy to overlook as a parade of visually commanding images appears upon the screen.

For much of *Prisoner Without a Name, Cell Without a Number* (1983), the 'prison' is the house of Jacobo Timerman (Roy Scheider), editor of an Argentinian newspaper, who, in 1977, began to question the actions of the right-wing military government. After imprisonment and torture Timerman was placed under house arrest and spent several months living in one room of his home while police guards roamed the rest of the building intimidating his family and destroying his belongings.

Both Jacobo Timerman and Ed Horman, the character played by Jack Lemmon in *Missing*, are real people and their stories are true but the Timerman film fails to grip and involve the audience in the way that audiences responded to Ed Horman's search for his son and his slow realization that the government of his own country is behind the horrors he sees in this frighteningly foreign land. Timerman's story demanded more than the slack direction it received and, Roy Scheider apart, it also deserved a better cast.

Kiss of the Spiderwoman (1985) is the story of two prisoners in a South American jail who cling on to their sanity and hope in a curious way.

Although one of the prisoners, Valentin Arregui (Raul Julia), is a political prisoner the story quickly widens out into a strange fantasy world created by his cellmate's habit of hauntingly recounting the plot of his favourite movie. Luis Molina (William Hurt) is a homosexual hair-dresser imprisoned for corrupting the morals of a minor.

The threat of torture and death which hangs over Arregui is everpresent, but the edges of reality blur for him as he is seduced by Molina's dreamy fantasies. The relationship between the two men warms and deepens as each takes refuge from reality in Molina's movie (a strange mixture of brutality and eroticism set in German-occupied France during World War II). This bond is further strengthened when Molina lovingly cares for Arregui when he is stricken by poison administered by the authorities.

Molina is playing a dangerous double game, convincing the authorities that he will help them unearth Arregui's secrets while persuading them to send expensive food into their squalid cell. He eventually convinces the authorities to release him so that Arregui will reveal his secrets. On their last night together Molina tells Arregui the story of another movie, about a Spider Woman who falls in love with a shipwrecked sailor, and then confesses to his cellmate that he is in love with him. The two men make love and in the morning, as Molina is about to released, Arregui gives him a message for his insurgent comrades.

The film ends with Molina shot to death by Arregui's friends who think he has betrayed him, while back in the prison, thanks to a painkilling injection in the prison hospital, Arregui escapes into the fantasy world of the Spider Woman, becoming the shipwrecked sailor of Luis Molina's dream movie.

Fantasy filled the world of TV's *The Prisoner*, a series that eventually became a cult, in which a man of conscience struggles against the shifting faces of authoritarian figures, constantly echoing the universal cry of prisoners of conscience and victims of political extremism: 'I am not a number, I am a free man.'

Pushed to the limits of numbered captivity are the prisoners in the Siberian labour camps.

In *One Day in the Life of Ivan Denisovich* (1971) the central character (portayed by Tom Courtenay) is followed through one day in the hard, repetitive life he endures as a prisoner in a remote gulag. Survival is all that counts in this bleak, forbidding world. In order that he shall survive, Ivan Denisovich has to ensure certain basic necessities – enough food and enough clothing – but as his day passes he must also ensure other human needs. He must share the little he has with others, whether those things he shares are practical or spiritual, and he must accept that to make the day a 'good' one he need not achieve anything positive; it is enough not to achieve something negative. The

Just staying alive is a kind of victory for James Maxwell (l) and Tom Courtenay in One Day in the Life of Ivan Denisovitch **(1971).**

simple fact that he is not punished on this day is a reason for celebration.

The camps represent just one facet of 'treatment' available for use on political dissenters in the Soviet Union; others are injection with neuroleptic drugs, Sulfazin, insulin shock, electroshock, restraint in 'wetpacks', and solitary confinement. Given the choice, the labour camps might almost be seen as a soft option.

For all its setting and the political imperative surrounding the story's origins (the author of the novel, Alexander Solzhenitsyn, had himself served a term of imprisonment in a Soviet camp) there is a disturbing universality about

One Day in the Life of Ivan Denisovich. Ivan's story acclaims the spirit of mankind, sustaining the optimistic belief that man is indomitable even if there are often examples of the human spirit being conclusively crushed in Soviet and Third World penal systems and, occasionally but too often for complacency, in those of America and Britain.

Another example of misplaced Soviet zeal occurs in *The Fixer* (1968). Based upon Bernard Malamud's novel and set in Tsarist Russia, the tale, based upon real events, traces the imprisonment of Yakov Bok (played by Alan Bates), a Jew accused of the ritual murder of a Gentile child. Pressurized to deny his race and take responsibility for a crime he did not commit, Yakov undergoes fearful privations during his imprisonment but overcomes them by drawing upon a seemingly bottomless well of dignity and strength. As Yakov's lawyer, Bibikov (Dirk Bogarde), realizes, his client's imagined crime is merely an excuse for the State to lend spurious justification to its malicious persecution of the Jews.

A perverted form of 'justification' filled the pre-World War II propaganda spewed out by the National Socialist regime in Germany.

The concentration camps set up by the Nazis were initially declared to be places of confinement for political dissidents and those whose religious beliefs conflicted with the aims of the State. But the camps quickly became the means of pursuing a policy of religious persecution to its ultimate end, in this case the extermination of the Jews, gypsies and other individuals cruelly deemed as sub-human in the first step of brainwashing an all-too readily co-operative nation.

The existence of the concentration camps was known several years before the beginning of World War II. The governments of several European countries, including Britain and America, also knew what was being done in these camps. Even the Red Cross knew, and by late 1942 also understood the extent of the horrors. Yet virtually no steps were taken to bring them to an end. By the closing years of the war it was too late to do anything and millions had already been slaughtered.

A Russian film, *Concentration Camp* (1939), gave a Soviet view of the fascist threat, and if its one-sided approach seemed extreme at the time, later events gave it a considerable measure of justification (although the same nation's refusal to acknowledge its own persecution and wholesale slaughter of racial and religious minorities has yet to find adequate cinematic representation).

Until America joined the war in 1942, Hollywood took a fairly distant view of things. There were, however, some exceptions. As early as 1934 *Little Man, What Now?* adopted a positively anti-Nazi stance and, as Europe rumbled into war, a string of Hollywood films cottoned on to the box-office possibilities of anti-German movies even if, for the most part, they tended to be fairly immature espionage stories. The fate of the British, defending their tight little island against the Nazi threat took the fancy of some film-makers and a handful of strongly pro-British movies appeared, among them *Mrs Miniver* (1940). Even the Russians were viewed with a benign eye in *Mission to Moscow* and *North Star* (both 1943, and both getting their makers into a lot of post-war red hot water). In *The Mortal Storm* (1939) concentration camps are mentioned as is the fate of the Jews (and the film is also the first Hollywood movie to mention Adolf Hitler by name); *Escape* (1940) centres upon an attempt by Countess von Treck (Norma Shearer), a young woman, to free her mother from a camp, but such examples are rare.

A British film of the same period, *Pastor Hall* (1940), traces the true story of Pastor Niemöller who was sent to the camps in 1934 for speaking out against the fascists. Helped to escape by a 'good' SS man, Pastor Hall (Wilfrid Lawson) cannot restrain himself and when he again raises his voice in protest his death is assured.

Generally speaking, however, the camps remained a vaguely distasteful, almost subliminal image, and were generally avoided. They were mentioned, however, in Ernst Lubitsch's brilliant hard-black comedy, *To Be Or Not To Be* (1942), which stars Jack Benny, who delivers the line, 'So, they call me concentration camp Ehrhardt.' Criticized at the time of its release for its presumption that war was something to joke about, *To Be Or Not To Be* can be seen today as a superbly constructed film. Even the acquisition of knowledge of what was really happening at the time in Poland, where the film is set, cannot entirely unseat admiration.

The Seventh Cross (1944) takes a serious view of the subject but uses it not so much for protest but as a jumping-off point for an escape yarn as seven Germans escape from a camp and are hunted down and executed by the Nazis.

The hunting down and persecution of Jews took a movingly personal turn in one of the first post-war stories to have a great international impact. This was the true story of a young Dutch girl whose fate became known to the world when her diaries were discovered and published long after she had died in Auschwitz.

Anne Frank and her family had hidden in the attic above an office building in Amsterdam, remaining there for two years before their discovery by the Germans and transportation to the camps. The pressures on the family, incarcerated in a prison of their own making, give the movies based upon Anne's diaries a misleading feel of universality yet can anyone fully empathize with what befell the Franks? They were completely normal in all respects and had committed no crime; their fate and their fears were founded in the fact that they were Jews in a country invaded by a race hell-bent on destroying Jews. There is little there that smacks of true universality.

The two screen versions of Anne's story, both based upon the play by Frances Goodrich and Albert Hackett, are generally commendable. In *The Diary of Anne Frank* (1959) the outstanding acting performances come from Joseph Schildkraut, who was in the original stage play, as Anne's father, Otto, and Shelley Winters as Mrs Van Daan, although it is plagued by the inappropriate pretentiousness of CinemaScope.

The Diary of Anne Frank (1980), a TV movie, has good performances from Maximilian Schell, as Otto, and Millie Perkins, as Anne, yet neither this nor the earlier version carries the weight and authority the subject matter de-

mands in their depiction of the tension and constraints of a family imprisoned by their own hand in order to avoid extermination because of their racial origins.

Another television treatment, in 1988, took the viewpoint of those who hid the Frank family and their friends. *The Attic: the Hiding of Anne Frank* starred Mary Steenburgen as Miep Gies who risked her life by her humanitarian actions.

Susan Strasberg had played the role of Anne Frank in the Broadway stage production of *The Diary of Anne Frank* and also played the role of a young Jewish girl caught up in the Holocaust in a European co-production, *Kapo* (1960).

Edith (Strasberg) is 14 when she is taken from Paris to a camp where her parents are killed. Saved by the camp doctor who gives her a new identity, as 'Nicole' a non-Jew, she is transported to a camp in Poland. Edith barely escapes death, collaborates with the Germans, and becomes a kapo, a prisoner placed in charge of other prisoners. She abuses this position of authority and becomes the focus of the hatred of her fellow prisoners for her cruelty. Later, Edith falls in love with Sacha (Laurent Terzieff), a young Russian, and eventually sacrifices herself so that he and others can escape.

There is an uncomfortably simplistic crudity about *Kapo*; for every good deed there is a bad one, there are good Germans and bad, Edith is good then bad then good again. It is almost as if the film's makers (it was directed by Gilles Pontecorvo for a Franco-Italian production company) were desperately anxious not to offend anyone.

The failings of *Kapo* underline the problems facing feature film-makers wishing to deal with the Holocaust. Occasionally, a measure of success was attained when sequences depicting life in the camps were used to counterpoint contemporary actions and motivations in films which were not, on their surfaces, about this subject. Thus, *The Pawnbroker* (1965) and *Sophie's Choice* (1983) made an impact on their audiences as they demonstrated the harrowing effect of the concentration camps on survivors.

During the 1960s and on through the next two

decades television film-makers, some working in drama, others in drama-documentaries, and still others in straight documentaries, took up the subject and to their everlasting credit some of them came close to achieving success.

According to the Rules, part of a 1964 trilogy, *The Seekers*, is one example; another is *The Joel Brand Story* (1965), which dealt with the wartime efforts of Brand to persuade the Allies to accept Adolph Eichmann's offer to trade a million Jews for 10,000 trucks. This true story has an uneasily evasive quality that hints that the Allies' failure to accept the deal (in hindsight reprehensible) somehow lets the Germans off the hook. In 1985 *Mengele* pursued the story of the evil medical experimenter, while the same year saw the screening of *A Painful Reminder*, shot at the end of the war by Sidney Bernstein but suppressed so as not to damage attempts to put Germany on its feet again.

Some film-makers found themselves on more comfortable ground when blending the factual background into largely fictional accounts. *QB VII* (1974) tells the story of a writer, Abe Cady (Ben Gazzara), whose latest novel is based on events in the life and death of his father. The book becomes the centre of a libel case brought by an internationally famous Polish-born doctor, Adam Kelno (Anthony Hopkins), who believes the book has defamed him by levelling unsubstantiated accusations that he was responsible for medical atrocities committed in a concentration camp. The first half of this six-hour film traces Kelno's life from the end of the war as he rises to prominence, eventually being knighted in Britain, his new homeland. The second half of the film looks at Cady's life and what motivated him to write the novel. The closing stages are set in court as Kelno makes his case, eventually driving himself almost wilfully into a corner from which there is no escape but to admit the truth of Cady's accusations.

Although powerful enough in its way, *QB VII* (the title, incidentally, refers to the courtroom in London in which the trial takes place) did not take hold of the nettle of attempting to show, on prime-time television, a realistic picture of life in the camps. The same failing was detrimental to *Holocaust* (1978), a nine-and-a-half-hour TV mini-series, which, even so, managed to arouse extraordinary emotions wherever it was shown, not least in Germany.

Holocaust interweaves fiction with fact as it traces the lives of fictional persecutors, like Erik Dorf (Michael Moriarty), who rises unemotionally through the ranks as he helps put the Final Solution into effect, and fictional victims, like Karl Weiss and Inga Helms Weiss, a young married couple (played by James Woods and Meryl Streep) whose fate is determined by the fact that he is a Jew while she is not. They are riven apart by the persecution of the Jews in Germany while other members of the Weiss family face persecution and extermination in other parts of Europe.

Among the real figures who flit through the nightmare world of *Holocaust* are Reinhard Heydrich (David Warner), Heinrich Himmler (Ian Holm) and Adolph Eichmann (Tom Bell).

Playing for Time (1980) generated some of its impact from the acute contrast between the sights and the sounds of Auschwitz. This TV movie was based upon the experiences of Fania Fenelon (played by Vanessa Redgrave), a musician who was a member of the Auschwitz orchestra formed from inmates and ordered to play cheerful melodies, such as gay Strauss waltzes, in order to lull any suspicions new arrivals might harbour.

Escape from the death camps was rare but the story of an extraordinary exception is told in *Escape from Sobibor* (1987). Approximately 300 prisoners, among them Jews and Russians, were led to freedom in a mass breakout.

The chief problem for the makers of these TV films and of such feature films as *The Pawnbroker*, *Sophie's Choice*, or even the earlier *Judgement at Nuremberg* (1961), which originated as a TV play, is that of effectively convey-

In Sophie's Choice **(1982), the horrors of the concentration camp reached out over the years to claim Meryl Streep (with Kevin Kline).**

ing through visual imagery something which is incomprehensible to all normal human minds – the savage physical destruction of several million people. A cynical remark attributed to Joseph Stalin, that a million deaths is merely a statistic, highlights the problems for a film-maker. If it is impossible to show the reality of these horrific events how can they begin to imply it?

Interestingly, the two documentary film-makers who came closest to achieving the impossible chose not to attempt visual imagery but adopted instead a largely verbal approach. For all this similarity of approach, they were otherwise very different in their methods.

Shoah (1986) was made by French-born documentary film maker Claude Lanzmann and in the course of its nine and a half hours running time builds a relentless, overwhelming and eventually numbing picture of the manner in which one nation set out to eliminate another (the word *shoah* is Hebrew for annihilation).

Lanzmann interviewed survivors of the camps, onlookers, and surviving perpetrators of the crimes for whom human justice has been unable to devise a satisfactory penalty. Lanzmann's technique varies but most often he simply points his camera, asks his questions and then waits as, haltingly, evasively, stories tumble out. The still casually indifferent attitude of the farmers whose land borders Auschwitz lays bare reality for those who claim that such a thing could never happen again.

Lanzmann was not afraid to go over the same ground time and time again, with differences whose subtlety slowly builds a picture of staggering inhumanity. Beneath shimmers another picture of the astonishing capacity for endurance of the human race.

One after another, faces loom before Lanzmann's camera, bearing witness to events in the ghettoes, on the trains taking prisoners to the camps, inside the camps, and even into the crematoriums themselves. Men like Filip Muller, who was assigned to the special detail making victims ready for the gas chambers; Rudolf Vrba, who tried to organize a rebellion at Auschwitz but then escaped when it became clear to him that rebellion was impossible; Franz Grassler, the Nazi Deputy Commissioner of the Warsaw ghetto who can still glibly excuse his behaviour by claiming that he did not know then what he knows now.

Part of Lanzmann's considerable achievement is the manner in which he builds a detailed picture of the workings of the Final Solution. In the process, he also goes some way to enabling his audience to place themselves in a seemingly impossible position – that of imagining what it was all really like.

In a curious way, a British documentary film-maker who took a different approach to that adopted by Lanzmann came just as close to achieving this impossible task. Peter Morley made *Kitty: Return to Auschwitz* (1979) for Yorkshire Television.

As a child Kitty Hart, who now lives and works in Birmingham, England, was taken with her mother to Auschwitz. Morley makes no use of newsreel pictures, nor even a still picture of Auschwitz as it was then. All that is seen is Auschwitz as it is now when Kitty returns with her grownup son, David, to the place where her family and friends died and where her own astonishingly resilient character was formed. As Kitty walks among the empty huts, only her words are heard, describing the events that occurred here all those years before, and only occasionally faltering as her memories flood back.

For most of this time her son plays little part, simply accompanying his mother and looking on, awkward and mostly uncomprehending, as she recounts what happened to her in this place. Then, in a moment of vivid drama, Kitty tells David that where they are now standing, a patch of waterlogged marshy ground, is where the ashes from the ovens were buried. David digs the toe of his shoe into the ground and he can see ashes; this is all that remains of his forebears. Quite suddenly, and obviously for the first time in his life, the son, an ordinary man like most of those in the audience for this remarkable film, understands the horror to which his mother was subjected and what his people endured.

Liberation for some victims of the Holocaust as John Wayne (l) and Kirk Douglas (c) stride into a concentration camp in Cast a Giant Shadow (1966).

No dramatized account of the Holocaust could ever hope to compete with either the relentless build up of evidence brought before the camera in *Shoah* or the simple, understated eloquence of the story of Kitty Hart.

In the aftermath of the Holocaust it may be difficult to agree unreservedly with the words Anne Frank wrote in her diary: 'In spite of everything, I still believe that people are really good at heart.' But looking into the eyes of survivors like Kitty Hart it is almost possible to believe that the human spirit is capable of overwhelming nobility.

10

Prisoners of War in Europe

'It is the sworn duty of officers to try to escape, to
harass the enemy to the best of their advantage.'
(The Great Escape)

If the problems surrounding an accurate representation of life and death in the concentration camps of World War II inhibited film-makers, there was no similar hesitancy when it came to making movies about another kind of wartime prison camp. Quite the reverse, in fact, for prisoner-of-war camp movies proliferated in the post-war years and, as Korea and Vietnam came and went, this sub-genre of the war movie gained in popularity.

Like those movies set behind bars, some of those located behind wire were good, others bad, and a few captured the reality. There was one marked difference from the civil prison movie which helped film-makers. Prisoners of war were quite definitely the heroes and the guards were positively the villains of the piece.

World War I had inspired a few prison camp movies including one, *La Grande Illusion* (1937), generally regarded as being among the best of the genre. Directed by Jean Renoir, the film stars Jean Gabin, Pierre Fresnay and Marcel Dalio as Maréchal, de Boldieu and Rosenthal, three captives held in a camp commanded by Captain von Rauffenstein (Erich von Stroheim). *La Grande Illusion* is not just about captivity, nor even war (there are no battle scenes), but is a profound study of the human condition. The principals, de Boldieu and von Rauffensein, are offered as men who belong to an outdated caste of officers and gentlemen, the implication being that theirs is a dying race and has no role to play in modern warfare.

Seen today, the philosophical sub-text of *La Grande Illusion* appears to be more than a trifle outdated as attitudes and practices of war have long left behind ideas that warfare bears within it any moral imperative.

Officers and gentlemen were still breathing rarified air in World War II, not only on the battlefield but also in prison camps. The most notable British-made prisoner-of-war movies came in the first dozen years after the ending of World War II when moviegoers were still filled with wartime zeal and fellowship. It was also before British audiences realized with dismay that the enemy whose defeat had cost them dear was racing ahead in the post-war world of industry and commerce.

Although there was no hard and fast style for prisoner-of-war movies, there were noticeable differences between those that depicted the lifes of Allied servicemen and women imprisoned by the Germans and those held captive by the Japanese, differences which in part arose from the different cultures of the two nations temporarily holding the upper hand.

If the majority of British-made prisoner-of-war movies are to be believed then the war with Germany was conducted much like a sporting contest between neighbouring communities. If they didn't actually like each other, they were certainly a long way from hating one another. Officers on both sides were gentlemen indulging in mutual admiration; the other ranks were peopled by good-hearted Tommys or Fritzs who shared similar backgrounds, mutual mistrust of officers and displayed an 'if it was up to us we'd call it all off, have a few beers and go back home tomorrow' attitude towards the war.

In some ways this crudely drawn picture of the societies engaged in the war in Europe is not completely inaccurate. Both Britain, particularly England, and Germany had clearly-drawn social barriers which were carried over into their respective armed forces and through which few were allowed to pass. (These social distinctions in Germany were one of the reasons for the distrustful lack of understanding between the high command of the *Wehrmacht* and what they saw as Hitler's gang of lower-class thugs.)

When British soldiers were captured they were allowed to retain the authority of their rank although the frequent separation of officers and other ranks into different parts of a camp or even into different camps served a dual purpose. It gave the captors a sense of security that they were not guarding a potentially dangerous body of men with properly organized leadership; and it saved the captives from the unpleasant task of learning how to live in close proximity with their social superiors or inferiors.

Tensions arising from these inherent differences in the nature of the captives allowed some film-makers to explore deeper philosophical areas than was usually possible in tales set in civil prisons wherein blue-collar prisoners dominated their white-collar cousins. For the most part, however, the movies that materialized out of this potentially rewarding vein tended to be Ripping Yarns for hearty, rugby-playing public school types, most of whom suffered from near-terminal stiff upper lips.

If the basic premise of *The Captive Heart* (1946) appears more than a trifle unlikely on the surface it does have the merit of a sound screenplay, by Angus Macphail and Guy Morgan, and sympathetic direction by Basil Dearden. Like so many other war movies of its time *The Captive Heart* also benefits from a cast of strong British character actors all the way down to the smallest roles, among them Jimmy Hanley, Gordon Jackson, Mervyn Johns, Guy Middleton, Basil Radford and Jack Warner. Heading this impressive list is Michael Redgrave who plays the role of Captain Karel Hasek, a Czechoslovak soldier who has taken the identity of a dead British officer as a means of escaping almost certain execution by the Germans. Suspected by the British prisoners in Oflag 27 of being a spy, Hasek eventually admits the truth but is then suspected by the Germans.

Obliged to reply to a letter from the wife of the man whose identity he has assumed, Hasek goes to extreme lengths to preserve his cover even to the extent of allowing his hand to be crushed so that his handwriting cannot be identified. The ensuing romance that develops with Celia Mitchell (Rachel Kempson), the unknowing widow in England, whose marriage was on the rocks strains credulity but overall the movie is an effective drama.

Life in the camp follows a curiously English Home Counties pattern as a narrator solemnly intones a verbal impression to match the music being played on the piano by one of the prisoners: 'It tells of men emerging from the twilight turning their faces inward from the wire, creating in miniature a world of their own.' As we listen to this the camera flits over men gardening, boxing, painting, reading, rehearsing a pantomime, and taking up choral singing.

Although escaping is barely hinted at in *The Captive Heart* there is defiance of a sort. As the loudspeakers blare German martial music the lads sing a rousing chorus of 'Roll Out the Barrel', eventually drowning out the enemy. (Hold on, isn't that song based on 'The Beer

Barrel Polka', an old Bavarian drinking song? Maybe the Germans thought they'd won this particular musical battle for their captive hearts.)

Stereotypes abound (even if they were not yet so well established as they now appear), not least the chirpy Cockney (Hanley) who, on giving up his chance for repatriation to allow Hasek to get out before the Germans discover his real identity is told, 'You are a sportsman.' The captors don't get much of a look in but those that do are also recognizable types, with Karel Stepanek as the villainous Gestapo officer out to nail Hasek, and Frederick Schiller as an easily fooled camp medical officer.

At the end of *The Captive Heart*, Hasek visits Celia Mitchell and an implied romance is in the air, an improbable happy ending which suited the mood of the first post-war year. (This is a problem that afflicts most prisoner-of-war

Sing-song in the showers in The Wooden Horse **(1950), just one way of keeping spirits up in the curiously public school-like world of a prisoner-of-war camp movie. (l to r) Leo Genn, Philip Dale, Anthony Steele.**

movies; seeing them at the time memories were sharp and freshened by immediate post-war euphoria is very different to seeing them 40 years later when cynicism has had time to build a hard shell.)

The problem of stereotyping afflicted Jean Renoir who tried to recapture some of the spirit of *La Grande Illusion* with *La Caporal épinglé* (1962), which pits a comical French escape artist against a collection of dim-witted German oafs.

Given the nature of the subject matter, prisoner-of-war movies were often centred more upon attempts to escape rather than on an examination of the reality of life in the camps.

Several of these escapes had all the appearance of a screenwriter's pipe dream yet many, even some of the least likely, were based upon fact. True or false, escape movies served as a means of combining the intense drama possible where men are in captivity with often simple-minded suspense and excitement.

An atmosphere reminiscent of *Boys' Own Paper* melodramatics suffused *The Wooden Horse* (1950) in which a group of imprisoned

officers use German assumptions about the British as a means of concealing their tunnelling operations. Faced with an impossibly long tunnel from the barrack-room to the far side of the wire, the would-be escapers are carried inside a wooden vaulting horse into the middle of the exercise area from where they dig their tunnel to freedom. Presumably the guards tolerated the daily appearance of a crowd of keep-fit fanatics because it matched their stereotypical view of the British as a nation of sporting nutcases. In the event, the three escapees, played by Leo Genn, Anthony Steele and David Tomlinson, make it to neutral shores.

The cover for escapees in *Albert RN* (1953) is a dummy carried on parade to be counted by presumably short-sighted guards. Disbelief is readily suspended thanks to Guy Morgan's script (from his own stage play) and effective playing by Jack Warner, as Captain Maddox, and Anthony Steele, as Lt Geoffrey Ainsworth, among the good guys and lip-curling Anton Diffring, as Hauptmann Schultze, heading the baddies. Suspense is maintained as the first escapee is caught, the second bid is foiled at the last minute, and the third man pauses to eliminate the new, vicious camp commandant before flitting away.

Were it not for the fact that it is a true story, disbelief would be hard to suspend in *Reach for the Sky* (1956), a bio-pic of the remarkable life of Douglas Bader. Starring Kenneth More as Bader, the movie, which is based upon Paul Brickhill's book, traces the pre-war experiences of a compulsive flier whose life is threatened and career apparently destroyed when, following an air crash, he has both legs amputated. Eight years after this accident, war is declared and against all odds Bader wangles his way into the Royal Air Force, becomes a squadron leader, and, after being shot down, ends up in a prisoner-of-war camp.

Post-war TV appearances by Bader revealed him as a much pricklier and far less endearing individual than he is made to appear in the movie and it is through images of the real Bader's aggressive bull-headedness rather than Kenneth More's amiable screen presence,

that his subsequent experiences ring true. These included repeated escape bids and his eventual incarceration in Colditz Castle, an 'escape-proof' prison in Saxony. The unnaturally forced gaiety that attends many of the prison camp sequences weakens the film but for all its failings *Reach for the Sky* is solid entertainment.

Similarly unlikely to outsiders in the almost cheerful interaction of captors and captives is *The Colditz Story* (1957), based upon the best-selling book by P. R. 'Pat' Reid (played in the film by John Mills). Colditz was the prison of last resort for inveterate escapers of many nationalities. German claims that it was escape-proof were eagerly challenged by the prisoners almost as if it were an invitation to a sporting contest. For all its often seemingly schoolboy heroics, the film stays fairly close to Reid's book, which is a careful and accurate account of life in the castle. The determination and courage displayed by Reid and his fellow captives is uplifting in the pages of his book but is not fully realized in the filmed account.

If *The Colditz Story* did not do Reid and his comrades full justice, ample compensation came in the 1972 BBC TV series *Colditz*, which was also based upon Reid's book.

The series, which starred Edward Hardwicke in the Reid role and featured numerous excellent British actors, examined many more cases than was possible in the film and also took rather more heed of the potential for disaster and tragedy inherent in some of the crazier escape bids. In one uncomfortably memorable episode a prisoner, played by Michael Bryant, feigned madness in order to escape only to sink into real psychiatric disorder after his repatriation to England.

Escape from Colditz (1977) is a theatrical release of sequences edited from the TV series designed to star Robert Wagner and David McCallum, both of whom were better known to American audiences than were their fellow cast members.

If only a few escaped from Colditz (among them Pat Reid himself), rather more escaped from the camp in *Danger Within* (released in

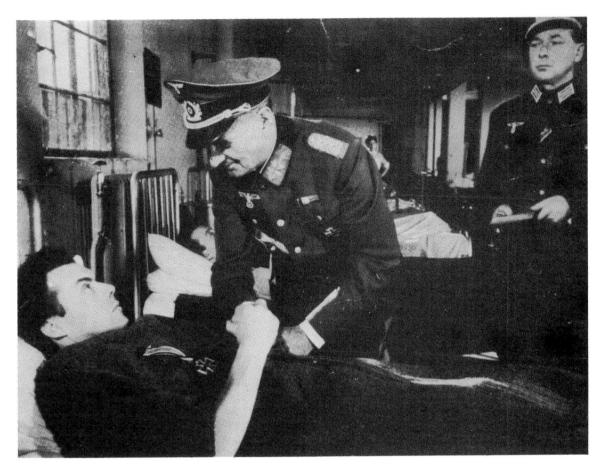

So good were his escape disguises in The Password is Courage **(1962) that at one point Dirk Bogarde (l) found himself the startled recipient of the Iron Cross.**

the United States as *Breakout*) (1959) wherein British prisoners were held by Italians. The film is briskly performed by a superior cast including Richard Todd, Bernard Lee and Richard Attenborough, with Peter Arne as the villainous Italian commandant, Capitano Benucci. With a strong Bryan Forbes-Frank Harvey screenplay, the main suspense of this tale stems from the prisoners' realization that their plans are being passed on to the guards by one of their own number. The discovery and elimination of the informer, Captain Tony Long (William Franklyn) and the eventual mass breakout is well-handled by director Don Chaffey. Neverthe-

less, the lingering impression is not of captured soldiers enduring grim imprisonment but of endless stereotypes playing rugger, lounging in the sunshine, and rehearsing scenes from *Hamlet* in the camp theatre.

The tendency towards tongue-in-cheek comedy that mars the reality of so many prisoner-of-war movies, while undoubtedly adding to their entertainment value, was almost out of control in *The Password Is Courage* (1962) in which Dirk Bogarde takes the role of a real life escaper, the inaptly named Charles Coward. Unlike most other movies on this theme *The Password Is Courage* has the merit of being about a member of the other ranks. Charles Coward was a sergeant-major whose exploits should have put paid to the assumption of most movie-makers that a commission was a necessary attribute if a man was to escape the

clutches of the enemy. However, such a positive factor was persistently undermined by writing in most of the enemy as being short-sighted, witless nincompoops among whom the camp's Unterofficer (Reginald Beckwith) is the worst offender.

Coward's sidekick, Corporal Cope (Alfred Lynch), is a bright spark and is actually a composite of several real-life associates of the inveterate escaper. Towards the end, Coward attempts to link up with the Polish underground, an episode upon which doubts have been cast and is, in the context of the movie, the least interesting.

A study of escape was clearly the prime motivator in the making of The Great Escape (1963), a big budget movie with an international all-star cast.

James Clavell, himself a former prisoner of war, and W. R. Burnett based their screenplay on Paul Brickhill's book and the result is a largely factual account of an attempt in 1942 to stage a mass breakout from Stalag Luft North, a camp for hardened escapees.

Shot at Geiselasteig, near Munich, The Great Escape centres upon the plans of two British prisoners, Bartlett and Ramsay (Richard Attenborough and James Donald), to get 250 men out of three tunnels, code-named 'Tom', 'Dick' and 'Harry'. Also in the camp, but with plans of his own, is American Virgil Hilts (Steve McQueen), the 'Cooler King', who has already clocked up 18 failed escape bids. When his cellmate is machine-gunned by guards, Hilts agrees to help the mass escape by getting out and allowing himself to be recaptured in order to bring back valuable topographical information.

One of the tunnels is discovered (in the movie, not in real life) and various anecdotal side issues are pursued before the break out takes place. Altogether 76 men make it, but the price paid is high: as a reprisal 50 prisoners are executed.

Hilts makes his final break for freedom, steals a motorcycle, and heads for the Swiss border. In a spectacular (and also fictitious) chase, he is pursued through beautiful rolling countryside until he tries, but fails, to leap his machine over the barbed wire border fence. Disentangled from the wire, Hilts is brought back to the camp as the disgraced commandant is replaced.

As a youth, Steve McQueen served time at Junior Boys' Republic, a reform school at Chino, California. He failed to escape from there, too, and when the school's movie-going privileges were suspended in reprisal he was beaten up by his fellow inmates. In later years he regularly returned to the school to help demonstrate that a graduate was not necessarily doomed to failure in life.

The Great Escape is given a more adventurous side than most European-set movies by the behaviour and attitude of the American prisoners who, apart from Hilts, include Hadly and Velinski (James Garner and Charles Bronson).

There is the usual tendency towards stereotyping, particularly among the Germans, although the commandant, von Luger (Hannes Messemer), is given an interestingly layered character as is Werner (Robert Graf), a guard who views the events he is obliged to witness with a troubled eye. Among the more elaborately drawn prisoners is Blythe (Donald Pleasance) who is slowly going blind and is thus facing another kind of imprisonment. (The blind prisoner sub-plot had also been used in *The Captive Heart* but with rather unnecessary sentimentality.)

In yet another form of stereotyping, the Americans generally disapprove of the patient burrowing beneath the wire undertaken by the British preferring instead to swashbuckle their way to freedom.

The American prisoner as swashbuckler was not universally adopted by movie-makers although this was the principle that drove *Von Ryan's Express* (1965) in which Frank Sinatra masterminds a wholesale escape bid, nobly sacrificing himself at the end so that others might live. Uninspired though this movie might be, the use of a railway train was at least a little more believable than the elephant used by Oliver Reed and Michael J. Pollard in *Hannibal Brooks* (1969).

The award for unbelievability must be granted, however, to *Escape to Victory* (1981). This incredible saga concerns a group of Allied prisoners of war whose numbers just happen to include several world class soccer players. Under the tutelage of former West Ham United star John Colby (Michael Caine), they form a team to play a German side at the behest of camp commandant Major Karl von Steiner (Max von Sydow), who also just happens to be a former international player. The great match will take place in Paris and instantly an escape plan is put into operation. The French Resistance will dig a tunnel into the dressing-room through which the entire Allied team will escape at half-time. This is arranged by American prisoner Robert Hatch (Sylvester Stallone) who escapes, fixes up the plot and then allows himself to be recaptured.

On the day of the big match, the Allied team (which includes such noted soccer stars as Bobby Moore, Ozzy Ardiles and Pele, with Sylvester Stallone as one of the goalposts, sorry, the goalkeeper) discovers that the dastardly Germans have bribed the referee because they cannot afford the loss of face that will result if they lose the match.

Comes half-time and the lads repair to the dressing-room smarting under a two-goal deficit. Now what do you suppose happens? Right, they turn their backs on the tunnel and return to the field and equalize. A last-minute penalty for the Germans is saved by Robert Hatch (Stallone, remember) and the massed crowds of Frenchmen promptly break into a rousing version of 'La Marseillaise'. There isn't a soccer hooligan in sight. Unbelievably, this tosh was directed by John Huston; the great man had a few off days in his career but this took the palm. Perhaps his latent anti-British feelings got the better of him.

Considerably more sober in its approach is

William Holden (r) trying to buy his way out of trouble by forcing fags on a startled Sig Ruman in Stalag 17 **(1953).**

Stalag 17 (1953), which is set in a German camp for Americans. Thanks to the inherent cynicism of Billy Wilder, who directed and collaborated on the screenplay, the movie has much less of the irritating romanticism which afflicted practically all of the British and most American entries in this sub-genre although it has far too many moments of rowdily coarse comedy.

Stalag 17 stars William Holden as Sefton, a sergeant in the American army, whose profit-motivated wheeling and dealing earns him a curious mixture of contempt and respect from his comrades together with the mistaken belief of his captors that such a self-centred individual must be a potential collaborator.

When it becomes apparent that there is an informer in the camp, suspicion falls on Sefton. Two of his fellow prisoners, Hoffy and Price (Richard Erdman and Peter Graves), convince the others and when Dunbar (Don Taylor) is

beaten up by the guards Sefton is attacked. Realizing that he must find the real informer or risk dying at the hands of his fellow countrymen, Sefton investigates and eventually unmasks Price as the spy. An escape bid is arranged and Sefton and Dunbar make the break, taking Price along with them having ensured that he will be shot in the process.

Among the stereotypes on display are a pair of American jokers, Stosh and Harry (Robert Strauss and Harvey Lembeck), and a dopey German guard named Schulz (Sig Ruman). Film director Otto Preminger makes one of his occasional appearances in an acting role as the villainous, domineering Oberst von Scherback. (Judging from comments by actors who worked with Preminger over the years this looks like typecasting; maybe this was Billy Wilder's best joke in the movie.)

In fact, German-born Wilder's usually stiletto-sharp spearing of American hypocrisy doesn't always find its mark here, but for most of its length *Stalag 17* works as a portrait of the different ways in which men behave in captivity and under constant pressure to survive.

William Holden was also the star of *The Counterfeit Traitor* (1962), a movie about a real-life American-born naturalized Swede, Eric Erickson, who was able to convince the Germans of his allegiance and so pass on details of their oil refineries. In a grim, dramatic scene, Erickson watches helplessly from a cell where he is temporarily held by the Germans as his girlfriend, Marianne Mollendorf (Lilli Palmer), is executed by firing squad.

A variation on the theme of captivity in wartime Germany appears in *Situation Hopeless – But Not Serious* (1965). Two American fliers, Lucky Finder and Hank Wilson (played by Mike Connors and Robert Redford) are found by an elderly German when their aircraft is shot down in 1944. The old man, Wilhelm Frick (Alec Guinness), hides them in his cellar, but when the war ends he is unable to contemplate the

William Holden watches in anguish as his girlfriend is executed in The Counterfeit Traitor **(1962).**

loneliness he is sure will ensue if his unwilling guests depart. He conceals from them the fact that the war is over and the years pass with Frick concocting spurious war reports to keep Finder and Wilson where they are.

After being taken ill and briefly hospitalized, Frick is desperate to return to his starving friends and in his haste attracts the attention of the police. Unable to take the risks he has been running any longer (it is now 1950) but equally unwilling to confess his deception to the American fliers, Frick urges them to 'escape' to Switzerland. Before they learn the truth, the Americans endure several nerve-racking moments evading non-existent pursuers.

However fanciful the storyline might seem, it generally holds up well until the denouement, which finds Frick working as Finder's butler and gaily recounting his part in events to guests at the fliers' belated victory party.

Contrasting with the seemingly constant stream of British and American servicemen escaping from prisoner-of-war camps in Germany, official records appear to substantiate the claim inherent in the title of a movie about German servicemen imprisoned in camps in Britain. *The One That Got Away* (1957) was a *Luftwaffe* pilot, Oberleutnant Franz von Werra (Hardy Kruger), whose persistent attempts to escape brought him the guarded respect of his British captors, much as his counterparts, Douglas Bader, Charles Coward and others earned unwilling respect from the Germans.

Von Werra's Messerschmitt fighter-plane crash-landed in Kent and after capture he was determined to find his way back to Germany. A personable individual, von Werra impersonated a Dutchman (rightly assuming that to the British all foreigners sound alike), in an attempt to steal an airplane. If anything, von Werra is given rather more credit than he earned in real life. In one scene he spots a hidden microphone in the room he shares with another prisoner; leaning out the window so that they can talk freely, he spots another mike. In reality it was three days before he found the second instrument, the first being planted on the assumption he would spot it easily.

Despite such allowances, the Germans are generally put down in the movie – especially in a scene where, on the eve of embarkation to Canada, they have a rousing get-together which ends in a chorus of Sieg Heils. As silence falls, the British adjutant laconically interjects, 'Collect your sandwiches on the way out.'

Once in Canada, von Werra tries again, leaping from a train. This time he is successful and he heads for America which at the time was still neutral. The film ends here, leaving the flyer to find his way first to Mexico and then home where he resumed his career.

The One That Got Away undermines the tacit assumption that enemy soldiers captured by the British didn't really want to escape, an assumption that was more openly directed against the Italians, who were generally regarded with contempt by the British Army. Despite this long-lasting impression, the lives of Italian prisoners of war in Britain were touched upon with great sympathy in *Another Time, Another Place* (1983).

Set in Scotland in 1944 *Another Time, Another Place* centres upon the bleak life of Janey (played by Phyllis Logan), the wife of a farmer in whose barn are billetted three Italian prisoners. The slowly developing relationship between Janey and the Italians is compassionately realized, and her eventual affair with one of them, Luigi (Giovanni Mauriello), is authentically grubby and unsatisfying to Janey, although it does serve to underline for her the even greater dissatisfaction with which she regards the drab, hard, emotionally imprisoned life she leads.

The role of women in wartime has often caused more than a handful of problems for film-makers. Just as women in civil prisons were potential minefields, so too were women in wartime captivity. In many instances, the women were on the outside, as wives or girl-friends seen in flashback sequences, but occasionally the nature of the story called for them to be imprisoned. This did not happen

German flying ace, Hardy Kruger assesses his chances of being The One That Got Away **(1957).**

too often in the movies' interpretation of the European theatre of World War II but there have been exceptions of which *Odette* (1950) and *Carve Her Name with Pride* (1958) are fine examples.

Both films are based upon the activities of real life secret agents, Odette Churchill and Violette Szabo (played respectively by Anna Neagle and Virginia McKenna).

In *Odette* the star's slightly regal air puts a shield between her character and the audience but there are still many powerful moments especially during Odette's imprisonment and torture. Overall, however, the movie is just too stately and adopts an air of detachment akin to that of the star, which is only momentarily relieved by Peter Ustinov as Arnaud and Trevor Howard as Peter Churchill.

Shortly before the outbreak of World War II, Anna Neagle had played a similar role to that of Odette Churchill. This was the title role in *Nurse Edith Cavell* (1939), the true story of a British nurse executed for spying against Germany during World War I whose story had already been told in *Dawn* (1930). The star's distant manner is somehow more appropriate here, perhaps as a consequence of the armour-plated bearing implied by the sternly-corsetted figure of an Edwardian nurse. A broadly similar but fictional tale was told in *I Was a Spy* (1933).

There was no similar distancing from the audience in Violette Szabo's story, thanks to one of the best performances of McKenna's career. Despite her performance, however, and while having all the ingredients necessary for a major movie, *Carve Her Name with Pride* is uneven and never really begins to flow.

Violette becomes a secret agent after the death of her husband, Etienne (played by Alain Saury). After extensive training she is parachuted into France with Captain Tony Fraser (Paul Scofield) for a successful first mission. On her second mission she is captured and interrogated before being executed at Ravensbrück with two other female agents.

In an ending which is, perhaps understandably, rather sentimental, Violette's daughter,

Tania, collects a posthumous George Cross from the King at Buckingham Palace.

The imperfections of both *Odette* and *Carve Her Name with Pride* serve to underline the fact that all too often, when confronted by real life stories, film-makers suffer from an attack of nerves. In the case of these heroic women such nervousness is understandable, and their respect is even commendable, but it doesn't help the end result. A measure of respectful detachment might have produced rather better memorials to the many brave men and women who served their country in the manner exemplified by these two great ladies.

As its title implies, considerably more ladies featured in *2,000 Women* (1944), which took as its premise the internment by the Germans of the many foreigners in France when that country fell to the invader. Held in the Grand Hotel at Marneville, this valiant bunch behave as if they have just been told that the cucumber sandwiches are off, treating their captors with dismissive contempt. When three Allied airmen parachute from their burning plane and take refuge in the hotel, the ladies rally round the flag. Even Parisian nightclub ex-stripper Bridie Johnson (Jean Kent), whose morals are far more suspect than British movie-makers usually allowed in those days, helps out. However, when called upon to delay the Germans by enticingly performing her act at the end of a concert, she is laid low by a traitor in the camp. As there is a plot afoot to let the airmen escape this is a disastrous state of affairs but into the breach steps brave novice nun Rosemary Brown (Patricia Roc) who volunteers to take Bridie's place on the stage. Surely this is going too far; a novitiate baring her all in the service of her country sounds like New World material not Gainsborough. But no, all is safe; Rosemary, demure as can be in a full-length evening gown, sings a little song until the airmen are away and then leads all the ladies, and just about every British actress available for duty was assigned to this morale-boosting tale, in a rousing chorus of 'There'll Always Be An England'.

Many war movies, including most of those

about prisoners of war, implied that war brings out the best in people by creating comradeship which, forged in fire, will survive and add to the inherent nobility of mankind. Indeed, an entire generation of the British still clings on to the quaint belief that they were all better people during the early 1940s. A moment's cold thought reveals that this was clearly the opposite of reality, nevertheless it is an ideal which pops up often enough to warrant paying attention to those films that show just how badly people could treat their friends and brothers-in-arms.

In *The Hill* (1965) the prisoners are British soldiers in North Africa held captive neither by the Germans nor the Italians but by their own side. The fact that some of these men are malcontents, backsliders, deserters and other misfits does not alter the fact that the treatment they receive is far worse than that meted out to enemy prisoners. In many respects, not least the fact that prisoners and guards come from the same background as one another, *The Hill* more closely resembles civil prison movies than the prisoner-of-war movies to which it is

ostensibly kin. Its wartime setting, however, gives it a greater philosophical resonance. *The Hill* deserves considerably more attention than it received at the time of its release and its virtual disappearance from sight, seemingly never turning up on even the latest of late shows, is unfortunate. Crisply directed by Sidney Lumet and with powerful performances from a strong cast of mainly British actors, *The Hill* offers a microcosmic view of man's capacity for inhumanity towards his brothers.

At its heart, *The Hill* is a contest of wills between RSM Williams (Harry Andrews), who does everything by the book (in this case King's Regulations), and Joe Roberts (Sean Connery), a former sergeant major who refused orders that he believed would needlessly send him and his men to their deaths. Thus, the man who believes in the system is set against the man who believes that men's lives matter more.

In its relatively narrow field, *The Hill* is a summation of the futility of wars and unflinchingly demonstrates the hollowness of the accord and camaraderie which suffuses most prisoner-of-war films with an unreal glow.

Prisoners of Other Wars

'These things have been a part of our lives.
We will never quite forget.'
(Rohan D. Rivett)

It is inappropriate to suggest that some wars are worse than others; such a statement carries with it the corollary that some wars must therefore be 'better'.

Nevertheless, there is a particularly unsettling background to civil wars. Mankind can, and usually does, find excuses for fighting wars against neighbouring countries. It is even easier to build a nation's belligerence against some far-off foe, especially if the enemy can be given a non-specific name: the Yellow Peril, the Red Menace, the Evil Empire. But when kinsmen fight it is difficult to assume anything other than mankind's inherent instability and blood lust; a deep-seated desire to fight and kill for the sake of fighting and killing.

In the American Civil War the divide not only pitted state against state, county against county, but divided the smallest communities and even split families. Cousin fought cousin; brother took up arms against brother.

The war is generally regarded as the first 'modern' war, a term which conveys the wholesale slaughter and the fact that the killing spilled over from the battlefields and engulfed non-combatants, bringing with it a massive death toll. More Americans died as a result of the Civil War than in World Wars I and II combined.

It may be difficult to understand why a nation would inflict such punishment upon itself on the battlefields. But it becomes utterly incomprehensible that appalling treatment should be carried over into prison camps after hot blood had cooled. Andersonville was one such incomprehensible blight upon the nation.

Andersonville was an American prison located near the little town of Andersonville, which is in Sumter County, Georgia. It was here that the Confederate army built a camp to house up to 50,000 captured Union soldiers. Brought in to organize and run the camp was a Swiss-born administrator named Henry Wirz whose single-minded dedication to the logistics of his task, allied as they were to an apparently complete ability to ignore the manner in which the men under his charge were being treated, made him a forerunner of countless latterday bureaucrats in uniform who excused their behaviour with the cry, 'I was only doing my duty.'

Under Wirz's command Andersonville became a place of sickness and death. Through mistreatment, inadequate food, almost non-existent medical care, and conditions of utter squalor in which disease spread like a forest fire, hundreds died.

In fairness, but not in exculpation, it should be mentioned that although more than 22,000 Union soldiers died in Southern prison camps, the number of Confederates to die in Northern camps exceeded 26,000.

R. Randolph Stevenson, a surgeon in the Confederate army, had declared that if 'revolting crimes...have indeed been committed, the perpetrators must be held accountable. Be they of the South or of the North, they can not escape history.' In fact, foreign-born Henry Wirz of Andersonville was the only man to stand trial for war crimes committed during this most uncivil of encounters.

One of the earliest movies to touch upon prison was *Escape from Andersonville* (1909) which took a brief look at the Andersonville story. In the late 1950s plans were announced for a movie bearing the same title, which was to be directed by Stanley Kramer, but nothing came of the project.

However, America is a nation which sometimes displays an almost desperate need to examine in public its own shortcomings, and a 1972 TV documentary drama, *The Andersonville Trial* (produced by Kramer and directed by George C. Scott), proved that there are still aspects of the war between the states that cause acute embarrassment to Americans.

In striking contrast with the war between the states, that part of World War II fought by the Allies against Japan fulfilled the criteria of 'understandable' wars: the foe was foreign, far-off, and a part of the yellow peril.

The war against Japan was very different from the war in Europe in the terrain in which it was fought and in the manner of fighting. It was also different in the way in which the opposing sides perceived one another. The average British soldier thought that he understood his German counterpart, and vice versa; there was never any hint that the British, the Australians, New Zealanders, Americans, or anyone else for that matter, had even the remotest idea of what made the Japanese tick.

To use a mild cliché, this was a clash of cultures; but there was nothing mild about the manner in which cultural differences affected the behaviour of the Japanese towards any prisoners they took.

For centuries warriors had been held in special regard by the Japanese and among many preconceptions regarding behaviour was one which severely affected the lives of Allied prisoners of war. Although in certain circumstances capture might be inevitable, it was incumbent upon a true warrior to resist, to fight on even if it was to certain death; surrender was ignoble. When, early in 1942, on the orders of their commanding officers, more than 10,000 Allied soldiers, mostly British, surrendered at Singapore, an impression was created in Japanese military minds of their enemy as inferior beings. One ordinary British soldier has recounted how, when faced with execution he inexplicably burst into uncontrollable laughter. His captors, ordinary Japanese soldiers, were so impressed with his apparent bravery they spared his life.

Incorrect impressions were not confined to the Japanese side. Until the fall of Singapore, and in some quarters for a long time afterwards, the Allies regarded the military ambitions of the Japanese as a joke. When they proved to be a determined fighting machine, adept at jungle warfare and capable of moving fast in appalling terrain, the Allies were taken by surprise. They had fallen into the trap of believing their own propaganda, which portrayed the Japanese soldier as a short-sighted, bullet-headed, bicycle-riding imbecile weighed down with swords and other medieval regalia.

In certain other respects, notably claims that the Japanese could behave in a brutal and 'uncivilized' manner, some of the propaganda became a harsh and unpleasant fact.

Towards the end of the war, prison camps were overrun and the manner in which Allied soldiers had been treated became known. For cinema audiences in Britain the reality of the treatment of Allied prisoners of war was less well-publicized than was that of prisoners in German concentration camps. It was left to ex-prisoners who were capable of recounting their experiences on paper to bring the facts to a wider audience.

Notable among these writers were two Australians, Rohan D. Rivett and Russell Braddon whose books, respectively *Behind Bamboo* and *The Naked Island*, shocked public opinion.

It was not just soldiers who suffered in captivity at the hands of the Japanese. The civilian populations of the countries through which the

Japanese army sped in the early months of the war were harshly treated with hundreds of thousands being forced to labour on construction work and in maintaining supply routes. Foreign civilians were also caught up in the conflict and either killed or captured. These might be businessmen or civil employees of foreign governments and, as it was common for such individuals to have their wives and families with them, many women and children were also picked up and taken prisoner as the Japanese swept through South-East Asia in a seemingly unstoppable tide.

One woman taken captive in Borneo in 1941 was writer Agnes Newton Keith and her published account of her experiences formed the basis for a movie, *Three Came Home* (1950), which stars Claudette Colbert as the writer and Patric Knowles as her husband, Harry. The movie lacks tension and does not make as much as might have been possible from a story that

Life behind barbed wire is only bearable for Peter Finch when he dreams of A Town Like Alice **(1956).**

was certainly not lacking in human suffering. Good performances from Florence Desmond (as Betty Sommers) and Sessue Hayakawa (as Colonel Suga) did not rescue *Three Came Home* from undeserved ordinariness.

One element of this tale is the stereotypical Japanese officer caught up in an internal moral conflict. Colonel Suga was educated at an American university, a distinction which, it is implied, makes it hard for him to act in a manner acceptable to his ancestors. It is possible only to speculate what the colonel's ancestors would have thought of the actions of a group of Japanese soldiers who, on capturing twins decided to conduct a 'scientific' experiment. They beat one to death before his brother's eyes just to see what effect it has on him.

The special problems of women in these times, which did not have a precise counterpart in the European war, continued to attract writers and film-makers. *A Town Like Alice* (1956), based on Nevil Shute's novel, is one such tale. With often harrowing attention to detail, the film follows a group of women as they are marched from one place to another

without reason or plan but simply because their captors don't really know what to do with them. Because of this meaningless meandering through the jungle, the film suffers by appearing as a string of unconnected anecdotes. For all its structural drawbacks, however, *A Town Like Alice* effectively conveys the privations suffered by Jean Paget (Virginia McKenna), Mrs Horsfall (Jean Anderson), and others as they drag themselves wearily along. Their lives are fleetingly brightened by the appearance of Joe Harman (Peter Finch), an Australian soldier taken prisoner and employed by his captors as a truck driver-mechanic, duties he uses to inflict sabotage whenever he can. Harman's activities are eventually uncovered and he is crucified by the Japanese.

The fate of the women here is a curious offshoot of the war in South-East Asia. When their single, ailing guard eventually dies no one knows where they are and so they stay in a Malayan village, eking an existence helping the villagers grow rice in the paddy fields.

At the end of the war Jean Paget discovers that Joe survived and she travels to his home town, Alice Springs in the heart of Australia, to find him; only to discover that he is in London looking for her. Their eventual reunion brings a happy ending to a (supposedly true) story of captivity.

A version of *A Town Like Alice* made for Australian television in 1981 has a better shape because it draws upon more of the novel and is thus better able to frame events in the jungle in the overall context of the love story that is the main strength of the book. This version stars Helen Morse and Bryan Brown in the roles originally played by McKenna and Finch. A BBC TV series, *Tenko*, which is on broadly similar lines, proved to be extremely popular with audiences in 1981 with sequels in 1982 and 1984 and a post-war reunion in 1985. *Tenko*'s success demonstrates that the theme of women in captivity in the hands of an unspeakably awful foe is still a box-office winner, even if the majority of the people watching the series are doing so on television sets made in Japan.

Among the earliest prisoner-of-war movies

involving American forces in Japanese hands is *The Purple Heart* (1944), an apoplectic and one-sided assault on the stiff-necked, fiercely militaristic Japanese hierarchy. This attitude, allied to a delight in senseless cruelty removes any chance of survival for eight fliers captured after a bombing raid on Tokyo. The key to the fliers' fate rests on demands from the Japanese to reveal whether or not they flew their mission from an aircraft carrier. The fliers, led by Captain Harvey Ross (Dana Andrews), stick it out through grim imprisonment, torture, and a medieval trial. In the end, they go to their deaths having ensured that no member of the audience was in any doubt that the enemy with whom the nation was at war was less than human and deserved anything the Americans could, and soon would, throw at them.

The manner in which captured soldiers were treated by the Japanese was most widely seen by movie audiences in *The Bridge on the River Kwai* (1957). Although the most exciting action sequences befall Jack Hawkins and William Holden as Warden and Shears, members of a commando unit sent behind Japanese lines, the scenes with the greatest dramatic impact centre upon a prison camp in the middle of the jungle. The camp is under the command of Colonel Saito (played by Sessue Hayakawa, lending a measure of iconography to this second appearance as a Japanese commandant) but the soldiers imprisoned here respect only their own commanding officer, Colonel Nicholson (Alec Guinness in an Academy Award-winning performance). Conflict between Saito and Nicholson arises initially through the British officer's insistence that he and his brother officers should not work alongside the other ranks on the building of a bridge across the River Kwai. The treatment to which Nicholson is then subjected, he is placed in a 'hot box' without shelter from the sun and with almost no food and water, closely resembles that meted out to a real life prisoner whose story is told in Rohan Rivett's book.

In the book, Captain Bill Drower refused to fill a bucket of water for a Japanese private soldier and as a result was beaten, then,

Sessue Hayakawa tries to stand higher than his captives but Alec Guinness remains indomitable in The Bridge on the River Kwai **(1957).**

together with three fellow officers, was compelled to stand in front of the guard house for three days. Following this, Captain Drower was put into a hole in the ground that was partially filled with water. For the first three days he was given no food but thereafter received two small balls of rice and a little water each day for the next six and a half weeks. After this, Captain Drower was placed in a cell in the guard house for a further three weeks by which time the war had ended.

Like the real-life Drower, Nicholson's resistance to the Japanese commander is a triumph of the spirit and he is allowed to rejoin his men. From this point Nicholson co-operates in the building of the bridge but only because he sees the task as a means of occupying his men in a manner that will help keep them fit and maintain their morale. As theoretical therapy it makes a kind of sense but Nicholson becomes obsessed with the bridge, scrapping all the work that has been done so far and bringing to bear on the task the best possible design and workmanship. His commitment is so strong that when the commandos arrive to destroy the bridge he tries to stop them. At the last moment he realizes what he is doing and as the bridge is destroyed the valedictorian line, delivered by the British medical officer, sums up all that has happened: 'Madness, madness.'

The Bridge on the River Kwai **(1957)**
**demonstrated how understandable pride in
the achievements of Allied prisoners of war
could lead their commanding officer (Alec
Guinness) to the brink of collaboration.**

With its strong combination of dramatic prison camp scenes, the psychological development of the character of the magnificently obsessed Colonel Nicholson, and the activities of the commando unit intent on destroying the bridge, *The Bridge on the River Kwai* is a powerful movie and generally deserves the many awards it won (five Oscars apart from Guinness's).

The screenplay by Carl Foreman changes the ending from Pierre Boule's novel wherein the lethal idiocy of all that has happened is underlined when the attempt to destroy the bridge fails. The new, upbeat ending no doubt fits better the grandeur of director David Lean's concept but in some respects it is a weakness, displaying as it does an element of inappropriate glory.

Nowhere in *Kwai* does any hint arise that the 'Death Railway' was built at the cost of 18,000

Allied lives (many at the hands of Korean guards who aided their Japanese allies with sadistic delight) and countless more Asian deaths (some estimates put these as high as 150,000).

Decidedly dubious is the manner in which the ill-treatment handed out by the Japanese was used as the main attraction of such films as *The Camp on Blood Island* (1958). Ostensibly based on a true incident, the main strand of tension in this movie, which connects various acts of atrocious brutality, is the fear that the camp's commandant will slaughter all the inmates if Japan loses the war. The movie's credibility suffers from a blanket stereotyping of the Japanese as murderous villains, a failing exacerbated by the fact that Colonel Yamamitsu and Captain Sakamura are played by non-Japanese actors Ronald Radd and Marne Maitland.

King Rat (1965) is an interesting examination of how one particular character sets out to survive in a Japanese prison camp. Corporal King (played by George Segal) is an American who wheels and deals his way through his confinement in Singapore's Changi Jail. The movie's depiction of everyday life in the prison, and the mingled hatred and envy with which King is regarded by his comrades, are among many creditable factors in a generally strong movie.

Few prisons offered a life as grim as that suffered behind the wire by Allied soldiers captured by the Japanese in World War II. Michael Goodliffe (l) and Andre Morell (second from l) in The Camp on Blood Island **(1958).**

King Rat is based upon a novel by James Clavell who was himself a prisoner of war. It is well-directed by Bryan Forbes with good performances from Segal and a strong cast of mainly British actors including Tom Courtenay, Denholm Elliott, John Mills and James Fox.

In real life, Changi Jail, which was designed to house 600 inmates, was crammed with 15,000 Allied prisoners, 1,000 of whom did not survive.

Survival was the central theme of *Escape to Mindanao*, a 1968 TV movie starring George Maharis as a man quite prepared to stay in a POW camp and put all his energies to merely surviving. When an enemy decoder falls into his hands he is persuaded to make an escape bid. He boards a Dutch merchant vessel and thereafter the story is a routine adventure yarn.

A ship is used for very different reasons in *Prison Ship* (1945). Packed with American pri-

soners, soldiers and civilians, the ship carries only a skeleton crew and is ablaze with lights. This leads two of the prisoners, Tom Jeffries and Anne Graham (Robert Lowery and Nina Foch) to guess that they are being set up as a target to lure American submarines into a trap. A riot is quelled with wholesale reprisals but the prisoners manage to send out a radio message and all ends in victory for the good guys, a fact which appears to be all that concerned makers of this kind of movie. Simplistic or not, at least no one had any doubt about the message such movies conveyed.

The main concern of *Merry Christmas, Mr Lawrence* (1982), which is set in Java in 1942, is much less readily defined and its message difficult to decode. Based upon the novel *The Seed and the Sower*, and other stories by Laurens van der Post, which are in their turn based upon his own wartime experiences, this is not a simple tale of reality. The author's intentions were not factual recall but a spiritual examination of the ties that bind people of different cultures and which can, even in the crucible of war, produce understanding and potentially lasting benefits to mankind.

Conveying a philosophical angle such as this is by no means a difficult problem in a movie but in this instance the makers of the film have taken on board other qualities of their own choosing which serve mainly to confuse, at least for Western audiences. In the hands of Japanese director Nagisa Oshima, who also co-wrote the screenplay (with Paul Mayersberg), the spirituality of the story becomes extremely diffuse, bringing in aspects of Buddhism that are obscure to most non-Eastern audiences.

The structural core of the tale revolves around two pairs of characters. One pair is Major Jack Celliers, a rebellious New Zealander (played by British pop star David Bowie), and Captain Yonoi, the camp commandant (played by Japanese pop star Ryuichi Sakamoto), who gradually forms an attachment for his prisoner. The other pair, more readily identifiable with characters in other prisoner-of-war movies, are Colonel John Lawrence (Tom Conti), a Japanese-speaking Englishman

who serves as interpreter for his comrades and also as narrator to the film, and Sergeant Gengo Hara (played by Takeshi, a Japanese stand-up comic), a brutal guard.

Celliers proves to be a disturbing influence on the rest of the camp, inside and outside the wire, and as unrest grows Yonoi finds that his control both of the camp and himself is slipping. Scenes of Celliers' early life are interwoven but serve mainly to add to the confusion over his later actions where there is an uneasy simplicity in the manner in which Celliers, who has for years nursed feelings of guilt over the fact that as a schoolboy he failed to protect his younger brother, eagerly embraces his own death.

Aware of the Japanese commandant's implicitly homosexual interest in him, Celliers deliberately intervenes to interrupt the execution of the senior officer among the prisoners, Group Captain Hicksley (Jack Thompson). Celliers' action, he kisses Yanoi in full view of prisoners and guards, leads to the disgrace of the Japanese and to Celliers' own death. Celliers is buried up to his neck on orders from a new camp commandant and is left to die.

The interrelationships, particularly that between Celliers and Yonoi, spread a surreal patina across the surface of the film through which the maker's intentions gleam only fitfully.

The poetic spirituality of *Merry Christmas, Mr Lawrence*, and its unconvincing use of implicit homosexual attraction between prisoner and captor in a Japanese camp, places the film a considerable distance outside the norm and leads any member of the audience with the historical perspective of life endured by the Braddons, Rivetts and Drowers of that evil world to question the use of this particular *milieu* for a story that has very little to do with its reality.

Similarly uneasy, although much more orthodox and simplistic, is an Australian movie which tells the true tale of Z Special Force, a group of Commonwealth commandos who destroyed enemy vessels in Singapore harbour. *The Highest Honour* (1982) traces the attacks, led by Lieutenant Colonel Ivan Lyon (Stuart

Tom Conti (c) faces his captor, Takeshi, in Merry Christmas, Mr Lawrence **(1982).**

Wilson), and when a further assault is carried out the subsequent capture of most of the unit.

A bond builds between Captain Bob Page (John Howard) and a civilian interpreter, Minoru Tamiya (Atsuo Nakamura), but this does not spare the prisoners their fate. Found guilty of the acts they are granted the 'highest honour' of being sentenced to death so that they will be remembered as heroes by their families and fellow countrymen. If this obscene abstraction of the Japanese code of honour is not enough, death will be in accordance with the tradition of Bushido. They will be beheaded.

The revulsion felt by the ten prisoners is well conveyed although, heaven knows, it isn't difficult to induce horror in a Western audience at such a fate.

As the execution commences, shots of the Japanese interpreter are intercut as he races on a motor cycle to the execution site. Any innocent in the audience who thinks this might be the signal for a last-minute reprieve is soon put straight. Minoru Tamiya has come to pay the highest personal honour he can bestow upon his friend Captain Page; he will wield the sword. With friends like this, who needs enemies?

The reverse of the Japanese-American coin, the internment of Japanese-born American citizens and their descendants during World War II, is a subject barely touched upon by filmmakers. When Japan attacked Pearl Harbor in 1941, Americans suddenly woke up to the fact that the West Coast was liberally studded with communities of Issei and Nisei (first and second generation immigrants), particularly among the California fishermen. Amidst sudden panic measures, which were not so panic-stricken that they affected the even greater numbers of Italian-Americans and German-Americans living in other parts of the country, laws were passed that permitted mass internment, wholesale deprivation of property, and abrogation of the civil rights of people who had never given the least indication that they represented a threat of any kind whatsoever. Designated as aliens, the Issei and Nisei were arrested and transported, their homes left behind to rot, their businesses to founder and in many cases to be taken over by competitors who had long grumbled at the success of these hard-working immigrants. The alacrity with which some of these takeovers occurred might lead a cynic to assume that localized self-interest was at work in prompting some of the moves against the Japanese-Americans.

It is hard to find many Hollywood feature films that so much as mention the Japanese-Americans. Two exceptions are *Go For Broke* (1951), a war movie about a Nisei division fighting in Italy, and *Bad Day at Black Rock* (1955), about the aftermath of the murder of an old Japanese-American while his son, a soldier in the US Army, was fighting in the war and winning a medal for gallantry. Neither of these films, however, concern themselves with the internment of innocent people whose only offence was their ancestry.

A small gesture towards righting a longstanding wrong occurred in 1976 with the appearance of a TV movie, *Farewell to Manzanar*, made by Jeanne Wakatsuki and her husband, James D. Houston. *Farewell to Manzanar* tells the story of Jeanne Wakatsuki's family through her own eyes; as a little girl she and her parents were among the internees and her subsequent book and film recall those events with sensitivity and understanding and a commendable absence of bitterness.

Of more substance, but over 40 years too late to be of any real use, 1988 saw a formal apology made to the former internees by the United States government.

Long before that date, America had been involved in two more wars in South-East Asia although the first of these, in a triumph for go-vernmental euphemism, was officially described as a 'police action'.

The police action in Korea, which also involved British and Commonwealth troops, did not inspire film-makers in the way that they were inspired by World War II. There were exceptions, notably Samuel Fuller's energetic and erratic *The Steel Helmet* (1951), made soon after the war began, and Lewis Milestone's *Pork Chop Hill* (1959), which ostensibly tells a true story of the war.

If movies about the actual fighting in Korea were pretty sparse then movies set in prisoner-of-war camps were even rarer. The fate of prisoners lurked in the background of *The Rack* (1956) in which Captain Edward W. Hall Jr (Paul Newman) is court-martialled for broadcasting propaganda messages for the North Koreans, an action he took to save fellow prisoners from being tortured or killed.

The treatment of prisoners also plays a part in *The Manchurian Candidate* (1962), an improbable, occasionally hysterical but always entertaining account of the effects of brainwashing.

A group of prisoners is systematically conditioned so that they can return to America unaware that one of their number, Raymond Shaw (Lawrence Harvey), has been induced to become a killer who will be triggered by the sight of the queen of diamonds. When another of the repatriated soldiers, Bennet Marco (Frank Sinatra), discovers that his bad dreams are matched by similar bad dreams experienced by Corporal Melvin (James Edwards) he takes his fears to the army high command. Subsequently a plot is uncovered which will result in Shaw assassinating a presidential candidate so that his running-mate, a Communist-backed senator, will become president. All this is controlled by Shaw's mother (the red queen).

The movie thus simultaneously parodies red scare movies of the 1950s and reveals its own belief in a Communist-backed conspiracy, while consistently upholding director John Frankenheimer's belief that fanaticism of the far right and far left are, in essence, exactly the same thing.

The Manchurian Candidate was re-released in 1987 and attracted big audiences as America moved towards a real life presidental election which saw the end of the Hollywood presidency (for the time being).

In fact, the retiring president had done his own movie share of prison camp time. This came in *Prisoner of War* (1954), a shallow tale in which Web Sloane (Ronald Reagan) parachutes behind enemy lines in order to infiltrate a prison camp to see if stories of atrocities are true. He discovers that they are (surprise, surprise), learns that the two senior officers on the enemy side, Russian Colonel Nikita I. Biroshilov and Korean Colonel Kim Doo Yi (Oscar Homolka and Leonard Strong) are comic-opera bemedalled baddies, and escapes to report the truth.

Presumably no one was dumb enough to think that *Prisoner of War* was based on fact. But if they did, it would help prove that the men who give orders in real wars can be just as fatuous as those movie-makers who show it all to be a kind of glorified fun and games for grown up schoolboys.

Latterday interest in *Prisoner of War*, if any, lies in the fact that its star later went on to demonstrate the effects of self-induced brainwashing by imagining he had done in real life some of the things he actually did only in the movies. This characteristic reared its head most offensively when, as President of the United States, Ronald Reagan visited Europe, which he appeared to believe he had visited as either a soldier landing on the beaches or as a photographer entering the concentration camps.

While, for the most part, the Korean war slipped past film-makers in America they more than made up for it with America's next adventure in South-East Asia.

The war in Vietnam prompted a succession of movies, many of the early ones being simple-minded, rally-round-the-flag-boys efforts which culminated in the abysmal right-wing pretentiousness of *The Green Berets* (1968). These movies, and most of what followed, proved just how little film-makers understood about either the reason for the conflict or what the Americans were doing there in the first place. They

Robert De Niro and John Savage up to their knees in water and up to their necks in trouble in The Deer Hunter **(1978).**

hadn't done much better either with the earlier films depicting the struggles of the French in Vietnam in the years before America's involvement. Such titles as *A Yank in Indo China* (1952) and *A Yank in Viet-Nam* (1963) give some clue to the depths of their integrity.

After John Wayne had made the world a safer place for all good capitalists in *The Green Berets* the climate began to change with the drop-out, see-America-first, view of *Easy Rider* (1969). Then a string of movies emerged that took a much more cynical view of the war in Vietnam. These movies ranged from *Taxi Driver* (1976), and its returned mixed-up vet, to *Apocalypse Now* (1979), with its impressively doomed view of American involvement in the region. Of course, these movies looked at war with a detachment made possible by hindsight and a realization of the losses the American nation had suffered in terms of human life, international prestige, and money.

Only rarely did prison camps feature in these movies. An exception is *The Deer Hunter* (1978) in which American prisoners are subjected to particularly unpleasant treatment by their North Vietnamese captors.

Held in a bamboo cage suspended in a river which runs grey with rats and the remains of dead comrades, three buddies, Michael, Nick and Steven (Robert De Niro, Christopher Walken and John Savage) are subjected to a lethal gambling game by guards who are uniformly sadistic, depraved villains. The game they play is Russian roulette and the fact that this scene is shot in a powerfully dramatic, suspenseful manner in an atmosphere of all-stops-out hysteria conceals the hollowness of its basis not in fact but in the imagination of the movie's maker.

Neither does real life have very much to do with the third major batch of Vietnam movies, which took hold in the early 1980s. Although this was still too early for the wounds, physical, material and to national pride, to have fully healed, the worst of the damage was at least growing a thin shield. Sensing this, and taking heart from the gung-ho, right-wing politicizing of the Reagan years, some film-makers began making Vietnam movies depicting a fantasy world in which America's crushing defeat becomes merely a temporary set-back. The central theme of these movies is built upon the belief held by some members of the public and unaccountably fostered by some sections of the military establishment, that many hundreds of American soldiers have not been killed but are only Missing In Action. The next step in this assumption is, of course, that these MIAs are held captive in prison camps scattered throughout Vietnam and neighbouring Laos and Cambodia.

Having cottoned on to the potential public appeal of movies about the MIAs all that remained for film-makers to decide was whether or not to treat the subject in a calm and carefully considered manner, sympathetically examining the possible plight of men held in captivity for a decade or more. Although there were occasional movies that tried to take a sympathetic stance, the fact that film-makers inhabit the same imperfect world that is home to the rest of mankind ensured that for the most part they chose the opposite approach and a steady stream of slam-bang, let's-get-'em-out movies began to appear.

An early entry in the field, and one which tries to keep the lid on hysteria and the ammunition box for most of its running time is *Uncommon Valour* (1983). Directed by Ted Kotcheff from a screenplay by Joe Gayton, the story develops out of the belief held by a retired soldier, Colonel Jason Rhodes (played by Gene Hackman), that his son is still alive and in captivity in Laos 11 years after he went MIA. Rhodes wants the government to help but is told that negotiations are in hand and interference by individuals may be damaging. Rhodes decides he will make his own bid to find his son and seeks financial backing from Hugh MacGregor (Robert Stack) whose own son is also MIA. Rhodes recruits a team of 'experts' drawing mainly upon survivors of his son's former unit, trains them at a dummy Laotian camp he has constructed deep in the heart of Texas, ignores governmental attempts to persuade him to call off his mission, and eventually heads for South-East Asia.

In Thailand, the group's weapons and transport are impounded by the local authorities, who have been alerted by the US government, but Rhodes buys replacements on the black market. Guided into Laos by a local drug smuggler and his two daughters, Rhodes and his team find the camp where he believes his son is being held. They attack the camp, bringing to bear on it an astonishing amount of fire power and high explosive, to say nothing of several helicopters they have stolen along the way. After killing off a substantial number of the 'enemy' Rhodes and his men free four American prisoners, one of whom is MacGregor's son who tells Rhodes that his son died recently. The helicopters clatter off towards freedom, no one having appeared to notice that in order to get these four men out of captivity almost the same number of the rescue party have lost their lives. If *Uncommon Valour* has a message, it presumably is that it is better for a free American to be valorously dead than that a fellow countryman should be a forgotten prisoner of an alien state.

Uncommon Valour chose not to offer a feasible façade but it did at least have as its star an actor who made his non-action scenes look as if they might have some connection with reality. *Missing in Action* and its prequel *Missing in Action 2-The Beginning* (both 1984) did not have even that small merit.

In fact, the second film of this pair was made first and is more concerned with prison camp life under the Vietnamese than are any of the other MIA movies. The usual array of stereotypes are paraded across the screen: sadistic camp commandant, a prisoner who is a collaborator but who later assures his place in heaven by sacrificing his life for a comrade, a tragicomic prisoner who might be going crazy, and a stalwart hero who survives all the enemy's attempts to break his spirit and eventually leads a successful escape bid. This latter character, destined for a long movie life, is Colonel James Braddock (played by Chuck Norris, popular star of countless rock bottom violent actioners, who first attracted Hollywood's attention thanks to his success as a karate champion).

Unlike *Missing in Action 2-The Beginning*, which drew its values, such as they are, from World War II prison camp movies, *Missing in Action* is a straightforward MIA movie in which James Braddock returns to Vietnam several years later to prove to his government that many Americans really are still being held in captivity by the simple expedient of finding and rescuing some of them. To do this Braddock has to invade Vietnam by boat, something he achieves with the assistance of just one old buddy. The fact that two men alone manage to achieve what the US government with all its might cannot accomplish directs rather more light upon the minds of the film's makers than it truly reflects any reality which might lurk beneath the movie's soggy surface.

The success of these two James Braddock movies was such that the colonel was brought back for *Braddock: Missing in Action III* (1988). This time Braddock returns to Vietnam in 1987 after being told that his Vietnamese wife, Lin (Miki Kim), and son, Van (Roland Harrah III),

are still alive. He finds them but is captured and tortured by the regulation sadist, General Qoc (Aki Aleong), who kills Lin. Braddock eventually triumphs and leads his son and a horde of Amerasian children, the result of countless overfriendly liaisons between American troops and Vietnamese women, to freedom. That such tragic offspring of war really exist barely excuses this kind of exploitation.

The reason behind the decision to release *Missing in Action 2-The Beginning* and *Missing in Action* in reverse order was because the MIA movie had suddenly become big business. This came as a result of another sequel, this time to the hugely successful *First Blood* (1982), which stars Sylvester Stallone as John Rambo, a Vietnam veteran who single-handedly lays waste to the quiet American town of Hope after the local sheriff upsets him and triggers memories of his wartime experiences.

Rambo: First Blood, Part II (1985) takes John Rambo back to Vietnam on a mission to discover if reports of American soldiers being held in prison camps are true. Rambo is offered a pardon for destroying Hope (you bet there's symbolism in this) but there is never any doubt that he would take on this new task without reward of any kind. Any excuse for wasting a few score Viet Cong would serve just as well for this homicidal maniac.

Setting aside for a moment the content of *Rambo: First Blood, Part II* the movie is well made, structurally sound, and the hardware impressive. Unfortunately, the content keeps intruding and the wholesale destruction of human life that Rambo carries out creates the inescapable impression that the movie is intended as a kind of celluloid catharsis for years of biting on the bullet of defeat. The villains here include the Vietnamese, the Russians, and American governmental bureaucracy; the heroes, or rather hero because this is another of Rambo's single-handed assaults, is the traditional American loner who has dominated the movies from their very beginnings.

Unfortunately, apart from his monsyllabic dialogue, there is not the slightest resemblance between the acting style, if that is the right phrase to use, of Sylvester Stallone and such earlier loner heroes of the movies as Gary Cooper and James Stewart. As for his physical appearance; next to this muscular hero even Chuck Norris looks as though a puff of wind would blow him away. Just why men with physiques closely resembling button-studded leather armchairs have become some of the biggest box-office stars in the world is a matter for eternal wonderment. There must be an awful lot of people in the world who are constantly having sand kicked in their faces and dream of waking up one day looking like one or another of these latterday inflated supermen.

The slogan implicit in earlier MIA movies turned up in the dialogue of *POW The Escape* (1986) in which Colonel Jim Cooper (David Carradine, who had once been an avowed opponent of the crass nationalistic values displayed here) leads a mission to rescue prisoners still being held by the North Vietnamese as the end of the war looms. 'Everybody goes home' is Cooper's declared aim and so they do, except those who are blown up, shot, stabbed, impaled, and otherwise disposed of in the course of Cooper's adventures.

Sadly, Vietnam was a tragedy not an adventure. The effects of this war are still present for many Americans, whether former combatants or relatives of the dead, wounded and missing.

Those who are missing, and little hard evidence has emerged that they exist in substantial numbers, surely deserve something better than rally-round-the-flag-boys movies which glorify wholesale slaughter. What is worst about these movies is that they make no appeal to those in government who might do something about surviving victims of past wars but appeal instead to those who might well become the victims of future wars. That future encounters are a possibility is demonstrated convincingly by recent American attitudes in Central America, which show that neither the Pentagon nor the White House learned any lessons from Vietnam.

As movies dealing with the fate of hostages held by terrorist factions, particularly in the Middle East, begin to pepper cinema and televison screens of the late 1980s, the need for mature movie-making is just as important. If the Rambo school of thought prevails, the odds are that maturity will be in short supply.

Going Straight ... Over the Wall

'It's a good world outside.'
(Call Northside 777)

One day, someone with time on his hands, a lifetime maybe, might try tracing all the movies that have begun outside prison gates. Using nothing more reliable than a blurred memory of endless iron gates clanging and studded doors slamming, a hazarded guess would put the answer in the high hundreds if not the low thousands. As often as not these opening sequences show the star of the movie – Alan Ladd, say, in *Hell on Frisco Bay* (1956) or Robert Redford in *The Hot Rock* (1972) – coming out to breathe free air for the first time in one, ten, twenty-five or fifty years, and determined to go straight, find the loot from the last job, plan the next job, or take revenge on the cop, judge, stool pigeon, or ex-girlfriend who put him inside.

As often as not, such movies have very little to do with prison and those opening shots might well be the last we see of the joint. Occasionally, thanks to those movie-makers with a cyclical sense of structure who like to end up where they began, we may later see prison gates clanging shut behind whomever the hero has battled against in his struggle to go straight, take revenge, etcetera.

Formal release of the kind enjoyed by Ladd and Redford in the named movies does have its drawbacks; for one thing, it isn't very exciting. Escape, on the other hand, offers all the same possible storylines plus the fact that our hero also has to avoid the guards, dig the tunnel, scale the walls, whatever, all of which helps kick the movie off with a high adrenalin count.

Those film-makers who were either unwilling or intellectually incapable (as many were) of working within the physical limitations of prison began exploring ways of escaping with as much enthusiasm as real life prisoners, and often with rather more success. The escape bid, its plotting and mechanics, and the excitement of the breakout itself quickly became essential ingredients of the prison movie. So much so that in many cases the escape is used as little more than the jumping off point for an adventure movie.

Nevertheless, the prison itself in all such movies can be a significant part of the motivation for what follows, usually in the form of a powerful impulse for the protagonist to avoid going inside again. Sadly, for those who believe in the efficacy of prison, it is only rarely that this determination means the ex-con has been rehabilitated. Usually, it means that he has spent his time inside figuring ways to avoid being caught next time.

Most of the movies already touched upon in these pages have featured escape. Even a film like *Birdman of Alcatraz*, which deliberately concerned itself with the dreary routine of prison life, has its moments of excitement in its depiction of the attempted breakout by Bernie Coy and his comrades. Many movies, among them *I Am a Fugitive from a Chain Gang*, carry the notion of escape in their titles while scores incorporate the magic word 'escape' itself.

That practically all the prisoner-of-war camp movies concern themselves with escape bids is only natural – given the fact that it is a part of every soldier's commitment to his trade – that he should attempt to escape. Subsequently he should do all he can to harrass the enemy while behind the wire or when he is loose on the enemy's side of the lines.

Among the movies that use an escape from prison as the starting point for a tale that otherwise has little or nothing to do with confinement are such classic tales of derring-do as the novels by Alexandre Dumas.

The Count of Monte Cristo is set during the Napoleonic era and features an heroic patriot named Edmond Dantes who falls foul of scheming enemies and is imprisoned in the Chateau d'If, an impregnable castle on an island off the southern coast of France. Dantes languishes in his cell for many years, growing steadily more resigned to remaining there for the rest of his life, but a fellow prisoner, attempting to tunnel out, breaks through the wall of Dantes' cell and the two men strike up a cautious friendship. The other prisoner, Abbe Faria, has been incarcerated here for even more years than Dantes and appears to have lost his reason, babbling crazily about a vast treasure he claims he has hidden on the island of Monte Cristo. Dantes finally gets his chance to escape when the old man dies. Knowing that dead prisoners are wrapped in a shroud and tossed into the sea, Dantes changes places with the old man just before the jailers come to dispose of the body.

Dantes survives this desperate escape bid, goes in search of the old man's treasure and finds that his tales were not insane ramblings but nothing less than the truth. Now immensely rich, Dantes returns to society, which thought it had long ago seen the last of him, determined to take his revenge.

The romantic appeal of Edmond Dantes' tale is such that it has appeared many times in motion picture form, not always with acknowledgement to its source. John Gilbert played the count in 1922 but the best version of *The Count of Monte Cristo* is that made in 1934 starring Robert Donat as Dantes. Confronting

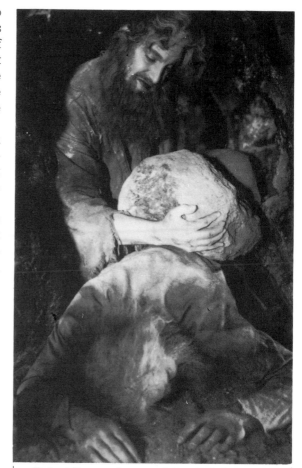

Robert Donat takes a weight off O. P. Heggie but the old man has left it too late to escape from the Chateau D'If in The Count of Monte Cristo **(1934).**

Dantes are a fearsome array of villains, including De Villefort (Louis Calhern), Mondego (Sidney Blackmer) and Douglas (Raymond Walburn). Dantes' true love, Mercedes (Elissa Landi), eventually finds her way back into his affections although she is, understandably, a little shaken at his return from the living dead.

Subsequent remakes, including a French film in 1955 starring Pierre-Richard Wilm and that of 1977 starring Richard Chamberlain, tried their best but failed to measure up to the high standards of the earlier film. *Return of Monte Cristo* (1946) stars Louis Hayward as a descendant of Edmond Dantes who is sent to Devil's Island when he tries to claim his inheritance.

Another tale by Dumas, of a mysterious prisoner in an iron mask, has proved even more fascinating for film-makers and for scholars because there seems reason to believe that its origins lie in a real case. Recent intensive research has established with little room for doubt that a masked man really was held in various prisons in France during the eighteenth century, being moved from place to place, often with the same senior prison officer moving with him.

The romantic legend perpetuated by Dumas is that the king of France, Louis XIV, has an identical twin brother, Philippe, who is hidden away so that he can never compete for the throne.

In *The Man in the Iron Mask* (1939), which stars Louis Hayward in the dual role, Philippe's existence is suspected and an elaborate plan developed that will free him so that he may replace his evil brother thus bringing peace and contentment to the country. With D'Artagnan (Warren William) leading his Musketeer friends, Athos, Porthos and Aramis (Bert Roach, Alan Hale and Miles Mander) to the rescue, everything zips along at swashbuckling pace until the imprisoned brother can be freed and his evil sibling locked inside the iron mask there to remain for the rest of life.

The tale popped up under the same title as a 1977 TV movie starring Richard Chamberlain and again in 1978 as *The Fifth Musketeer* with Beau Bridges. Although the passage of time had not allowed film-makers to improve upon the earlier version, the 1978 fling did have the mildly engaging gimmick of showing D'Artagnan and the Three Musketeers as ageing swordsmen. Employed in the role are iconographic actors from past swashbuckling epics including Cornel Wilde as D'Artagnan and Alan Hale Jr in the role his father had played in the 1939 version.

Escaped prisoners of the twentieth century have appeared so often in the movies it seems as though the overpopulation of prisons we hear so much about is fantasy. With so many cons on the run, most prisons must be half empty.

The Siege of Pinchgut (1960) traces an unsuccessful attempt by four convicts to escape from prison only to find themselves trapped on an island in Sydney Harbour, Australia. The fact that they find on the island a long-range gun with which they threaten to blow up an ammunition ship thus laying waste to a fair slice of the city allows them to drag out the suspense rather longer than this slim tale can withstand. The fact that the leader of the gang, Matt Kirk (Aldo Ray), wants a retrial (he is a hardened criminal but claims to be innocent this time) suggests he has an improbable faith in human nature. Does he really think a Sydney jury will believe anything he says after he's threatened to send them into orbit?

The Desperate Hours (1955) stars Humphrey Bogart as escaped convict Glenn Griffin who takes over a private house as a temporary hideout for himself and his companions. The movie takes place in or around the house, which is located in a middle-class residential area in Indianapolis, but this entirely normal setting soon becomes a prison for the Hilliard family. As time passes and the convicts' getaway plans misfire, the house turns into a prison for the gang that is just as claustrophobically confining as the one from which they have escaped.

A real life jail break in December 1947 was whisked onto the screen by midsummer the following year. *Canon City* tells the story of 12 cons who skipped from the Colorado state pen in Canon City only to be killed or recaptured. Told with brisk urgency, the movie benefited from a quasi-documentary style, its proximity in time to the real events and also to the appearance of Warden Roy Best who played himself.

Prison Break (1938) features an example of the noble con. This time he is Joaquin Shannon (Barton MacLane) who has taken the rap for a murder he thinks his brother committed. When he learns that his sibling is as innocent as he is (but not, presumably, quite so dumb), he takes off in pursuit of bad guy Red Kincaid (Ward Bond).

In *Crashout* (1955) Van Duff (William Bendix) and five cronies escape from jail intent on recovering loot stashed after the last job. The cons hide out in an old mine, thus replacing one man-made prison for another, and are whittled away by accident or murder until only the leader and young Joe Quinn (Arthur Kennedy) are left. With Joe clearly the intended hero of this yarn it comes as no surprise to anyone when Van Duff wraps things up neatly by falling off a mountain.

Exchanging one kind of imprisonment for another is a common movie routine and it pops up in a British thriller, *Escape By Night* (1965). Here, convict Bart Rennison (Tom Bowman) is rescued from a prison bus along with several other cons. Taking refuge in a barn along with a handful of guards as hostages, the cons douse the place in paraffin and threaten to torch it if the police move in. Unfortunately for this plan, one of the cons is Victor Lash (Peter Sallis), a psychotic killer with a liking for starting fires and he happily sends the cons' hopes of freedom up in smoke.

Charles Bickford leads the mass breakout in Brute Force **(1947) knowing it is doomed to bloody failure.**

Tiring of the word 'escape', several movies have used 'breakout' in their titles including at least three which use nothing else (four, if the American release title of *Danger Within* is included).

Breakout (1959) centres upon George Munro (Lee Patterson), a harmless clerk whose spare time is gainfully employed in devising escape plans for criminals. George's wife, Rose (Billie Whitelaw), is understandably concerned at the way her housekeeping allowance is being supplemented and domestic conflict develops alongside the escape. The fact that the bid involves a getaway in a grocery van suggests that George is alarmingly one-track minded.

Breakout (1971) is a TV movie about Joe Baker (James Drury), a con who, after several unsuccessful attempts, eventually breaks out from behind the walls of Folsom prison. Baker's motivation is simple; he wants to rejoin his wife (Kathryn Hays) and the loot from his last job. When the fugitives head for the hills, the movie becomes fairly interesting both for its action and the scenery.

Breakout (1975) features the implacable Charles Bronson as Nick Colton, a professional escape organizer who is here called upon to put his talents to helping a prisoner escape from a Mexican jail.

The prisoner is Jay Wagner (Robert Duvall) who is there on a phony rap concocted by his grandfather, Harris Wagner (John Huston), whose plans for the family's multi-million dollar business empire do not include Jay.

Harris has done a deal with the organizers of an existing escape system, which uses corrupt warders who usually take the money and shoot the cons. Meanwhile, Jay's wife, Ann (Jill Ireland), has hired Nick who makes several airborne attempts at getting Jay out before hiring a helicopter complete with a pilot who doesn't want to take any risks as the day of his wedding approaches. The reluctant pilot, Harvey (Alan Vint), is actually the least of Nick's worries because his other assistants include a pair of over-the-top exhibitionists, Hawk Hawkins and Myrna (Randy Quaid and Sheree North), who infiltrate the prison by pretending to be a Mexican whore and a rape victim (respectively; yes, really).

Nick eventually succeeds in lifting Jay from the joint, and even saves him from a hitman sent in by granddaddy, which is really rather noble of him because by now, inevitably, Nick has fallen for Ann.

It's all jokey nonsense, of course, but it has a curiously engaging persuasiveness even if Nick's use of a helicopter has since seen real life imitators in various parts of the world including an escape from a prison in England. A con was lifted from the middle of the exercise field by a hijacked chopper while inmates and prison officers looked on, apparently under the impression that they were seeing the arrival of an important visitor – or maybe they thought someone was making a movie.

Break Out (1984) is a pleasing tale directed at the younger element of the contemporary audience (the film was produced in Britain for the Children's Film and Television Foundation). Prison here is only in the unseen background as two young brothers find themselves entangled with a pair of escaped convicts and slowly develop a curious and entirely believable bond of friendship with one of them.

Entirely unbelievable is the motivation that drives a trio of cons in *The Devil at 4 O'Clock* (1961). The perennial script standby of having these men redeem themselves by humanitarian gestures even at the cost of their own lives is used.

Father Matthew Doonan (Spencer Tracy), a brandy-soaked priest on a Pacific island, has a deal with the island's governor (Alexander Scourby) which allows him free use of convict labour. Three hardnuts are in transit to face trial and are simmering slowly in the prison's sweat box. The three, Harry, Marcel and Charlie (Frank Sinatra, Gregoire Aslan and Bernie Hamilton), are taken by Doonan to repair a church at a hospital up in the mountains. Shocked to discover they are at a leper colony, the three are eventually won over (because, of course, they really have hearts of gold). Harry falls for a young woman who helps run the colony, not noticing at first that Camille (Barbara

Luna) is blind.

Later, the island's rumbling volcano erupts when Doonan and the cons are down by the harbour. The priest persuades them to help him bring the kids down before the mountain explodes. They weigh in willingly, even though the risk of death is high; in fact, it's quite certain because it's that kind of movie. Marcel drowns in a mud pool, Charlie is crushed by a collapsing bridge, and Doonan and Harry (whom the priest had earlier and inexplicably married to Camille) are still philosophizing about God, man and the meaning of life when the island disintegrates with a bang that is almost loud enough to awaken the audience.

A personal quest for justice motivates the protagonist of *State Penitentiary* (1950) when Roger Manners (Warner Baxter), an aero-engineer sentenced for embezzlement, escapes to hunt down the real transgressor, his erstwhile partner Stacy Brown (Robert Shayne). It is all pretty routine stuff and more than a mite dated.

An unusual angle on a prison break is taken in *House of Numbers* (1957) in which Jack Palance plays brothers Arne and Bill Judlow. One brother is bad and suitably locked away but his sibling cannot see the warning signs and breaks *into* prison in order to make the escape plans. When a romance develops between good brother Bill and his sister-in-law the ending is telegraphed. The love of a good woman lifts the veil from Bill's eyes and he realizes his brother is a psycho and promptly hands him over to the cops.

A motivation that is both personal and unusual, not to say improbable, urges the protagonist of *Five Days from Home* (1978). T. M. Pryor (played by George Peppard) breaks out of prison in Louisiana when he has less than a week of his sentence left to serve. Pryor's motive for this seemingly crazy act is that his son has been critically injured and he has to see him. By making Pryor an ex-lawman, convicted on a manslaughter rap for killing his wife's lover, the film gains rather more depth than is usual for this fairly routine sort of drama. Neville Brand, who must have done more movie 'time' than any other actor (except

Barton MacLane) adds his iconographic presence to the tale as Inspector Markley who grimly purses Pryor across country to Los Angeles.

Ex-cons trying to go straight but being confounded at all sides have long been a feature of prison movies. Apart from films already touched upon, there have been such riveting sagas as *The Convict's Sacrifice* (1909), in which an ex-con is shunned by all except one man. Sent back inside he escapes, finds that his friend is destitute and cannot care for his sick child. Nobly the con insists that his friend hand him over to the law and claim the reward. When the man refuses the con makes a fight of it so that when the cops arrive the reward will be forthcoming. But he then makes the mistake of being shot for his trouble. (This tale bears a striking resemblance to *A Convict's Heroism* [also 1909] in which an escaped con insists that the destitute family that feeds him turn him over to the law so that they can claim the reward. 1909 was obviously a good year for noble convicts.)

More recently, cons trying to go straight have provided the spur for scores of movies including *Fool's Parade* (1971) to *Straight Time* (1978) to *Tough Guys* (1986), to say nothing of (and we won't) *Jailhouse Rock* (1957).

Fool's Parade stars James Stewart as Mattie Appleyard, a former miner who has just completed a long sentence for murder. Set in 1930s America the tale concerns Mattie's attempts to recover the money he has earned during his stay in prison and which has been placed in the care of the local crooked banker. There is rather a lot of money at stake, more than $25,000, and it was hard earned. As Mattie replies when asked what a man has to do to earn money like that: 'Forty-seven years.'

The fact that prison is where Mattie earned his money is all that connects this tale with imprisonment as the banker and his crooked associate, Uncle Doc Council, the captain of the prison guards (George Kennedy in bottle-bottom spectacles and a set of very bad teeth), do their best to bring Mattie and his companions to a sticky end. As the movie's British alternative title, *The Dynamite Man from Glory Jail*, suggests, Mattie Appleyard has a highly explosive way of dealing with his enemies.

The problems for a young man on parole trying to keep his nose clean is a popular theme for movie-makers. *Parole* (1936) was one such saga, but in those days youthful parolees tended to be rather pleasant if greatly misunderstood souls with whom audiences could readily identify. No such identification was likely with the protagonist of *Straight Time*, the story of Max Dembo (Dustin Hoffman), an unpleasant loser who resists every attempt to persuade him to go straight. At the start of the movie, with Max freshly out of jail, he crosses swords with his parole officer, Earl Frank (M. Emmet Walsh). Out after six years in the joint, Dembo spends his first night at a Los Angeles hotel. This directly contravenes the conditions of his parole; he is supposed to stay at a halfway house. This gets him off on the wrong foot with Frank and when an ex-con junkie pal, Willy Darin (Gary Busey), shoots up in Dembo's room and the parole officer finds traces, both feet are quickly off the ground as Dembo is thrown back in the tank. Dembo refuses to name Willy and then, taking exception to Frank's admittedly insulting attitude towards him, Dembo hijacks the car they are travelling in. He leaves Frank handcuffed to the safety fence in the middle of the highway with his trousers around his ankles and takes off.

As the film progresses it soon becomes apparent that behaviour like this is as good as Max is capable of offering as his contribution towards society. Despite having found a clean-living but remarkably naïve girlfriend in Jenny Mercer (Theresa Russell), Dembo now embarks upon a renewal of the career of petty crime which landed him in jail in the first place. With his sidekick Jerry Schue (Harry Dean Stanton), a thick-witted loser, he is soon heading for disaster. Taking Willy along as getaway driver adds to the pressing evidence that Dembo is no judge of people. Willy panics and leaves Dembo and Schue at the scene of the robbery. Schue is killed, Dembo then kills Willy before leaving town with Jenny.

The love affair has been intrusive, Jenny may be naïve but she certainly isn't dumb and a

Peter Sellers (r) temporarily behind bars in The Prisoner of Zenda **(1979) as the rascally Jeremy Kemp (c) and a rather grubby Norman Rossington (l) consider his fate.**

three-time loser like Dembo should never have reached first base. The affair now provides an improbable ending as, from out of nowhere, Dembo produces a flicker of decency and drops Jenny off at a bus stop before driving towards certain arrest.

By this point in the movie this is the least that most members of the audience are hoping will come to him. *Straight Time* is the kind of movie that gives rehabilitation of prisoners a bad name.

Unlike Max Dembo, from whom anyone in his or her right mind would run a mile, a pair of ex-convicts anyone would welcome into his (or

her) home are Harry Doyle and Archie Long, the protagonists of *Tough Guys*. Engagingly played by Burt Lancaster and Kirk Douglas, Harry and Archie are released from prison after serving 30 years for robbing a train only to find that life outside has left them so far behind that their only chance at surviving, both financially and spiritually, is to rob the same train all over again. It is all done with effortless ease but the fact that the two stars have such a significant movie past suggests that this amiable piece of hokum could have drawn much more from its audience's accumulated memory banks than it chose to do.

Another actor with an amiable persona is Dennis Weaver, who stars in *Rolling Man*, a 1972 TV movie. Lonnie McAfee (Weaver), an inoffensive but hopeless ex-con, is trying to pick up the pieces of a wrecked life as he drifts around the country searching for his young sons who have been fostered out. Life for McAfee is one raw deal after another and his worthy attempts to make it, following as they do some vividly unpleasant scenes in prison, have the audience hoping he'll make out okay in the end.

A glance forward to a possible future for mankind comes in *Escape from New York* (1981), which is set in New York City as it might be in 1997. Manhattan Island has become one huge maximum security prison in which the State can conveniently dump and forget anyone it chooses. When the President's plane is hijacked on the way to an international peace conference, he bales out and lands slap in the middle of this gigantic joint. Fortunately for the President (Donald Pleasance), one of the cons is Snake Plissken (Kurt Russell), an all-purpose hard case who agrees to get him out in exchange for a parole.

The movie is all hokum, of course, and does not have much relation to prison movies as such but the central premise raises a tiny quiver of fearful doubt about how long we have before some bright spark decides that such a concept might be the way to solve the twin problems of a fast-increasing prison population and even faster-rising inner-city crime rates all in one fell swoop.

As was suggested in earlier pages of this book, the vast majority of crime is committed by the poor and disadvantaged. Some observers of the social scene in America have gone so far as to suggest that society needs a visible prison population in order to describe the bounds behind which the non-criminal population is shielded. What better way than a city full of transgressors?

Another way, already making an appearance in America, is the new high technology prison, which dehumanizes relationships in such a manner that a prisoner might well make no contact with non-prisoners during his incarceration.

An Australian movie, *Ghosts . . . of the Civil Dead* (1988), ventures an impression of how such an establishment might develop. It is a frightening image of violent unrestrained psychopathic behaviour in which most of the prisoners run their own lives with unlimited access to alcohol, drugs and sex. More serious offenders are restricted and thus become more dangerous than they were when they came in. As for the men decreed to be already dangerous, they are locked in solitary confinement with no light and no sound with the inevitable outcome that they go slowly and frighteningly insane.

That such an establishment as the Central Industrial Prison of *Ghosts . . . of the Civil Dead* appears in a fictional film should not obscure the fact that most of the incidents in this powerful and alarming film are based upon real events at two American prisons, the new high-technology prison at Marion, Illinois, and the New Mexico State Penitentiary.

Just how bad these real life events were can be gleaned from comments made by John Hillcoat and Evan English, the makers of *Ghosts . . . of the Civil Dead*. 'What you see is in fact greatly toned down . . . If we had not exercised restraint our film would be too horrific to be shown.'

13

Death and Other Endings

'...there must be another way.'
(Warden Cabana)

If society does need a visible prison population in order to define its own boundaries then it might be rewarding to consider how individual members of that society might respond if sent down themselves. Would they, perhaps, move the boundary markers?

It is similarly speculative to suggest that if classes of society other than the poor were subjected to real prison rather than the version offered by the movies one result might be an improvement in prison conditions.

Among the statistics quoted earlier was the fact that more than 90 per cent of the population have probably committed crimes punishable by prison but remain unapprehended. The reason for the failure of law enforcement departments to bring these criminals to book may well lie in a matter of class.

Today, prison might be regarded as a last bastion separating the poor from the rich. If this is true, and statistics would suggest it is becoming increasingly so, then it is a state of affairs which dramatically affects the progress of prison reform because the would-be reformer comes from a social group with little or no direct experience of doing time.

Even when the rich do fall foul of the law their punishments tend not to match the crime but to reflect a curious leniency in the judiciary. A survey of crimes and punishments conducted in America in the early 1970s revealed that the average sentence for men convicted of robbery was more than ten years; add in the lesser crimes of burglary, larceny and theft and the average still stands high at six years. Contrasting with this is the average penalty for those convicted of such 'middle-class', white-collar crimes as embezzlement, fraud and income tax evasion where those found guilty can expect an average sentence of under two years.

Specific cases show that the amount of money stolen has no bearing on the sentence: A judge of the Supreme Court of New York state, convicted of receiving $800,000 was given a year in prison and fined $10,000. A man who stole $10 million from investors collected six months (with five more on probation). Mark Rifkin, who in 1980 ripped off more than $10 million from a Los Angeles bank by computer fraud, received comparatively severe treatment when he was given an eight-year sentence. Much more in line with the general trend was a man who swindled stockholders out of $200 million; he went to jail for one year. In 1988 in England, Harvey Michael Ross picked up a 14-year sentence, which sounds pretty stiff in comparison; but he had committed a £14 million fraud.

The sentences of Rifkin and Ross apart, these terms of imprisonment are plainly ludicrous when set against a petty thief who steals the equivalent of the price of a loaf of bread. Of course, they may strike a blow with fist or knife or even gun; but is the difference really so great? Come to think of it, with or without time off for good behaviour, both Rifkin and Ross might even consider that one year per million stolen, be it in dollars or pounds, amounts to a pretty good deal.

The phrase used by Jeffry Reiman for the title of his book, *The Rich Get Richer and the Poor Get Prison*, sounds much less jokey as such facts are unreeled.

One conclusion that is hard to avoid drawing is that such reforms as do take place rarely get to the heart of the problem because the section of society in positions of authority are rarely on the receiving end of punishments and hence neither understand the reality of prison nor care enough to make effective changes to the conditions to which prisoners are subjected.

To a great extent prison reform over the years has proved to be a futile exercise. Certainly, in America and Britain the worst excesses have been replaced with more humane methods but the essential ingredients remain: men and women are locked away from society in order to protect society from further depredations and as a form of punishment. Any hope that imprisonment of criminals might act as a warning to others is dashed by rising crime rates (with a marked increase in violence). The other reason for prison, rehabilitation, really is a joke.

But reformers keep on trying and however cynically the outsider might view their efforts this is certainly better than nothing. After all, without them prisons might still be using the lime cell and wetpack, or confining men in solitary for decades.

How might reformers really succeed in reforming the prison system? If the recent batch of stock market swindlers in America and Britain are sent away for sentences which bear a more realistic relationship to their crimes perhaps a previously privileged section of society close to the seat of power will learn at first hand the harsh reality of life in the slammer. Provided, of course, that they go into the joint and not into an open prison where they might awaken to the sound of birdsong and not the clangour of cell doors and the stench of slopping out.

Without the protection of either wealth or influence and without the comforting benefit of the distancing effect created by watching such things on their cinema and television screens,

they might be forced into action.

That movement in previously entrenched, or at least protected, attitudes is possible can be seen from views expressed by two individuals already mentioned in these pages.

In the 1940s Los Angeles District Attorney Asa Keyes, who had a successful career sending thousands to San Quentin, including some to the gas chamber, was convicted of taking a bribe. As a result, Keyes found himself in San Quentin. Typically enough, the prison authorities offered Keyes an easy job in the administration building but to his eternal credit Keyes decided to take his medicine. He emerged from prison a changed man, declaring:

> 'Prison doesn't help any man. It's a poison, degrading all but the strongest. I don't know what to substitute for penitentiaries, but if I were a district attorney again, I would hesitate about sending so many men to prison. It is far more terrible than people realize, and the sentences are too severe.'

If more people in high places were faced with the threat of prison they might realize the truth of Asa Keyes's statement and begin devising ways of solving the problem of finding a substitute for prison.

In Britain, four decades after Asa Keyes's salutory lesson, when Judge Stephen Tumim was appointed HM Chief Inspector of Prisons in 1987 his duties entailed personal visits to prison establishments of all levels in many parts of the country. He encountered overcrowding, insanitary conditions, massive boredom, overworked prison officers, the mixing together in enforced idleness of violent criminals, the mentally subnormal, and those whose crimes required understanding rather than punishment. Writing of this experience in the *Daily Telegraph* in November 1988, Judge Tumim pondered:

> A question for me is whether I am learning anything, as a judge, from this job. Would it affect my approach in court?
> Never again will I look at a husband waiting at the back of the court between two prison officers, obviously brought from prison, and think he is no hurry and can wait happily till the end of the list. Nor will I keep dock officers, where

there is no security risk, hanging about. Prison officers' time is far too valuable.

And never again will I sentence someone to custody without an image of the sort of life to which he is being consigned, whether the Gothic spikiness of the Victorian urban local prison, the mists of Dartmoor or the low-ceilinged huts of badly built prisons of the 1960s.

Earlier, the question was asked, shouldn't people like Asa Keyes and Judge Tumim have known what prison was really like before they were appointed to posts that required them to send their fellow citizens to such places? Of course, it isn't their fault that they were not made fully aware. The system doesn't require it. Indeed, it frequently doesn't allow it. But it should. Forty years elapsed between Asa Keyes's experience and that of Judge Tumim, forty years in which little change seems to have taken place. No one in high places (and, whether we like it or not, in Britain and to a significantly lesser extent in America, our laws are made and enforced by an unelected elite) appears to know, or if they do, to care. Their ignorance is hard to swallow; after all, they only had to go to the movies to see what was happening beneath their carefully deflected noses. To be realistic, however, no one in his right mind would suggest that establishment attitudes should be moulded by the movies. Too often, the makers of movies have got it wrong.

Undoubtedly, movie-makers who have used prison as a setting for movies of infinitely variable content and quality could help more than they have. More to the point, they should make it an important issue because there will be as much need in the twenty-first century for a socially conscious prison movie as there ever was in the past.

If they take the challenge and succeed in changing the world then one day, undoubtedly far off in another century, the prison movie in all its forms might be seen as a curiosity, a depiction of a society that no longer exists and which has been replaced by one of which mankind can be proud and no longer ashamed.

The trouble is, such hopes require a civilized

attitude towards wrongdoers and while few would condone leniency for vicious and unrepentent thugs, rapists and killers, the powers-that-be seem unable to find a balanced attitude towards levels of punishment, prison conditions, or any other element in the threadbare fabric of what passes for law and order policies in either Britain or America.

Politicians have long been aware that the fastest way to popular success is to find the lowest common denominator. They, like the gutter press, find it easier to scream for heavier penalties than to whisper for those that are more appropriate and more likely to be of benefit to society.

The extreme form taken by this section of the political establishment and its fellow thinkers of the Fourth Estate periodically makes an appearance in cries for the return of capital punishment as a means of eliminating certain crimes.

The fact that no statistics are to hand to support their belief does not deaden their appeal to the unreasoning among us. And they are succeeding, at least in America where, since January 1983, capital punishment has returned to more than two-thirds of the states. So far, Britain has avoided this return to the Dark Ages but no one can have failed to notice that the periodic clamour for its return comes from the far right. As the right wing of the political spectrum continues to grow in strength how long will it be before the ultimate sanction returns – even if it is only for certain crimes that someone deems most heinous.

Capital punishment is a subject that seems difficult for even the most rational and no one ever seems swayed from his or her original viewpoint, even by the most persuasive argument. It isn't surprising, therefore, that when movie-makers have confronted the subject they have, for the most part, done so with cautiously averted gaze.

An exception is a latterday horror film, *Prison* (1987), which has no truck with social conscience but takes violent revenge as its theme.

The blending of the horror genre with the prison movie is a good idea and if not entirely original (among a handful of others, back in 1936 Boris Karloff was revived post-electrocution in *The Walking Dead*) it is certainly fresh enough to provide diversion.

The makers of *Prison* go about their aims with such commendably single-minded intensity that they carry along all but the most hardened sceptic in their audience.

The 'reality' of the storyline centres upon Creedmore Penitentiary, Wyoming, recently reopened by the authorities who are desperate to ease overcrowding in the state's prison system. Control of the prison is placed in the hands of reactionary Ethan Sharpe (played with twitchy intensity by Lane Smith) who was formerly a guard here in the bad old days. Two of the new prisoners are put into solitary after an escape attempt goes wrong and are languishing there when two other cons, Connie Burke and Sandor (Viggo Mortensen and Andre De Shields), are ordered to break through into the old execution chamber.

As Burke smashes a hole through the wall a malevolent force is released into the already grim atmosphere of the prison.

In a prologue we have already seen an execution on the prison's electric chair. This was back in 1964, when Charlie Forsythe was executed for the murder of a fellow con who had in fact been killed by Ethan Sharpe.

The spirit of Forsythe is now free to roam the prison, killing guards and convicts with progressively more gruesome relish. The fact that the film-maker's ingenuity can cap an early scene in which one of the cons in solitary is roasted alive in his cell shows that there are still new twists to give to old horror tales.

The manner in which the ghost of Charlie Forsythe eventually rises from the ground to destroy Ethan Sharpe is satisfyingly gruesome but, of course, does nothing to disturb the balance of pro and con in the argument over capital punishment.

Many of the prison movies already touched upon have a Death Row sequence, on-camera or off, but for the most part audiences saw the condemned man walking stoically to his fate with only rare outbursts of hysteria as in *We*

Who Are About to Die (1937), supposedly a tale based upon real happenings in San Quentin, in which a character named Kwong (played by Willie Fung) steps way outside Hollywood's usual stereotype and becomes anything but an inscrutable Oriental as he is dragged screaming to the death chamber.

Accusing Finger (1936) is an early, and somewhat blatant, plea for abolition with its awkward anecdotal tale of a hotshot prosecuting attorney, Douglas Goodwin (Paul Kelly), whose 100 per cent conviction record has seen several men off by way of the electric chair. When he finds himself heading in that direction he undergoes a sudden and not entirely unexpected change of mind.

Also anecdotal, and suffering from an absence of narrative thread, is *Now Barabbas . . .* (1949), a British film which looks at a random selection of offenders serving their time. Among them is Tufnell (Richard Greene), a murderer whose progress towards the hangman's rope is watched gloomily by the governor (Cedric Hardwicke).

Attitudes towards death house scenes affected the ending of *Double Indemnity* (1944). Director Billy Wilder shot two versions, one of which shows Walter Neff (Fred MacMurray) going to the gas chamber. In the event, the alternative ending, which has him die from gunshot wounds, was used, thus sparing audiences from thinking too deeply about what the State was doing in its name.

Two important movies about women facing the death sentence, *I Want to Live* and *Yield to the Night*, have already been mentioned at some length. Of this pair, *I Want to Live* is notable in showing the State's victim going to the chamber. Indeed, there have been few movies in the following 30 years that went this far.

Attention to detail in the death scene was meticulous, with director Robert Wise reluctantly attending a real exection in the interests of verisimilitude. However, as he later observed, one aspect was fudged. Death comes much more slowly to the condemned than is shown in the movie. A sideways reference to this is made when one of the officials tells Barbara

Graham (Susan Hayward) that her death will be easier if she takes a deep breath as the gas rises around her. This prompts her to ask: 'How would *you* know?'

A similarly facile premise is the inspiration for *Two Seconds* (1932), which opens and closes in the death house as John Allen (Edward G. Robinson) is led to the electric chair. The prison doctor mournfully explains to the assembled journalists that within two seconds the brain is paralysed but in that time the brain is still active and the dying man's whole life flashes before him. No one asks *him* how he knows and the movie thereafter occupies itself with flashing back through John Allen's life.

Among the crimes most likely to bring calls for continuation or reintroduction of corporal or capital punishment are acts of terrorism, those against children, and sex crimes. Yet, in the 1950s the case of a convicted sex criminal produced a remarkable international outcry against capital punishment. The man at the centre was Caryl Whittier Chessman.

Chessman was arrested in Los Angeles in 1948 and charged with a series of sex attacks against women. His trial was conducted under a California statute known as the 'Little Lindbergh' law. This statute related to kidnapping in which the victim suffered bodily harm. The maximum penalty under this law was death even though, in Chessman's case, no one had been murdered. Found guilty without recommendation for leniency, the maximum penalty was automatic. Chessman was sentenced to die in the gas chamber and his execution was eventually scheduled for 28 March 1952.

Chessman was housed in Cell 2455, Death Row, at San Quentin where he began a battle for his life. Apart from undertaking an intensive study of the law, Chessman also wrote a book, entitling it *Cell 2455, Death Row*, which became a runaway international best-seller.

The movie based on the book, *Cell 2455, Death Row* (1955), stars William Campbell as Whit, a convicted man. Like the book upon which it was based, the movie carries a considerable punch with little of the special pleading that might have been expected from a criminal in the author's circumstances.

The screenplay does not explore or explain Whit's motivation; neither does it excuse his crimes, which begin in childhood (the young Whit is played by Robert Campbell) and escalate in seriousness accompanied by sometimes vicious violence.

The question of guilt is not central to Chessman's case, although he recanted his original confession claiming it to have been made under duress. The nature of the crimes for which he was convicted do have an important bearing, especially three decades on when rape and other sexual attacks on women are increasing in most Western countries while suitable punishment lags far behind the brutality of the crime. Nevertheless, the most important factor in the Chessman case is the remarkable change which took place in the man himself. From being a petty criminal of apparently limited intellectual capacity, Chessman developed into a literate, thoughtful, compelling individual clearly capable of contributing to the society he had previously wronged. In short, Caryl Chessman was rehabilitated. The system, however, was not geared to accommodate this fact.

Despite the success of Chessman's book (and three other books he wrote later), despite the movie, despite appeals and petitions from many famous men and women, heads of state and ordinary people (the number of signatories

in Brazil ran into millions), the justice machine rolled on. After eight stays of execution Chessman's time finally ran out on 2 May 1960.

Although too late for the movie, which had long been released, Chessman's final moments contained the kind of event movie-makers have milked for dramatic effect on countless occasions. A judge granted a 30-minute stay to allow Chessman's attorneys to make a further plea; due to an incorrect telephone number being used the call did not reach San Quentin until after the prisoner was gassed.

This final event in Chessman's life eventually appeared on the screen in a 1977 TV movie, *Kill Me If You Can*, starring Alan Alda as the condemned man. Much more strongly anti-capital punishment than the earlier movie, *Kill Me If You Can* took a polemic stance which the case, with its unavoidable implications of sexual malevolence, does not easily withstand. Yet for all such misgivings, there are elements of doubt in Chessman's case, elements that are now merely footnotes in history. He isn't around to share in any benefits which might have accrued since his time, benefits which, as the 1980s draw to a close, are disappearing once more into medieval darkness.

Stays of execution such as those enjoyed for a time by Caryl Chessman do at least offer a benefit of sorts to condemned prisoners. Nevertheless, there is a marked imbalance in the manner in which prisoners are most likely to succeed in gaining stays. Quite clearly, those with good lawyers stand a better chance than those without. As good lawyers usually cost a lot of money those who benefit are those with the fattest wallets, a story we have heard before. At the time of writing, the man enjoying the longest stay in an American prison is Henry R. Anderson, who was sentenced to death early in 1960. He is an exception to the rule in that he is an attorney and hence will never be faced with a bill for his lawyer's services.

The Quare Fellow (1962) is a British film set in Dublin prison and follows the days and nights that precede an execution. The Quare Fellow, Irish prison slang for the condemned man, is seen only at the end when, head hooded, he is

Stark shadows fall across the prison as the ritual of death begins in The Quare Fellow **(1962).**

prepared for the final drop. Before then the movie examines the lifestyle of the Quare Fellow's wife, Kathleen (Sylvia Syms), a promiscuous young woman who tells the new warder at the prison, Crimmins (Patrick McGoohan), that her husband killed his brother because he found the two of them in bed together (this is a screenplay addition to the original Brendan Behan stage play). An affair between Kathleen and Crimmins brings confusion to the young warder who tries to help with an appeal against the death sentence. He fails and has to assist at the execution, which is conducted by 'Himself' (Arthur O'Sullivan), the cynically sadistic hangman.

The balance of the film is at variance with Behan's play. In the film the death penalty is presented as an inappropriate punishment for a man who killed with 'good cause'; Behan's original work carried an impassioned attack on capital punishment *per se.*

It is not particularly easy to decide precisely what attitude towards capital punishment motivates a 1982 TV movie, *The Executioner's Song,* that relates a case that gave those who approved of the reintroduction of capital punishment further titillation. The reason for the excitement was that this particular case promised to come to a different conclusion to most.

In 1976 Gary Gilmore had just completed a 12-year sentence for armed robbery and was trying half-heartedly to make a go of normal life when he pulled a hold-up at a filling station and killed the attendant. The next night he killed a motel manager and was then turned in to the police by his cousin. His arrest and trial attracted no more than limited attention in the locality, around Provo, Utah, but when he was sentenced to death and formally requested that he be executed by firing squad the media moved in.

The Executioner's Song is from a screenplay by Normal Mailer whose book swelled public interest in this sordid criminal. Although Tommy Lee Jones, as Gilmore, effectively con-

veys a mixed-up character who, among other peculiarities, firmly believed in reincarnation, there is little of substance in either the story of this man or in the man himself. Indeed, the size of Mailer's massive book created an imbalance in the public mind. If the case warranted such a huge volume then maybe it was more important than it appeared. In fact, the case was not at all important; Gilmore was a semi-literate, rather unpleasant individual who stole because he was too lazy to work, who killed for no apparent reason. He certainly deserved punishment but not the memorial of a best-selling book by an internationally known writer.

And Gilmore certainly did not deserve the implied heroic stature he earned by asking to go out in a more spectacular manner than the gas chamber or electric chair allowed.

Gilmore's decision to fight attempts to have his sentence commuted to life imprisonment is one that remains shrouded in his mystical belief in reincarnation. The possibility that someone who had already spent 12 years in the penitentiary might simply believe that death was a better way is perhaps too simple and undramatic for a movie. It certainly was not dramatic enough for a man who appears to have conceived of his life in terms of a film script.

Gilmore's personal beliefs also led him to attempt an unsuccessful suicide pact with his girlfriend Nicole (played by Rosanna Arquette) and these events, along with his chosen method of execution, all helped in his bid for greater stature than he truly warranted.

When Gilmore finally goes to his death it is a very peculiar affair indeed. Maybe Gilmore was really like this, maybe it is Tommy Lee Jones's interpretation, but it all looks as if it is a part of some obscene TV quiz show in which the loser meets a somewhat worse fate than usual.

How much of Gary Gilmore's life was lived in a fantasy world is speculative but there remains a lingering suspicion that he lived his

life, and chose his way out of it, in the hope that one day, reincarnated as he expected to be, he could sit in a movie theatre or in front of a TV set watching his own strange tale and bizarre end.

Bizarre and improbable was the theme of an entirely fictional British movie, *Daybreak* (1946), which is one of the very few movies that centre upon an executioner. Here, the public hangman is Eddie Mendover (Eric Portman) whose secret occupation creates a serious moral difficulty for him.

Eddie, who has long ago abandoned his family name of Tribe, leads a dull private life as a barber. He has never married and shares his secret only with his hairdressing partner, Ron (Bill Owen). Eddie has been alienated from his father since he was a child but when the old man dies Eddie inherits the Tribe family business. As the new owner of a fleet of barges plying their trade on the River Thames, Eddie decides to resume the family name, give up his share in the barber shop, and retire as public hangman. When he meets a beautiful young woman, Frankie (Ann Todd), he thinks that his old life is behind him for ever. Eddie and Frankie marry, but he keeps from her his secret other life as Mendover the hangman, painfully working out the last few months of his duties. But then Eddie hires a handsome young Danish seaman to help out on the barges.

Olaf Thyson (Maxwell Reed) forces his attentions upon Frankie and, disturbed by Eddie's growingly paranoiac behaviour as he makes frequent unexplained trips to cities across the country, she responds. One night, returning unexpectedly when a condemned man receives a last-minute reprieve, Eddie catches Olaf and Frankie together. The two men fight and Olaf knocks Eddie into the river. Everyone believes that Eddie is dead and Frankie commits suicide, not knowing that Eddie has dragged himself from the water. Olaf is tried for murder and sentenced to death. When Eddie is called upon to execute Olaf his conscience gets the better of him and he reveals the truth.

With nothing left to live for, Eddie takes his

The public hangman rarely appears in movies but here Eric Portman steps briefly into the light for an assignment with Ann Todd in Daybreak **(1946).**

own life. Not surprisingly in the circumstances, he chooses to hang himself.

The American way of death appears in *The Travelling Executioner* (1970), which follows the peregrinations of Jonas Candide (Stacy Keach) who take his portable electric chair around prisons in the Deep South in the years after World War I. Essentially a likeable con-man, Candide charges $100 a shot for his services but runs into problems with Gundred (Mariana Hill), a young woman he is supposed to help into the hereafter along with her brother Willy (Stefan Gierasch). Candide deals with Willy but Gundred keeps on wangling stays of execution and as the executioner has made the tactical error of charging a joint fee he has to stick around until he can pull the switch on her.

Then he compounds his error by falling in love with her and if that were not enough he takes on an assistant, Jimmy (Bud Cort), a shy young undertaker. This last mistake proves fatal because when Candide is convicted of man-slaughter Jimmy is available to pull the switch on his boss.

No one is supposed to take *The Travelling Executioner* very seriously, and within its premise the movie works well and even provides a few slightly macabre laughs.

The real situation, however, is not a laughing matter.

Light-hearted con man Stacy Keach (r) has a profitable little sideline in executions in The Travelling Executioner **(1970).**

As has been the case rather too often for coincidence, television has shown a way that movie-makers might do well to follow in portraying the implications of capital punishment although, admittedly, in non-fictional terms.

In 1988, Paul Hamman, a British television producer, made a programme for the BBC about Edward Earl Johnson, a young black man held on Death Row in a Mississippi prison.

Johnson had been accused, tried and sentenced to die for the murder of a police officer. His case was taken up by Clive Stafford Smith, a lawyer with a passionate belief in the inhumanity of the death penalty. In this case, Smith was equally passionate in his belief that his client was innocent.

Hamman and his camera team followed the last two weeks in Johnson's life as attempts were made for stays of execution to allow appeals to higher and still higher authorities.

As the lawyer fought his way deeper and deeper into the legal jungle, officials at Parchman Penitentiary began their grim countdown. To be fair to the prison staff they did their job with no overt sign of relish even if, as Warden Cabana proved, they sometimes found the right words hard to come by. On one occasion he observed to the condemned man, 'We're going to get through this together.' Not so, because the options for Johnson eventually ran out and he was taken to the gas chamber.

Although firm in his belief that Johnson was guilty, Warden Cabana became progressively less sure that the state's method of dealing with convicted men was right, remarking at one point, 'When this is over I think I'm going to better understand that there must be another way.'

When it was over, Johnson's lawyer continued digging into his client's case, eventually turning up evidence that strongly supported his opinion and which even pointed a finger at the possible killer of the policeman. All this was, of course, much too late for Edward Earl Johnson.

Any capital case which carries with it even the merest whiff of a miscarriage of justice carries also the single most powerful practical argument against the death penalty. A wrong-fully convicted man or woman can be released from prison and even compensated, however trivially. But when you're dead, you're dead.

It is in this area that movie-makers, whether working in fact or fiction, could do so much more than they have. It is within their power to convey to a mass audience the undeniable fact that even the most open-and-shut cases can sometimes be seen to have cracks.

American documentary film-maker Errol Morris is one who has done his part by following the case of Randall Dale Adams, sentenced to die for killing a policeman and languishing for 12 years in prison, several of them on Death Row, while lawyers were arguing. Morris's film, *The Thin Blue Line* (1988), not only traces the case but also, like Hamman and Smith in the Edward Earl Johnson case, unearths the probable killer.

Treading a fine line between documentary and drama, unafraid to use dramatized reconstructions that blend, unannounced, into reality, Morris's film not only recounted a miscarriage of justice but generated a reappraisal of the case and unearthed the identity of the probable real killers. In March 1989 a local circuit judge in Texas not only recommended a retrial but also urged the immediate release of Randall Adams.

It is encouraging that film-makers like Hamman and Morris are doing what they can but so much more could be done.

The power of movies – whether fiction or fact – to convey great themes through the use of evocative and easily understood visual imagery, to display great depths of emotion, and to leave lasting impressions in even the most tightly-closed mind, should be exploited. They can carry a powerful argument appealing not to the practical side of mankind but to those instincts that are supposed to make man better than the animals.

Another prisoner on Parchman's Death Row summed this up before Paul Hamman's camera. All those who plan to make movies on this theme, and all those who believe in the virtue of the death penalty, would do well to consider it: 'We're supposed to be vicious and cruel but this goes beyond anything we would ever do.'

Death, in a different form to that administered by the State through electrocution, gas chamber, hanging, firing squad, or even lethal injection (by which the state authorities of Texas ended a condemned man's life in December 1988), might offer a solution to harrassed government officials wrestling with overcrowded prisons. The way things are going in America, and increasingly in certain parts of Europe, their lives may be made easier by the spread of AIDS.

Homosexuality is rife in prisons; the fact that many heterosexual prisoners adopt some form of homosexual practice while in prison only to return to their previous behaviour on release is well known. The spread of AIDS is encouraged by communal use of hypodermic needles; many prisoners are able to obtain and use drugs in prison.

The spread of AIDS within the American prison system is already causing grave concern. Figures released in September 1988 show that a similar problem exists in Spain with a Madrid prison currently estimating that 50 per cent of its inmates are infected. Surely no one can be naïve enough to think that America and Spain are isolated instances.

No figures are available for Britain because, incredibly, there is no compulsory testing of prisoners. But unofficial estimates by authoritative voices suggest that 30 per cent of the prison population might be infected. The Home Office, however, suggests that the figure is less than 1 per cent. A government spokesman appearing on a British TV current affairs programme in September 1988 was even more sanguine; he announced that, officially, there was only one case of AIDS in the entire British prison system.

Is this a typical head-in-the-sand attitude or is it a sign of something more sinister? Maybe the notion that a walled-off city full of prisoners might be the way of the future, has taken a more lethal turn. Maybe someone has decided that not only are prisoners to be kept in walled-off security but that they will be allowed to be decimated, or worse, by fatal disease. It would certainly solve the overcrowding problem.

But what about all those heterosexual prisoners who may have become infected and who, when they come out, return to wives and girlfriends, amateur and professional?

The prisons of the late twentieth century might be hiding behind their walls a catastrophe that will engulf us all. Now, wouldn't that make an exciting movie!

Bibliography

This bibliography contains books referred to in my research together with others that may well prove to be of interest to readers.

ADAIR, GILBERT, *Hollywood's Vietnam: from the Green Berets to Apocalypse Now*, Proteus, 1981

ARNOLD, WILLIAM, *Shadowland*, Jove, 1978

ARROWSMITH, PAT, *Breakout*, Edinburgh University Student Publications Board, 1975

BERGAN, RONALD, *Sports in the Movies*, Proteus, 1982

BURNS, ROBERT E., *I Am a Fugitive from a Georgia Chain Gang!*, Vanguard, 1932

CLARENS, CARLOS, *Crime Movies: From Griffith to the Godfather and Beyond*, Secker & Warburg, 1980

CLEMMER, DONALD, *The Prison Community*, Holt, Rinehart & Winston, 1958

COHEN, DAVID, *Broadmoor*, Psychology News Press, *c.*1981

CONNOR, JOHN E., Ed., *I Am a Fugitive from a Chain Gang*, (annotated screenplay) University of Wisconsin Press, 1981

CONSIDINE, DAVID, *The Cinema of Adolescence*, McFarland, 1985

CORLISS, RICHARD, *Talking Pictures*, David & Charles, 1975

DUFFY, CLINTON T., and JENNINGS, DEAN, *San Quentin: the Story of a Prison*, Peter Davies, 1951

FIELD, XENIA, *Under Lock and Key: a Study of Women in Prison*, Max Parrish, 1963

FOX, JULIAN, 'Four Minute Mile: an Interview with Michael Mann' *Films and Filming*, January 1980

GADDIS, THOMAS E., *Birdman of Alcatraz*, Victor Gollancz, 1985

GRUBB, DAVIS, *Fool's Parade*, Hodder, 1969

GUSSOW, MEL, *Darryl F. Zanuck: Don't Say Yes Until I Finish Talking*, Da Capo, 1971

HEFFERMAN, ESTHER, *Making It in Prison: the Square, the Cool, and the Life*, John Wiley, 1972

KESEY, KEN, *One Flew Over the Cuckoo's Nest*, Picador, 1973

LEAB, DANIEL J., *From Sambo to Superspade: the Black Experience in Motion Pictures*, Secker and Warburg, 1973

MCCOY, MALACHY, *Steve McQueen*, Robert Hale, 1974

MANVELL, ROGER, *Films and the Second World War*, J. M. Dent, 1974

MINDSZENTY, JÓZSEF, *Memoirs*, Weidenfeld & Nicholson, 1974

MITFORD, JESSICA, *The American Prison Business*, Allen & Unwin, 1974

ORWELL, GEORGE, *Nineteen Eighty-Four*, Penguin, 1987

PETTIGREW, TERENCE, *Bogart: a Definitive Study of His Film Career*, Proteus, 1981

PETTIGREW, TERENCE, *Raising Hell: the Rebel in the Movies*, Columbus, 1986

QUINNEY, RICHARD, *Criminology: Analysis and Critique of Crime*, Little, Brown, 1975

REIMAN, JEFFREY H., *The Rich Get Richer and the Poor Get Prison*, John Wiley, 1979

RIVETT, ROHAN D., *Behind Bamboo: an Inside Story of the Japanese Prison Camps*, Angus & Robertson, 1952

ROFFMAN, PETER, and PURDY, JIM, *The Hollywood Social Problem Film: Madness, Despair and Politics from the Depression to the Fifties*, Indiana University Press, 1981

SATCHELL, TIM, *McQueen*, Sidgwick & Jackson, 1981

SCHRODER, ANDREAS, *Shaking It Rough: a Prison Memoir*, Doubleday, 1976

SHERRILL, ROBERT, *The Saturday Night Special*, Charterhouse, 1973

SIFAKIS, CARL, *The Encyclopedia of American Crime*, Facts on File, 1982

TUMIM, JUDGE STEPHEN, 'Judging Our Jails: the Inside Story', *Daily Telegraph*, 12 November 1988

WRIGHT, ERIK OLIN, *The Politics of Punishment: a Critical Analysis of Prisons in America*, Harper & Row, 1973

Filmography

Most of the films appearing in the main text are detailed here together with others with prison content that may be of interest to readers. The information supplied here is culled from various sources including original press releases, *Halliwell's Film Guide* (published by Grafton), *Monthly Film Bulletin* and *Variety*.

Albert RN (1953) (US: **Break to Freedom**) 88 mins
Dial
Director Lewis Gilbert
Screenplay Guy Morgan, Vernon Harris (from play by Guy Morgan, Edward Sammis)
Photographer Jack Asher (b&w)
Music Malcolm Arnold
Leading Players Jack Warner, Anthony Steel, Robert Beatty, William Sylvester, Anton Diffring

Alcatraz: the Whole Shocking Story (1980)
2 x 96 mins
NBC TV
Director Paul Krasny
Screenplay Ernest Tidyman
Photographer Robert B. Hauser (color)
Music Jerrold Immel
Leading Players Telly Savalas, Ronny Cox, Michael Beck, Art Carney

Angels With Dirty Faces (1938)   97 mins
Warner
Director Michael Curtiz
Screenplay John Wexley, Warren Duff
Photographer Sol Polito (b&w)
Music Max Steiner
Leading Players James Cagney, Pat O'Brien, Humphrey Bogart, Ann Sheridan, The Dead End Kids

Another Time, Another Place (1983)   102 mins
Umbrella/Rediffusion/Channel 4
Director Michael Radford
Screenplay Michael Radford (from unpublished novel by Jessie Kesson)
Photographer Roger Deakins (Eastmancolor)
Music John McLeod
Leading Players Phyllis Logan, Giovanni Mauriello

Attica (1980)   104 mins
ABC, Circle
Director Marvin Chomsky
Screenplay James Henderson (from book *A Time to Die* by Tom Wicker)
Photographer Don Birnkraut (color)
Leading Players George Grizzard, Charles Durning, Anthony Zerbe, Roger E. Mosley, Henry Darrow, Joel Fabiani

Bad Boys (1983)   109 mins
EMI
Director Rick Rosenthal
Screenplay Richard Di Lello
Photographer Bruce Surtees (Technicolor)
Music Bill Conti
Leading Players Sean Penn, Reni Santoni, Jim Moody, Eric Gurry, Esai Morales, Ally Sheedy

Bedlam (1946)   79 mins
RKO
Director Mark Robson
Screenplay Val Lewton, Mark Robson
Photographer Nicholas Musuraca (b&w)
Music Rob Webb
Leading Players Boris Karloff, Anna Lee

Behind Locked Doors (1948)   61 mins
Eagle Lion
Director Budd Boetticher
Screenplay Malvin Wald, Eugene Ling
Photographer Guy Roe (b&w)
Music Irving Friedman
Leading Players Richard Carlson, Lucille Bremer

Big Bird Cage, The (1972)   88 mins
New World
Director Jack Hill
Screenplay Jack Hill
Photographer Philip Sacdalan (Metrocolor)
Music Kerry Magness
Leading Players Pam Grier, Anitra Ford, Candice
Roman, Teda Bracci

Big Doll House, The (1971)   93 mins
New World
Director Jack Hill
Screenplay Don Spencer
Photographer Freddie Conde (De Luxe Color)
Music Hall Daniels
Leading Players Judy Brown, Roberta Collins,
Pam Grier, Brooke Mills

Big House, The (1930)   88 mins
MGM
Director George Hill
Screenplay Frances Marion
Photographer Harold Wenstrom (b&w)
Leading Players Chester Morris, Wallace Beery,
Robert Montgomery, Lewis Stone

Big House USA (1955)   82 mins
United Artists/ Bel Air
Director Howard Koch
Screenplay John C. Higgins
Photographer Gordon Avil (b&w)
Music Paul Dunlap
Leading Players Broderick Crawford,
Ralph Meeker, William Talman, Lon Chaney Jr,
Charles Bronson

Birdman of Alcatraz (1962)   147 mins
United Artists
Director John Frankenheimer
Screenplay Guy Trosper (from book by Thomas
E. Gaddis)
Photographer Burnett Guffey (b&w)
Music Elmer Bernstein
Leading Players Burt Lancaster, Telly Savalas,
Karl Malden, Thelma Ritter, Betty Field,
Edmond O'Brien, Neville Brand, Hugh Marlowe

Birdy (1984)   120 mins
Columbia-EMI-Warner
Director Alan Parker
Screenplay Sandy Kroopf, Jack Behr (from book
by William Wharton)

Photographer Michael Seresin (Metrocolor)
Music Peter Gabriel
Leading Players Matthew Modine, Nicolas Cage,
John Harkins, Sandy Baron, Karen Young

Blackmail (1939)   81 mins
MGM
Director H. C. Potter
Screenplay David Hertz, William Ludwig
Photographer Clyde de Vinna (b&w)
Music David Snell, Edward Ward
Leading Players Edward G. Robinson,
Ruth Hussey, Gene Lockhart

Black Tuesday (1954)   80 mins
United Artists
Director Hugo Fregonese
Screenplay Sydney Boehm
Photographer Stanley Cortez (b&w)
Music Paul Dunlap
Leading Players Edward G. Robinson,
Peter Graves, Jean Parker, Milburn Stone

Blackwell's Island (1939)   71 mins
Warner
Director William McGann
Screenplay Crane Wilbur
Photographer Sid Hickox (b&w)
Music Leo F. Forbstein
Leading Players John Garfield, Victor Jory,
Rosemary Lane, Stanley Fields

Boys' Town (1938)   93 mins
MGM
Director Norman Taurog
Screenplay John Meehan, Dore Schary
Photographer Sidney Wagner (b&w)
Music Edward Ward
Leading Players Spencer Tracy, Mickey Rooney,
Henry Hull, Gene Reynolds

Breakout (1959)   62 mins
Independent Artists
Director Peter Graham Scott
Screenplay Peter Barnes
Photographer Eric Cross (b&w)
Leading Players Lee Patterson, William Lucas,
Terence Alexander, John Paul, Billie Whitelaw

Breakout (1975)   96 mins
Columbia/Persky-Bright/Vista
Director Tom Gries
Screenplay Howard B. Kreitsek, Frank Kowalski
(from their book *Ten Second Jailbreak*)
Photographer Lucien Ballard (color)
Music Jerry Goldsmith
Leading Players Charles Bronson, Robert Duvall,
Jill Ireland, Alan Vint, Paul Mantee, John Huston

Bridge on the River Kwai, The (1957)   161 mins
Columbia
Director David Lean
Screenplay Carl Foreman (from book by
Pierre Boulle)
Photographer Jack Hildyard (Technicolor)
Music Malcolm Arnold
Leading Players Alec Guinness, Sessue
Hayakawa, Jack Hawkins, William Holden, James
Donald

Brother Orchid (1940)   91 mins
Warner
Director Lloyd Bacon
Screenplay Earl Baldwin
Photographer Tony Gaudio (b&w)
Music Heinz Roemheld
Leading Players Edward G. Robinson,
Humphrey Bogart, Allen Jenkins, Donald Crisp,
Cecil Kellaway, Ann Sothern, Ralph Bellamy

Brothers (1977)   105 mins
Warners
Director Arthur Barron
Screenplay Edward and Mildred Lewis
Photographer John Morrill (Metrocolor)
Music Taj Mahal
Leading Players Bernie Casey, Vonetta McGee,
Ron O'Neal

Brubaker (1980)   130 mins
TCF
Director Stuart Rosenberg
Screenplay W. D. Richter (from book by
Thomas O. Murton, Joe Hyams)
Photographer Bruno Nuytten (De Luxe Color)
Music Lalo Schiffrin
Leading Players Robert Redford, Jane Alexander,
Yaphet Kotto, Murray Hamilton, David Keith

Brute Force (1947)   96 mins
Universal-International
Director Jules Dassin
Screenplay Richard Brooks
Photographer William Daniels (b&w)
Music Miklos Rozsa
Leading Players Burt Lancaster, Charles Bickford,
Hume Cronyn, Howard Duff, Ella Raines,
Yvonne De Carlo

Cabinet of Dr Caligari, The (1919)   90 mins
Decla-Bioscop
Director Robert Wiene
Screenplay Carl Meyer, Hans Janowitz (silent)
Photographer Willy Hameister (b&w)
Leading Players Werner Krauss, Conrad Veidt,
Lil Dagover

Caged (1950)   97 mins
Warner
Director John Cromwell
Screenplay Virginia Kellog, Bernard C.
Schoenfeld
Photographer Carl Guthrie (b&w)
Music Max Steiner
Leading Players Eleanor Parker, Hope Emerson,
Agnes Moorehead, Lee Patrick, Betty Garde,
Jan Sterling

Captive Heart, The (1946)   108 mins
Ealing
Director Basil Dearden
Screenplay Angus Macphail, Guy Morgan
Photographer Lionel Banes (b&w)
Music Alan Rawsthorne
Leading Players Michael Redgrave, Jack Warner,
Basil Radford, Mervyn Johns, Jimmy Hanley

Carve Her Name with Pride (1958)   119 mins
Rank/Keyboard
Director Lewis Gilbert
Screenplay Vernon Harris, Lewis Gilbert (from
book by R. J. Minney)
Photographer John Wilcox (b&w)
Music William Alwyn
Leading Players Virginia McKenna, Paul Scofield,
Sidney Tafler, Jack Warner, Alain Saury,
Noel Willman

Castle on the Hudson (1940)
(UK: **Years Without Days**) 77 mins
Warner
Director Anatole Litvak
Screenplay Seton I. Miller, Brown Holmes,
Courtney Terrett
Photographer Arthur Edeson (b&w)
Music Adolph Deutsch
Leading Players John Garfield, Pat O'Brien,
Ann Sheridan, Burgess Meredith, Jerome Cowan

Cell 2455, Death Row (1955) 77 mins
Columbia
Director Fred F. Sears
Screenplay Jack De Witt (from book by
Caryl Chessman)
Photographer Fred Jackman Jr (b&w)
Music Mischa Bakaleinikoff
Leading Players William Campbell, Kathryn
Grant, Harvey Stephens, Vince Edwards,
Robert Campbell

Chain Gang (1950) 70 mins
Columbia
Director Lew Landers
Screenplay Howard J. Green
Photographer Ira H. Morgan (b&w)
Leading Players Douglas Kennedy,
William Phillips

Colditz Story, The (1957) 97 mins
British Lion
Director Guy Hamilton
Screenplay Guy Hamilton, Ivan Foxwell (from
book by P. R. Reid)
Photographer Gordon Dines (b&w)
Music Francis Chagrin
Leading Players John Mills, Eric Portman, Lionel
Jeffries, Bryan Forbes, Ian Carmichael,
Anton Diffring, Theodor Bikel

Collector, The (1965) 119 mins
Columbia
Director William Wyler
Screenplay Stanley Mann, John Kohn (from book
by John Fowles)
Photographer Robert L. Surtees, Robert Krasker
(Technicolor)
Music Maurice Jarre
Leading Players Terence Stamp, Samantha Eggar,
Mona Washbourne

Concrete Jungle, The (1982) 99 mins
Ideal
Director Tom De Simone
Screenplay Alan J. Adler
Photographer Andrew W. Friend (CFI color)
Music Joseph Conlan
Leading Players Tracy Bregman, Jill St John,
Barbara Luna, Nita Talbot

Convict 99 (1938) 91 mins
Gainsborough
Director Marcel Varnel
Screenplay Marriott Edgar, Val Guest,
Ralph Smart, Jack Davies
Photographer Arthur Crabtree (b&w)
Music Louis Levy
Leading Players Will Hay, Graham Moffatt,
Moore Marriott, Googie Withers, Garry Marsh,
Basil Radford

Convicted (1950) 89 mins
Columbia
Director Henry Levin
Screenplay Seton I. Miller, Fred Niblo Jr (from
play by Martin Flavin)
Photographer Burnett Guffey
Music George Duning
Leading Players Broderick Crawford, Glenn Ford,
Millard Mitchell, Dorothy Malone

Cool Hand Luke (1967) 126 mins
Warner
Director Stuart Rosenberg
Screenplay Donn Pearce, Frank R. Pierson (from
book by Pearce)
Photographer Conrad Hall (Technicolor)
Music Lalo Schifrin
Leading Players Paul Newman, George Kennedy,
J. D. Cannon, Lou Antonio, Strother Martin,
Jo Van Fleet, Morgan Woodward, Dennis Hopper

Count of Monte Cristo, The (1934) 114 mins
Reliance
Director Rowland V. Lee
Screenplay Philip Dunne, Dan Totheroh, Rowland
V. Lee (from book by Alexandre Dumas)
Photographer Peverell Marley (b&w)
Music Alfred Newman
Leading Players Robert Donat, Elissa Landi, Louis
Calhern, Sidney Blackmer, O. P. Heggie

Crashout (1955)   83 mins
Standard
Director Lewis R. Foster
Screenplay Hal E. Chester, Lewis R. Foster
Photographer Russell Metty (b&w)
Music Leith Stevens
Leading Players William Bendix, Arthur Kennedy, Luther Adler, William Talman, Gene Evans, Marshall Thompson

Criminal, The (1960) (US: **The Concrete Jungle**)   97 mins
Merton Park
Director Joseph Losey
Screenplay Alun Owen
Photographer Robert Krasker (b&w)
Music John Dankworth
Leading Players Stanley Baker, Sam Wanamaker, Patrick Magee, Jill Bennett, Margit Saad

Criminal Code, The (1931)   96 mins
Columbia
Director Howard Hawks
Screenplay Seton I. Miller, Fred Niblo Jr (from play by Martin Flavin)
Photographer James Wong Howe, William O'Connell (b&w)
Leading Players Walter Huston, Phillips Holmes, Constance Cummings, Boris Karloff

Dance With a Stranger (1984)   102 mins
First Film/Goldcrest
Director Mike Newell
Screenplay Shelagh Delaney
Photographer Peter Hannan (color)
Music Richard Hartley
Leading Players Miranda Richardson, Rupert Everett, Ian Holm, David Troughton, Stratford Johns

Danger Within (1959) (US: **Breakout**)   101 mins
British Lion
Director Don Chaffey
Screenplay Bryan Forbes, Frank Harvey (from book by Michael Gilbert)
Photographer Arthur Grant (b&w)
Music Francis Chagrin
Leading Players Richard Todd, Bernard Lee, Michael Wilding, Richard Attenborough, William Franklyn

Daybreak (1946)   81 mins
GFD/Triton
Director Compton Bennett
Screenplay Muriel and Sydney Box (from play by Monckton Hoffe)
Photographer Reginald H. Wyer (b&w)
Music Benjamin Frankel
Leading Players Eric Portman, Ann Todd, Maxwell Reed

Dead Man Walking (1988)   85 mins
Granada/Citadel
Director Richard Pearce
Screenplay Ron Hutchinson
Photographer Michel Brault (color)
Music Cliff Eidelman
Leading Players Danny Glover, Ruben Blades, Tom Atkins, Larry Block, Sam Jackson

Deer Hunter, The (1978)   183 mins
Universal/EMI
Director Michael Cimino
Screenplay Deric Washburn
Photographer Vilmos Zsigmond (Technicolor)
Music Stanley Myers
Leading Players Robert De Niro, John Savage, Christopher Walken, Meryl Streep, John Cazale

Defiant Ones, The (1958)   96 mins
United Artists
Director Stanley Kramer
Screenplay Nathan E. Douglas, Harold Jacob Smith
Photographer Sam Leavitt (b&w)
Music Ernest Gold
Leading Players Tony Curtis, Sidney Poitier

Devil at 4 O'Clock, The (1961)   126 mins
Columbia
Director Mervyn LeRoy
Screenplay Liam O'Brien (from book by Max Catto)
Photographer Joseph Biroc (Eastmancolor)
Music George Duning
Leading Players Spencer Tracy, Frank Sinatra, Gregoire Aslan, Bernie Hamilton, Barbara Luna

Devil is a Sissy, The (1936)   92 mins
MGM
Director W. S. Van Dyke
Screenplay John Lee Mahin, Richard Schayer
Photographer Harold Rossen, George Schneidermann (b&w)
Music Herbert Stothart
Leading Players Freddie Bartholemew, Jackie Cooper, Mickey Rooney

Devil's Canyon (1953)   92 mins
RKO
Director Alfred Werker
Screenplay Frederick Hazlitt Brennan
Photographer Nicholas Musuraca (Technicolor, 3-D)
Music Daniele Amfitheatrof
Leading Players Dale Robertson, Virginia Mayo, Stephen McNally, Arthur Hunnicutt, Jay C. Flippen

Devil's Island (1939)   63 mins
WB
Director William Clemens
Screenplay Kenneth Gamet, Don Ryan
Photographer George Barnes (b&w)
Leading Players Boris Karloff, James Stephenson, Nedda Harrigan, Robert Warwick

Diary of Anne Frank, The (1959)   170 mins
TCF
Director George Stevens
Screenplay Frances Goodrich, Albert Hackett (from their play)
Photographer William C. Mellor (b&w)
Music Alfred Newman
Leading Players Millie Perkins, Joseph Schildkraut, Shelley Winters, Ed Wynn, Richard Beymer

Diary of Anne Frank, The (1980)   104 mins
TVM
Director Boris Segal
Screenplay Frances Goodrich, Albert Hackett (from their play)
Photographer Ted Voigtlander (color)
Music Billy Goldenberg
Leading Players Melissa Gilbert, Maximilian Schell, Joan Plowright, James Coco, Clive Revill

Double Indemnity (1944)   107 mins
Paramount
Director Billy Wilder
Screenplay Billy Wilder, Raymond Chandler (from novel by James M. Cain)
Photographer John Seitz (b&w)
Music Miklos Rozsa
Leading Players Barbara Stanwyck, Fred MacMurray, Edward G. Robinson

Dust By My Destiny (1939)   88 mins
Warner
Director Lewis Seiler
Screenplay Robert Rossen
Photographer James Wong Howe (b&w)
Music Max Steiner
Leading Players John Garfield, Priscilla Lane, Alan Hale, Frank McHugh, John Litel

Each Dawn I Die (1939)   84 mins
Warner
Director William Keighley
Screenplay Norman Reilly, Warren Duff, Charles Perry (from book by Jerome Odlum)
Photographer Arthur Edeson (b&w)
Music Max Steiner
Leading Players James Cagney, George Raft, George Bancroft

Escape (1940)   104 mins
MGM
Director Mervyn Le Roy
Screenplay Arch Oboler, Margeurite Roberts (from book by Ethel Vance)
Photographer Robert Planck (b&w)
Music Franz Waxman
Leading Players Norma Shearer, Robert Taylor, Conrad Veidt, Alla Nazimova

Escape (1980)   104 mins
TVM
Director Robert Michael Lewis
Screenplay Michael Zagar (from book by Dwight and Barbara Worker)
Photographer Isidore Mankofsky (colour)
Music James D. Pacuale
Leading Players Timothy Bottoms, Kay Lenz, Colleen Dewhurst

Escape from Alcatraz (1979)   112 mins
Malpaso
Director Don Siegel
Screenplay Richard Tuggle (from book by J. Campbell Bruce)
Photographer Bruce Surtees (De Luxe Color)
Music Jerry Fielding
Leading Players Clint Eastwood, Patrick McGoohan, Jack Thibeau, Fred Ward

Escape to Victory (US: **Victory**) (1981)   115 mins
Lorimar
Director John Huston
Screenplay Evan Jones and Yabo Yablonsky
Photographer Gerry Fisher (Panavision and Metrocolor)
Music Bill Conti
Leading Players Michael Caine, Sylvester Stallone, Max von Sydow

Executioner's Song, The (1982)   192 mins
TVM
Director Lawrence Schiller
Screenplay Normal Mailer (from his book)
Photographer Freddie Francis (color)
Music John Cacavas
Leading Players Tommy Lee Jones, Rosanna Arquette, Eli Wallach, Christine Lahti

Farewell to Manzanar (1976)   98 mins
TVM
Director John Korty
Screenplay Jeanne Wakatsuki Houston, James D. Houston, John Korty
Photographer Hiro Narita (color)
Music Paul Chihara
Leading Players Yuki Shimoda, Nobu McCarthy, Mako, Pat Morito

Fixer, The (1968)   130 mins
MGM
Director John Frankenheimer
Screenplay Dalton Trumbo (from book by Bernard Malamud)
Photographer Marcel Grignon (Metrocolor)
Music Maurice Jarre
Leading Players Alan Bates, Dirk Bogarde, Georgia Brown, Hugh Griffith, Elizabeth Hartman, Ian Holm

Fools' Parade (1971)   98 mins
(UK: **The Dynamite Man from Glory Jail**)
Columbia
Director Andrew V. McLaglen
Screenplay James Lee Barrett (from book by Davis Grubb)
Photographer Harry Stradling Jr (Eastmancolor)
Music Henry Vars
Leading Players James Stewart, Strother Martin, George Kennedy, Kurt Russell, William Windom, Anne Baxter

Fortune and Men's Eyes (1971)   102 mins
MGM/Cinema International/Canadian FDC
Director Harvey Hart
Screenplay John Herbert (from own play)
Photographer George Dufaux (Metrocolor)
Music Galt MacDermot
Leading Players Wendell Burton, Zooey Hall, Michael Greer

Frances (1982)   140 mins
EMI/Brooksfilms
Director Graeme Clifford
Screenplay Eric Bergren, Christopher De Vore, Nicholas Kazan
Photographer Laszlo Kovacs (Technicolor)
Music John Barry
Leading Players Jessica Lange, Kim Stanley, Jeffrey DeMunn, Christopher Pennock, Sam Shepard

Ghosts ... of the Civil Dead (1988)   90 mins
Correctional Services
Director John Hillcoat
Screenplay Gene Conkie, Evan English and John Hillcoat
Photographer Paul Goldman, Graham Wood and Evan English (color)
Leading Players Dave Field, Mike Bishop, Chris de Rose, Nick Cave, Kevin Mackey, Dave Mason

Glasshouse, The (1972)   91 mins
Tomorrow Entertainment
Director Tom Gries
Screenplay Tracy Keenan Wynn
Photographer Jules Brenner (color)
Music Billy Goldenberg
Leading Players Alan Alda, Vic Morrow, Clu Gulager, Billy Dee Williams, Kristoffer Tabori, Dean Jagger

Grande Illusion, La (1937)   117 mins
RAC
Director Jean Renoir
Screenplay Jean Renoir, Charles Spaak
Photographer Christian Matras, Claude Renoir, etc.
(b&w)
Music Joseph Kosma
Leading Players Pierre Fresnay, Erich von Stroheim, Jean Gabin, Marcel Dalio

Great Escape, The (1963)   173 mins
United Artists/Mirisch
Director John Sturges
Screenplay James Clavell, W. R. Burnett
(from book by Paul Brickhill)
Photographer Daniel Fapp (De Luxe Color)
Music Elmer Bernstein
Leading Players Steve McQueen, James Garner,
Richard Attenborough, James Donald,
Charles Bronson, Donald Pleasance

Hell's Highway (1932)   62 mins
Radio
Director Rowland Brown
Screenplay Samuel Ornitz, Robert Trask,
Rowland Brown
Photographer Edward Cronjager (b&w)
Music Max Steiner
Leading Players Richard Dix, Tom Brown

Highest Honour, The (1982)   143 mins
Southern International
Director Peter Maxwell
Screenplay Lee Robinson, Katsuya Suzaki, Takeo
Ito
Photographer John McLean (color)
Music Eric Jupp
Leading Players John Howard, Atsuo Nakamura,
Stuart Wilson

Hill, The (1965)   122 mins
MGM/Seven Arts
Director Sidney Lumet
Screenplay Ray Rigby (from his own play)
Photographer Oswald Morris
Music none
Leading Players Sean Connery, Harry Andrews,
Michael Redgrave, Ian Bannen, Ossie Davis,
Jack Watson, Ian Hendry

Holocaust (1978)   9 x 50 mins
NBC TV
Director Marvin Chomsky
Screenplay Gerald Green
Photographer Brian West (color)
Music Morton Gould
Leading Players Meryl Streep, Michael Moriarty,
Joseph Bottoms, Fritz Weaver, James Woods,
Tom Bell, Ian Holm, Marius Goring,
David Warner

Hoose-Gow, The (1929)   20 mins
Hal Roach
Director James Parrott
Screenplay Leo McCarey
Photographer George Stevens, Len Powers,
Glenn Robert Kershner
Music William Axt, S. Williams
Leading Players Stan Laurel, Oliver Hardy,
James Finlayson, Tiny Sandford

House of Numbers (1957)   90 mins
MGM
Director Russell Rouse
Screenplay Russell Rouse, Don M. Manciewicz
(from book *Cosmopolitan* by Jack Finney)
Photographer George J. Folsey (b&w,
CinemaScope)
Music Andre Previn
Leading Players Jack Palance, Barbara Lang,
Harold J. Stone

House of Women (1962)   85 mins
Warner
Director Walter Doniger
Screenplay Crane Wilbur
Photographer Harold Stine (b&w)
Music Howard Jackson
Leading Players Shirley Knight, Andrew Duggan,
Constance Ford

**I am a Fugitive
from a Chain Gang** (1932)   90 mins
Warner
Director Mervyn LeRoy
Screenplay Howard J. Green, Brown Holmes,
Sheridan Gibney (from book by Robert E. Burns)
Photographer Sol Polito (b&w)
Music Bernhard Kaun
Leading Players Paul Muni, Glenda Farrell,
Helen Vinson, Preston Foster, Allen Jenkins

**I Never Promised
You a Rose Garden** (1977)   96 mins
New World
Director Anthony Page
Screenplay Lewis John Carlino, Gavin Lambert
(from book by Hannah Green)
Photographer Bruce Logan (color)
Music Paul Chihara
Leading Players Kathleen Quinlan, Bibi
Andersson, Sylvia Sidney, Susan Tyrrell, Signe
Hasso, Diane Varsi

**Inside the Walls
of Folsom Prison** (1951)   87 mins
Warner
Director Crane Wilbur
Screenplay Crane Wilbur
Photographer Edward Du Par (b&w)
Music William Lava
Leading Players Steve Cochran, Ted de Corsia,
David Brian, Phil Carey

In the Custody of Strangers (1982)   95 mins
Orion
Director Robert Greenwald
Screenplay Jennifer Miller
Photographer Isidore Mankofsky (color)
Leading Players Emilio Estevez, Martin Sheen,
Jane Alexander, Kenneth McMillan

Invisible Stripes (1939)   82 mins
Warner
Director Lloyd Bacon
Screenplay Warren Duff (from book by
Lewis E. Lawes)
Photographer Ernest Haller (b&w)
Music Heinz Roemheld
Leading Players George Raft, Humphrey Bogart,
William Holden, Flora Robson

I Want to Live (1958)   120 mins
United Artists
Director Robert Wise
Screenplay Nelson Gidding, Don Mankiewicz
Photographer Lionel Lindon (b&w)
Music John Mandel
Leading Players Susan Hayward, Simon Oakland,
Virginia Vincent, Theodore Bikel

Jackson County Jail (1976)   84 mins
New World
Director Michael Miller
Screenplay Donald Stewart
Photographer Bruce Logan (Metrocolor)
Music Loren Newkirk
Leading Players Yvette Mimieux, Tommy Lee
Jones, Robert Carradine, Patrice Rohmer,
Frederick Cook, Severn Darden

Jericho Mile, The (1979)   104 mins
TVM
Director Michael Mann
Screenplay Patrick J. Nolan, Michael Mann
Photographer Rexford Metz (color)
Music Jimmie Haskell
Leading Players Peter Strauss, Roger E. Mosley,
Richard Lawson, Miguel Pinero

Johnny Dangerously (1984)   90 mins
TCF
Director Amy Heckerling
Screenplay Norman Steinberg, Bernie Kukoff,
Harry Colomby, Jeff Harris
Photographer David M. Walsh (DeLuxe Color)
Music John Morris
Leading Players Michael Keaton, Jo Piscopo,
Marilu Henner, Maureen Stapleton, Peter Boyle,
Griffin Dunne

Kapo (1960)   115 mins
Vides/Zebra-Francinex
Director Gilles Pontecorvo
Screenplay Gilles Pontecorvo, Franco Solinaro
Photographer Goffredo Bellisario,
Alexander Sakulovic (b&w)
Music Carl Rustichelli
Leading Players Susan Strasberg, Laurent Terzieff

Kill Me If You Can (1977)   104 mins
Columbia
Director Buzz Kulik
Screenplay John Gay
Photographer Gerald Perry Finnerman (color)
Music Bill Conti
Leading Players Alan Alda, Talia Shire,
John Hillerman, Barnard Hughes, Walter McGinn

King Rat (1965)   134 mins
Columbia
Director Bryan Forbes
Screenplay Bryan Forbes (from book by
James Clavell)
Photographer Burnett Guffey (b&w)
Music John Barry
Leading Players George Segal, Tom Courtenay,
James Fox, John Mills, Denholm Elliott

Kiss of the Spiderwomen (1985)   121 mins
HB Filmes/Island Alive/Palace
Director Hector Babenco
Screenplay Leonard Schrader (from book by
Manuel Puig)
Photographer Rodolfo Sanchez (color)
Music John Neschling, Nando Carneiro
Leading Players William Hurt, Raul Julia,
Sonia Braga

Kitty: Return to Auschwitz (1979)   88 mins
Yorkshire TV documentary
Director Peter Morley
Participants Kitty and David Hart

Ladies of the Big House (1931) 76 mins
Paramount
Director Marion Gering
Screenplay Louis Weltzenkorn
Photographer David Abel (b&w)
Leading Players Sylvia Sidney, Gene Raymond,
Wynne Gibson

Last Gangster, The (1937) 81 mins
MGM
Director Edward Ludwig
Screenplay John Lee Mahin
Photographer William Daniels (b&w)
Music Edward Ward
Leading Players Edward G. Robinson,
James Stewart, Lionel Stander, John Carradine,
Sidney Blackmer

Last Mile, The (1932) 78 mins
KBS
Director Sam Bischoff
Screenplay Seton I. Miller (from play by
John Wexley)
Photographer Arthur Edeson (b&w)
Leading Players Howard Phillips, Preston Foster,
Noel Madison, George E. Stone

Last Mile, The (1959) 81 mins
United Artists/Vanguard
Director Howard Koch
Screenplay Seton I. Miller, Milton Subotsky
(from play by John Wexley)
Photographer Joseph Brun (b&w)
Music Van Alexander
Leading Players Clifford David, Mickey Rooney,
Frank Conroy, Frank Overton, Leon Janney,
Alan Bruce, John Vari

Leadbelly (1976) 121 mins
Paramount
Director Gordon Parks Sr
Screenplay Gordon Parks Sr
Photographer Bruce Surtees (Eastmancolor)
Music Fred Karlin
Leading Players Roger E. Mosley,
James E. Brodhead, John McDonald

Lilith (1964) 126 mins
Columbia
Director Robert Rossen
Screenplay Robert Rossen (from book by
J. R. Salamanca)
Photographer Eugen Schufftan (b&w)
Music Kenyon Hopkins
Leading Players Jean Seberg, Warren Beatty,
Peter Fonda, Kim Hunter

**Loneliness of the Long Distance
Runner, The** (1962) 104 mins
British Lion/Bryanston
Director Tony Richardson
Screenplay Alan Sillitoe (from his own short story)
Photographer Walter Lassally (b&w)
Music John Addison
Leading Players Tom Courtenay, Michael
Redgrave, James Bolam

Longest Yard, The (1974)
(UK: **The Mean Machine**) 122 mins
Paramount
Director Robert Aldrich
Screenplay Tracy Keenan Wynn
Photographer Joseph Biroc (Technicolor)
Music Frank de Vol
Leading Players Burt Reynolds, Eddie Albert,
Ed Lauter, Michael Conrad

McVicar (1980) 112 mins
Polytel/Brent Walker
Director Tom Clegg
Screenplay John McVicar, Tom Clegg
Photographer Vernon Layton (color)
Music Jeff Wayne
Leading Players Roger Daltrey, Adam Faith,
Cheryl Campbell, Steven Berkoff

Manchurian Candidate, The (1962) 126 mins
United Artists
Director John Frankenheimer
Screenplay George Axelrod (from book by
Richard Condon)
Photographer Lionel Lindon (b&w)
Music David Amram
Leading Players Lawrence Harvey, Frank Sinatra,
Angela Lansbury, Janet Leigh

Man in the Iron Mask, The (1939)   119 mins
Edward Small
Director James Whale
Screenplay George Bruce (from book by
Alexandre Dumas)
Photographer Robert Planck (b&w)
Music Lucien Moraweck, Lud Gluskin
Leading Players Louis Hayward, Warren William,
Alan Hale, Bert Roach, Miles Mander, Joan Bennett,
Joseph Schildkraut

Mayor of Hell (1933)   87 mins
Warner
Director Archie Mayo
Screenplay Ed Chodorov
Photographer Barney McGill (b&w)
Leading Players James Cagney, Allan Jenkins,
Dudley Digges, Frankie Darro, Madge Evans

Merry Christmas, Mr Lawrence (1982) 120 mins
Palace
Director Nagisa Oshima
Screenplay Nagisa Oshima, Paul Mayersberg
(from book *The Seed and the Sower* by
Laurens van der Post)
Photographer Toichiro Narushima (Eastmancolor)
Music Ryuichi Sakamoto
Leading Players David Bowie, Tom Conti,
Ryuichi Sakamoto, Takeshi, Jack Thompson

Midnight Express (1978)   121 mins
Columbia/Casablanca
Director Alan Parker
Screenplay Oliver Stone (from book by Billy
Hayes)
Photographer Michael Seresin (Eastmancolor)
Music Giorgio Moroder
Leading Players Brad Davis, Randy Quaid,
John Hurt, Bo Hopkins, Pauolo Bonacelli,
Mike Kellin, Paul Smith, Miracle Sarons

Missing (1982)   122 mins
Universal/Polygram
Director Constantin Costa-Gavras
Screenplay Constantin Costa-Gavras,
Donald Stewart (from book by Thomas Hauser)
Photographer Ricardo Aronovich (Technicolor)
Music Vangelis
Leading Players Jack Lemmon, Sissy Spacek,
Melanie Mayron, John Shea, Charles Cioffi,
Richard Bradford

Missing in Action (1984)   101 mins
Cannon
Director Joseph Zito
Screenplay John Crowther, Lance Hool
Photographer Joao Fernandes (Metrocolor)
Music Jay Chattaway
Leading Players Chuck Norris, M. Emmet Walsh,
Leonore Kasdorf, James Hong, David Tress

**Missing in Action 2 –
The Beginning** (1983)   95 mins
Cannon
Director Lance Hool
Screenplay Arthur Silver, Larry Levinson
Photographer Jorge Stahl (TVC color)
Music Brian May
Leading Players Chuck Norris, Soon-Teck Oh,
Steven Williams, Bennett Ohta

Mutiny in the Big House (1939)   93 mins
Monogram
Director William Nigh
Screenplay Robert D. Andrews, Martin Mooney
Photographer Harry Newman (b&w)
Leading Players Charles Bickford, Barton
MacLane

My Six Convicts (1952)   104 mins
Columbia
Director Hugo Fregonese
Screenplay Michael Blankfort (from book by
Donald P. Wilson)
Photographer Guy Roe (b&w)
Music Dmitri Tiomkin
Leading Players John Beal, Millard Mitchell,
Gilbert Roland, Marshall Thompson, Regis Toomey

Nineteen Eighty-Four (1955)   91 mins
Holiday
Director Michael Anderson
Screenplay William P. Templeton, Ralph Bettinson
(from book by George Orwell)
Photographer C. Pennington Richards (b&w)
Music Malcolm Arnold
Leading Players Edmond O'Brien, Jan Sterling,
Michael Redgrave

Nineteen Eighty-Four (1984)   110 mins
Umbrella/Virgin/TCF
Director Michael Radford
Screenplay Michael Radford (from book by
George Orwell)
Photographer Roger Deakins (Eastmancolor)
Music Dominic Muldowney, Eurythmics
Leading Players John Hurt, Suzanna Hamilton,
Richard Burton

Numbered Men (1930)   65 mins
First National
Director Mervyn LeRoy
Screenplay Al Colin, Henry McCarthy (from play,
Jailbreak, by Dwight Taylor)
Photographer Sol Polito (b&w)
Leading Players Raymond Hackett, Bernice Claire,
Ralph Ince

Nurse Edith Cavell (1939)   98 mins
Imperator/RKO
Director Herbert Wilcox
Screenplay Michael Hogan (from book *Dawn* by
Reginald Berkeley)
Photographer Freddie Young, Joseph H. August
(b&w)
Music Anthony Collins
Leading Players Anna Neagle, George Sanders,
May Robson, Edna May Oliver

Odette (1950)   123 mins
British Lion/Wilcox-Neagle
Director Herbert Wilcox
Screenplay Warren Chetham Strode
(from book by Jerrard Tickell)
Photographer Max Greene (b&w)
Music Anthony Collins
Leading Players Anna Neagle, Trevor Howard,
Peter Ustinov, Marius Goring

**One Day in the Life of
Ivan Denisovich** (1971)   105 mins
Group W
Director Casper Wrede
Screenplay Ronald Harwood (from book by
Alexander Solzhenitsyn)
Photographer Sven Nykvist (Eastmancolor)
Music Arne Nordheim
Leading Players Tom Courtenay, James Maxwell,
Alfred Burke, Espen Skjonberg

**One Flew Over the
Cuckoo's Nest** (1975)   134 mins
United Artists/Fantasy
Director Milos Forman
Screenplay Laurence Hauben, Bo Goldman
(from book by Ken Kesey)
Photographer Haskell Wexler (De Luxe Color)
Music Jack Nitzche
Leading Players Jack Nicholson, Louise Fletcher,
Will Sampson, William Redfield, Brad Dourif,
Christopher Lloyd

One That Got Away, The (1957)   111 mins
Rank
Director Roy Baker
Screenplay Howard Clewes (from book by
Kendal Burt, James Leasor)
Photographer Eric Cross (b&w)
Music Hubert Clifford
Leading Players Hardy Kruger, Michael Goodliffe,
Colin Gordon, Alec McCowan

Ordeal of Dr Mudd, The (1980)   142 mins
CBS/Marble Arch/BSR
Director Paul Wendkos
Screenplay Michael Berk
Photographer Herbert Figueroa (color)
Music Gerald Fried
Leading Players Dennis Weaver, Susan Sullivan,
Richard Dysart, Michael McGuire, Arthur Hill,
Nigel Davenport

Papillon (1973)   150 mins
Papillon/Corona
Director Franklin Schaffner
Screenplay Dalton Trumbo, Lorenzo Semple Jr
(from book by Henri Charriere)
Photographer Fred Koenekamp (Technicolor)
Music Jerry Goldsmith
Leading Players Steve McQueen, Dustin Hoffman

Pardon Us (1931)   56 mins
Hal Roach
Director James Parrott
Screenplay H. M. Walker
Photographer George Stevens (b&w)
Music Marvin Hatley, etc
Leading Players Stan Laurel, Oliver Hardy,
James Finlayson, Walter Long

Password Is Courage, The (1962)　　116 mins
MGM
Director Andrew L. Stone
Screenplay Andrew L. Stone (from book by
John Castle)
Photographer David Boulton (b&w)
Leading Players Dirk Bogarde, Maria Pershcy,
Alfred Lynch, Nigel Stock

Penitentiary (1938)　　78 mins
Columbia
Director John Brahm
Screenplay Fred Niblo Jr., Seton I. Miller (from
play by Martin Flavin)
Photographer Lucien Ballard (b&w)
Leading Players Walter Connolly, John Howard,
Jean Parker, Marc Lawrence

Pete Kelly's Blues (1955)　　95 mins
Warner
Director Jack Webb
Screenplay Richard L. Breen
Photographer Harper Goff (Warnercolor)
Music Sammy Cahn, Ray Heindorf, Arthur
Hamilton, Matty Matlock
Leading Players Jack Webb, Edmond O'Brien,
Janet Leigh, Peggy Lee, Ella Fitzgerald

Playing For Time (1980)　　140 mins
TVM
Director Daniel Mann
Screenplay Arthur Miller (from book by
Fania Fenelon)
Photographer Arthur Ortiz (color)
Music Brad Fiedel
Leading Players Vanessa Redgrave,
Jane Alexander

Pot Carriers, The (1962)　　84 mins
Associated British
Director Peter Graham Scott
Screenplay T. J. Morrison, Mike Watts
(from play by Watts)
Photographer Edwin Hillier (b&w)
Music Stanley Black
Leading Players Ronald Fraser, Paul Massie,
Dennis Price, Paul Rogers, Carole Lesley

POW: The Escape (1986)　　89 mins
Columbia/Canon/Warner
Director Gideon Amir
Screenplay Jeremy Lipp, James Bruner,
Malcolm Barbour, John Langley
Photographer Yechiel Ne'eman (TVC color)
Music David Storrs, etc
Leading Players David Carradine,
Charles R. Floyd, Mako

Pressure Point (1962)　　91 mins
United Artists
Director Hubert Cornfield
Screenplay Hubert Cornfield, S. Lee Pogositin
(from book *The 50-Minute Hour*
by Dr Robert Lindner)
Photographer Ernest Haller (b&w)
Music Ernest Gold
Leading Players Sidney Poitier, Bobby Darin,
Peter Falk

Prison (1987)　　103 mins
Empire/Entertainment
Director Renny Harlin
Screenplay C. Courtney Joyner
Photographer Mac Ahlberg (color)
Music Richard Band, Christopher L. Stone
Leading Players Viggo Mortensen, Lane Smith,
Chelsea Field, Lincoln Kilpatrick

Prisoner, The (1955)　　91 mins
Columbia
Director Peter Glenville
Screenplay Bridget Boland (from her play)
Photographer Reginald Wyer (b&w)
Music Benjamin Frankel
Leading Players Alec Guinness, Jack Hawkins,
Wilfrid Lawson

Prisoner of Shark Island, The (1936)　　94 mins
TCF
Director John Ford
Screenplay Nunnally Johnson
Photographer Bert Glennon (b&w)
Music Louis Silvers
Leading Players Warner Baxter, Gloria Stuart,
Joyce Kay, John Carradine, Francis McDonald,
Ernest Whitman

Prisoner of War (1954)   81 mins
MGM
Director Andrew Marton
Screenplay Allen Rivkin
Photographer Robert Planck (b&w)
Music Jeff Alexander
Leading Players Ronald Reagan, Steve Forrest,
Dewey Martin, Oscar Homolka

Private Worlds (1935)   84 mins
Paramount
Director Gregory La Cava
Screenplay Lynn Starling (from book by
Phyllis Bottome)
Photographer Leon Shamroy (b&w)
Music Heinz Roemheld
Leading Players Claudette Colbert, Charles Boyer,
Joel McCrea, Joan Bennett

Purple Heart, The (1944)   99 mins
TCF
Director Lewis Milestone
Screenplay Jerome Cady, Darryl F. Zanuck
Photographer Arthur Miller (b&w)
Music Alfred Newman
Leading Players Dana Andrews, Richard Conte,
Farley Granger

QB VII (1974)   312 mins
Columbia/Screen Gems
Director Tom Gries
Screenplay Edward Anhalt (from book
by Leon Uris)
Photographer Robert L. Morrison and Paul Beeson
(color)
Music Jerry Goldsmith
Leading Players Ben Gazzara, Anthony Hopkins,
Leslie Caron, Lee Remick, Anthony Quayle

Quare Fellow, The (1962)   90 mins
BLC/Bryanston
Director Arthur Dreifuss
Screenplay Arthur Dreifuss (from play by Brendan
Behan)
Photographer Peter Hennessey (b&w)
Music Alexander Faris
Leading Players Patrick McGoohan, Sylvia Sims,
Walter Macken, Dermot Kelly

Rambo: First Blood, Part II (1985)   96 mins
Carolco/Columbia-EMI-Warner
Director George Pan Cosmatos
Screenplay Sylvester Stallone, James Cameron
Photographer Jack Cardiff (Technicolor)
Music Jerry Goldsmith
Leading Players Sylvester Stallone,
Richard Crenna, Julie Nickson

Reach for the Sky (1956)   135 mins
Rank/Pinnacle
Director Lewis Gilbert
Screenplay Lewis Gilbert (from book by
Paul Brickhill)
Photographer Jack Asher (b&w)
Music John Addison
Leading Players Kenneth More, Muriel Pavlow,
Lyndon Brook, Lee Patterson, Alexander Knox

Reprieve (1962) (UK: **Convicts Four**)   105 mins
Allied Artists
Director Millard Kaufman
Screenplay Millard Kaufman (from book by John
Resko)
Photographer Joseph Biroc (b&w)
Music Leonard Rosenman
Leading Players Ben Gazzara, Stuart Whitman,
Ray Walston, Broderick Crawford, Rod Steiger,
Vincent Price

Revolt in the Big House (1958)   79 mins
Allied Artists
Director R. G. Springsteen
Screenplay Daniel Hyatt, Eugene Laurie
Photographer William Margulies (b&w)
Leading Players Gene Evans, Robert Blake

Riot (1968)   98 mins
Paramount
Director Buzz Kulik
Screenplay James Poe (from book by Frank Elli)
Photographer Robert B. Hauser (Technicolor)
Music Christopher Komeda
Leading Players Gene Hackman, Jim Brown,
Mike Kellin

Riot in Cell Block Eleven (1954)   80 mins
Allied Artists
Director Don Siegel
Screenplay Richard Collins
Photographer Russell Harlan (b&w)
Music Herschel Burke Gilbert
Leading Players Neville Brand, Emile Meyer,
Leo Gordon, Frank Faylen

Rolling Man (1972)   73 mins
TVM
Director Peter Hyams
Screenplay Stephen Karpf, Elinor Karpf
Photographer Earl Rath (color)
Music Murray McLeod, Stuart Margolin
Leading Players Dennis Weaver, Don Stroud,
Agnes Moorehead, Jimmy Dean, Donna Mills,
Sheree North

San Quentin (1937)   70 mins
Warner
Director Lloyd Bacon
Screenplay Peter Milne, Humphrey Cobb
Photographer Sid Hickox (b&w)
Music Heinz Roemheld, David Raskin
Leading Players Pat O'Brien, Ann Sheridan,
Humphrey Bogart, Barton MacLane

Scum (1979)   97 mins
Berwyn Street Films
Director Alan Clarke
Screenplay Roy Minton
Photographer Phil Meheux (Eastmancolor)
Leading Players Ray Winstone, Mick Ford

Second Hundred Years, The (1927)   2 reels/silent
MGM
Director Fred L. Guiol
Leading Players Stan Laurel, Oliver Hardy,
James Finlayson

The Secret Fury (1950)   86 mins
RKO
Director Mel Ferrer
Screenplay Lionel House
Photographer Leo Tover (b&w)
Music Roy Webb
Leading Players Claudette Colbert, Robert Ryan,
Philip Ober, Jane Cowl, Paul Kelly

Shock Corridor (1963)   101 mins
Fromkess/Firks
Director Samuel Fuller
Screenplay Samuel Fuller
Photographer Stanley Cortez (b&w),
Samuel Fuller (color sequence)
Music Paul Dunlap
Leading Players Peter Breck, Constance Towers,
Gene Evans, Hari Rhodes

**Situation Hopeless –
But Not Serious** (1965)   97 mins
Paramount/Castle
Director Gottfried Reinhardt
Screenplay Silvia Reinhardt (from book
The Hiding Place by Robert Shaw)
Photographer Kurt Hasse (b&w)
Music Harold Byrne
Leading Players Alec Guinness, Mike Connors,
Robert Redford

Six Against the Rock (1987)   96 mins
Gaylord/Schaeffer, Karpf, Eckstein
Director Paul Wendkos
Screenplay John Gay (from book by Clark
Howard)
Photographer Philip Lathrop (color)
Music William Goldstein
Leading Players David Carradine, Charles Haid,
Howard Hesseman, David Morse, Richard Dysart,
Jan-Michael Vincent, Dennis Farina

Snake Pit, The (1948)   107 mins
TCF
Director Anatole Litvak
Screenplay Frank Partos, Millen Brand
(from book by Mary Jane Ward)
Photographer Leo Tover (b&w)
Music Alfred Newman
Leading Players Olivia de Havilland, Mark
Stevens, Leo Genn, Celeste Holm

Sounder (1972)   105 mins
TCF
Director Martin Ritt
Screenplay Lonnie Elder III (from book by William
H. Armstrong)
Photographer John Alonzo (De Luxe Color)
Music Taj Mahal
Leading Players Paul Winfield, Cicely Tyson,
Kevin Hooks

Stalag 17 (1953)   120 mins
Paramount
Director Billy Wilder
Screenplay Billy Wilder, Edwin Blum (from play
by Donald Bevan, Edmund Trzinski)
Photographer Ernest Laszlo (b&w)
Music Franz Waxman
Leading Players William Holden, Don Taylor,
Otto Preminger, Robert Strauss, Peter Graves

Stir Crazy (1980)   111 mins
Columbia
Director Sidney Poitier
Screenplay Bruce Jay Friedman
Photographer Fred Schuler (Metrocolor)
Music Tom Scott
Leading Players Gene Wilder, Richard Pryor

Straight Time (1978)   114 mins
Warner
Director Ulu Grosbard
Screenplay Alvin Sargent, Edward Bunker, Jeffrey
Boam (from book *No Beast So Fierce* by
Edward Bunker)
Photographer Owen Roizman (Technicolor)
Music David Shire
Leading Players Dustin Hoffman, Theresa Russell,
Gary Busey, Harry Dean Stanton, M. Emmet Walsh

Sullivan's Travels (1941)   90 mins
Paramount
Director Preston Sturges
Screenplay Preston Sturges
Photographer John Seitz (b&w)
Music Leo Shuken
Leading Players Joel McCrea, Veronica Lake,
Robert Warwick, William Demarest,
Franklin Pangborn, Jimmy Conlin

Take the Money and Run (1969)   85 mins
Palomar
Director Woody Allen
Screenplay Woody Allen
Photographer Lester Shorr (Technicolor)
Music Marvin Hamlisch
Leading Players Woody Allen, Janet Margolin,
Marcel Hillaire, Lonny Chapman, Mark Gordon

They Made Me a Criminal (1939)   92 mins
Warner
Director Busby Berkeley
Screenplay Sig Herzig
Photographer James Wong Howe (b&w)
Music Max Steiner
Leading Players John Garfield, Claude Rains,
Gloria Dickson, Billy Halop, Bobby Jordan,
Huntz Hall, Leo Gorcey

Three Came Home (1950)   106 mins
TCF
Director Jean Negulesco
Screenplay Nunnally Johnson

Photographer Milton Krasner (b&w)
Music Hugo Friedhofer
Leading Players Claudette Colbert, Patric
Knowles, Sessue Hayakawa, Florence Desmond

Town Like Alice, A (1956)   117 mins
Rank/Vic
Director Jack Lee
Screenplay W. P. Lipscomb, Richard Mason
(from book by Nevile Shute)
Photographer Geoffrey Unsworth (b&w)
Music Matyas Seiber
Leading Players Virginia McKenna, Peter Finch,
Tagaki, Marie Lohr, Jean Anderson

Travelling Executioner, The (1970)   94 mins
MGM
Director Jack Smight
Screenplay Garrie Bateson
Photographer Philip Lathrop (Metrocolor)
Music Jerry Goldsmith
Leading Players Stacy Keach, Mariana Hill,
Bud Cort, Graham Jarvis, M. Emmet Walsh

20,000 Years in Sing Sing (1932)   77 mins
First National/WB
Director Michael Curtiz
Screenplay Wilson Mizner, Brown Holmes
(from book by Lewis E. Lawes)
Photographer Barney McGill (b&w)
Music Bernhard Kaun
Leading Players Spencer Tracy, Bette Davis,
Arthur Byron, Lyle Talbot, Louis Calhern

2,000 Women (1944)   97 mins
GFD/Gainsborough
Director Frank Launder
Screenplay Frank Launder
Photographer Jack Cox (b&w)
Music Hans May
Leading Players Phyllis Calvert, Patricia Roc, Jean
Kent, Flora Robson

Two Way Stretch (1960)   87 mins
British Lion
Director Robert Day
Screenplay John Warren, Len Heath
Photographer Geoffrey Faithfull (b&w)
Music Ken Jones
Leading Players Peter Sellers, Lionel Jeffries,
Wilfrid Hyde White, Bernard Cribbins,
David Lodge

Unchained (1955)   75 mins
Warner
Director Hall Bartlett
Screenplay Hall Bartlett (from book *Prisoners Are People* by Kenyon J. Scudder)
Photographer Virgil Miller (b&w)
Music Alex North
Leading Players Chester Morris, Elroy Hirsch, Barbara Hale

Uncommon Valor (1983)   105 mins
Paramount
Director Ted Kotcheff
Screenplay Joe Gayton
Photographer Stephen H. Barum (Movielab Color)
Music James Horner
Leading Players Gene Hackman, Robert Stack, Fred Ward

Up the River (1930)   80 mins
TCF
Director John Ford
Screenplay Maurice Watkins
Photographer Joseph August (b&w)
Leading Players Spencer Tracy, Warren Hymer, Claire Luce, Humphrey Bogart

Up the River (1938)   75 mins
TCF
Director Alfred Werker
Screenplay Lou Breslow, John Patrick
Photographer Peverell Marley (b&w)
Music Samuel Kaylin
Leading Players Preston Foster, Arthur Treacher, Tony Martin

White Heat (1949)   114 mins
Warner
Director Raoul Walsh
Screenplay Ivan Goff, Ben Roberts
Photographer Sid Hickox (b&w)
Music Max Steiner
Leading Players James Cagney, Margaret Wycherly, Steve Cochran, Virginia Mayo, Edmond O'Brien

Women's Prison (1955)   80 mins
Columbia
Director Lewis Seiler
Screenplay Crane Wilbur, Jack De Witt
Photographer Lester H. White (b&w)
Music Mischa Bakaleinikoff
Leading Players Ida Lupino, Jan Sterling, Cleo Moore, Audrey Totter, Phyllis Thaxter, Howard Duff

Wooden Horse, The (1950)   101 mins
British Lion/Wessex/London
Director Jack Lee
Screenplay Eric Williams (from his own book)
Photographer C. Pennington-Richards (b&w)
Music Clifton Parker
Leading Players Leo Genn, David Tomlinson, Anthony Steele

Yield to the Night (1956)
(US: **Blonde Sinner**)   99 mins
ABP
Director J. Lee-Thompson
Screenplay John Cresswell, Joan Henry (from book by Joan Henry)
Photographer Gilbert Taylor (b&w)
Music Ray Martin
Leading Players Diana Dors, Yvonne Mitchell, Michael Craig

You Can't Get Away With Murder (1939) 78 mins
Warner
Director Lewis Seiler
Screenplay Robert Buckner, Don Ryan, Kenneth Gamet (from play *Chalked Out* by Lewis E. Lawes and Jonathan Finn)
Photographer Sol Polito (b&w)
Music Heinz Roemheld
Leading Players Humphrey Bogart, Billy Halop, Gale Page, John Litel

You Only Live Once (1937)   85 mins
Walter Wanger
Director Fritz Lang
Screenplay Graham Baker
Photographer Leon Shamroy (b&w)
Music Alfred Newman
Leading Players Henry Fonda, Sylvia Sidney, Barton MacLane